God Help Us

TOM HARPUR

God Help Us

M&S

Canadian Cataloguing in Publication Data

Harpur, Tom
God help us

ISBN 0-7710-3943-3

1. Christianity – 20th century. 2. Christian life – 1960-
3. Church and the world. I. Title.

BV4501.2.H37 1992 200 C92-094375-6

Typeset at McClelland & Stewart.
Printed and bound in Canada.
The paper used in this book is acid-free.

McClelland & Stewart Inc.
The Canadian Publishers
481 University Avenue
Toronto, Ontario
M5G 2E9

To all who labour and long for the healing of the planet,
for the coming of lasting peace and justice among
the nations, and for greater insight and
maturity in their own lives.

Contents

The Lord is my light and my salvation; whom shall I fear?
The Lord is the strength of my life; of whom shall I be afraid?
— Psalm 27

The crisis may be quiet, but it is urgent.
— John F. Kennedy,
Introduction to *The Quiet Crisis*

THE GLOBAL CRISIS

The Risks of Writing About Ethics and Related issues

While researching my book *Life After Death*, I came across the following epitaph from a gravestone in an English churchyard:

Sacred to the Memory of Capt. Anthony Wedgewood
Accidentally Shot by his Gamekeeper
Whilst out Hunting

Underneath was the date and this Bible quote:

Well done thou good and faithful servant

The humour was obviously unintentional. It illustrates, however, the perils inherent in any of our attempts to communicate with one another. One thing is said or written; frequently something quite different is understood.

Nowhere is this more readily observed than in the realm of ethical, religious, and spiritual ideas. I know from my own experience in the past as a parish priest that what is said from the pulpit and what is heard by the congregation are often two separate realities. I would, not uncommonly, have some earnest parishioner thanking me at the door of the church after the service for a remark, an emphasis, or even an overall message that I was certain I had never uttered and definitely did not intend.

In the twenty years since then, spent as a journalist and broadcaster concerned with the communication of spiritual and ethical beliefs in the mass media, I have had to learn to live with this ambiguity with total intensity. I have never deliberately set out to be controversial or provocative in my newspaper columns on ethics. At times, however, they have proven to be highly controversial simply because of the nature of the issues being tackled. You can't move an inch in the territory that most fascinates me – the religious and moral strivings of *Homo sapiens* – without treading on somebody's sensitivities, ideals, beliefs, prejudices, taboos, or pet hates. And when you add the problem of what is said (or written) not always being the same as what is perceived by the audience, the potential for truly heated debate escalates exponentially.

Nevertheless, I have never viewed the controversy that has so often attended my writing in a negative light. I agree with those who are convinced that the issues for humanity underlying all others at this time are precisely those that have to do with our spiritual and ethical growth and development. In a world almost completely dominated by a superficial or surface approach to life – particularly in the mass media – there is an urgent need for an engaged discussion about what it really means to be fully human, about the depth dimensions of living, and about the deeper questions of right and wrong.

Given the "info-glut" and the mental gridlock caused today by the vast outpouring of information (as opposed to knowledge), controversy has a key role to play: It gets people's attention. Unless you can do that, any chance of a meaningful change in human consciousness as a result of facing the spiritual and ethical implications of our current global situation simply evaporates by default. The contents of this book are meant to disturb and challenge the reader to fresh thinking. Hopefully, there is much that will also encourage and comfort the reader in his or her spiritual quest.

The Present Crisis

The essays in this book cover a very wide range of topics, from the effects of our over-consumption of meat on the environment to the euthanasia debate and the efficacy of prayer. They are united, however, by the author's fervent conviction that we are living at a time of unique global crisis. There are enormous, radical, and costly changes to be made if we are to weather the present world crisis and ensure human survival into and beyond the year 2000. This is the vital context in which these pieces are meant to be read.

Despite the recent, welcome, vast, and near-miraculous upheavals in Eastern Europe and the U.S.S.R., the virtual collapse of Communism, the end of the Cold War, the beginning of a Middle East peace process, and many other hopeful signs, we are now at a major, if not *the* major, turning-point of human history. The word "crisis" comes from a Greek verb with the root meaning of "to sift out" and hence to judge. This is a time of sifting out, of judgement, without parallel in the story of our evolution as a species. The old nineteenth-century myth of inevitable progress has been exposed as a fraud. It's very much an open question whether we can make the essential "quantum leap" forward that is needed or whether we'll end up instead as a failed experiment, much like the dinosaurs. The crisis has many symptoms, but it flows from a single source. We are ultimately, despite the cult of consumerism, spiritual animals (*Homo spiritualis*), and we suffer from a profoundly spiritual malady.

The environmental crisis

The industrial-technological age is coming to its end. Finally, after being "entranced" by technology (to quote cultural philosopher Fr. Thomas Berry) for decades, we are realizing that our fixation with this kind of illusory advancement is now shutting down all the basic life systems of the planet. Things simply can't go on as before or there'll be no future of any kind to worry about. This threat is global, and only a global response is capable of meeting it.

The temptation, of course – and there is abundant evidence of this happening on every side at present – is to play games with this whole issue. We'd like to burble on about ecology and government "green plans" while changing nothing fundamental. We still clamour for more development, more luxuries, more profits and pleasures, together with an ineluctably growing GNP, as though our debit-financing with the Earth itself had not reached its outer limits. According to columnist Gwynne Dyer, writing in *The Toronto Star*, we are still manufacturing motor cars at the rate of 100,000 a day worldwide, even though the automobile is a major depleter of non-renewable energy stocks, a major polluter of the atmosphere, and the single greatest destroyer of basic quality of life in all our key urban centres (not to mention the hundreds of thousands killed or maimed annually in auto accidents).

At stake in the whole crisis over the environment is whether or not we can square up to the global implications of where our "waste-world" attitude has brought us and make the inner and outer changes necessary if we are to relate, as a species, in a totally different way to the natural world. If we keep on abusing the Earth as if it were either our enemy or our dumb slave, it will close down and snuff us out. It's as simple as that.

At bottom, this is a spiritual problem, and no amount of surface tinkering will ever put it right.

War and Peace

It is a highly dangerous illusion to suppose that because the Cold War is over and the Soviet "Evil Empire" – to quote Ronald Reagan of old – is in almost total disarray, world peace is somehow now secure. Apart from ongoing, grave concerns over who exactly controls the nuclear weapons in the Soviet arsenal, it remains true that both the United States and its Soviet counterparts still possess many thousands of deadly ballistic missiles capable of wiping out civilization as we know it several times over. The risk of internecine nuclear war between the newly emancipated Soviet republics has been articulated, not just by the American Secretary of State, James Baker, but by no less knowledgeable a person than Mikhail Gorbachev. Add to this threat the many other nations that now have nuclear weapons – including Israel, with its so-called Samson Option in the case of overwhelming attack by Arab countries – and the real danger of fanatical terrorist cells one day holding the world to ransom with a nuclear device in a suitcase in central Paris, London, or Manhattan, and you have the scenario for near-certain, eventual holocaust.

As we saw in the 1991 debacle of the Gulf War, and as is manifest in dozens of war zones, potential and actual, around the world at this very moment – from Lebanon to Northern Ireland, Yugoslavia, East Timor, Sri Lanka, or various parts of Africa – once a group or nation decides its self-interest can best be served by violence, nobody can predict where the escalation will end. Unless we forsake the outmoded notion of a "just war," and unless war itself is outlawed and repudiated by all, the outlook for the future is extremely bleak.

The spiritual challenge to our species is enormous. Any truly new world order will come about not by the fiat or political will of this or that superpower but as the result of a spiritual leap forward by the human race itself. We need a universal acceptance of the ethic of non-violence, because the old alternative – no matter how it has been justified or blessed by both Church and state in the past – means eventual global suicide.

Injustice

As every thinking, caring person knows, it's a scandal of well-nigh cosmic proportions that in a world where some enjoy so much, many millions go to sleep every night starving, sick, homeless, or afraid for their very lives. Two-thirds of humankind lives in abject poverty while the minority suffer only the results of affluence – obesity, difficulty in parking their cars, and a pervasive sense of meaninglessness, particularly among the young.

In spite of all the high-tech wizardry of a computerized world, there is rampant injustice today on a scale scarcely imagined in earlier ages. The gap between rich and poor, even in the so-called First World, including the richest country of all, the United States – is still widening apace. This imbalance is morally outrageous, and it makes the chances of an enduring global peace even less likely. Injustice, in whatever shape, is the mother of eventual conflict. Peace, in the Judeo-Christian tradition (as the Hebrew word *shalom* makes clear), is much more than the mere absence of war.

It is the positive establishment of a human community based upon right-relatedness (righteousness) or absolute justice for every member. This is not some airy-fairy ideal. Without it, there can be no secure future for the planet.

A Global Ethic

In the light of the above, the central task of all those who care about our human destiny is to find and elucidate a global ethic as a foundation for global transformation. That is, we desperately need to transcend our past or present tribalisms, our racial, religious, and political ghettos, to a new vision founded upon basic ethical principles acceptable to and accepted by every citizen of Earth. Very specifically, this is a special challenge for the great world religions, which all preach compassion, justice, and peace but yet today are often themselves scandalously enmeshed in bitter, bloody strife. Whether the conflict is between Sikhs and Hindus, Muslims and Jews, Protestants and Roman Catholics, the cry rightfully goes up from the secular world: "Physician, heal thyself!"

Yet, at the same time, the vast numbers of secular folk who today on their own, non-transcendental grounds are committed to an ethic that also professes concern for peace, justice, and the healing of the Earth need to see beyond the failures of religion to the common values underneath. We need (as Catholic theologians Hans Küng and Leonard Swidler have recently pointed out in their call for a "global ethic") an immediate, worldwide dialogue between all religious and non-religious ethical groups and leaders to forge the announcement of a universal declaration on common ethical principles that would parallel the 1948 United Nations Universal Declaration of Human Rights.

What would such a universal declaration contain? The two theologians just cited (who, incidentally, have been joined by leading Muslim, Jewish, Buddhist, and Hindu scholars as well) suggest that since the "Golden Rule" appears in some form in all major religions, as well as in non-theistic or non-religious moral codes, it would make the obvious starting point. This is often stated in the negative – "Do not do unto anyone what you would not want done to yourself" – but the positive thrust of the Sermon on the Mount – "Love [respect and care for] your neighbour as yourself" – is better. The rule must be broadened, however, from its customary focus on humans alone to include animals and the whole of nature. There must be compassion and respect for every living creature and for the Earth itself.

The principle of non-violence, particularly the repudiation of war as a means of settling disputes, would be a necessary corollary to this first principle. If only this much were to be universally adopted as the minimum basis for global action by all peoples, tribes, and governments, the pathway to a major transformation would lie open before us.

Clearly, however, it is not enough to make agreements or declarations. As stated above, the reason we oppress one another, wage wars, permit injustice, and defile our only natural home is ultimately a spiritual matter. Only a profound change of consciousness, a new way of seeing ourselves, our neighbours, and our relationship with the environment will make a global ethic work. This transformation cannot and will not happen inevitably or by itself. We have to assent to it with our intellect and seek it with all our strength.

In the end, being the kind of creatures we are, the most powerful agent of transformation of consciousness (as religions have always known) is that which appeals to our right-brain, intuitive side. I'm referring to myth and symbolism. The new myth (a story with a deep spiritual meaning) for our time – one into which all other myths, religious or secular, can be inserted – is that now given to us by science. No matter what our race, religion, language, or clime, it asserts, we are all the offspring of the one universal story that began with the Big Bang and the birth of the cosmos itself. It is because of this common origin that we all belong intimately not just to each other but to the whole of creation.

The new symbol, under which all older symbols, from national flags and insignia to the Christian cross or figures of the seated Buddha, can be subsumed, is that of the image of Earth as seen from outer space. That warmly glowing, delicately fragile, purple ball, spinning on its silent axis, speaks to the heart of the matter as nothing else can. It is the single most powerful, non-verbal communication of what a global ethic must be all about. Viewed thus, as Joseph Campbell put it, "All the walls are down." Ideologies, faiths, denominations, sects, and nationalities pale to insignificance beside the overwhelming reality of our oneness, our interdependency, and our belonging to spaceship Earth. It is a synchronicity of the highest order that such a universal symbol has emerged just when our need for it is of paramount urgency.

With that in mind, I have a proposal to make. In the past, I have suggested a religious "summit" to be held in one of the world's trouble spots – for example, in the Middle East. Much could still be achieved that way. But the problems we currently face are much bigger than anything religion alone could ever hope to solve. So far, on all the various space missions, the wrong people have gone – technicians, scientists, or members of the military. What is needed now is for key religious leaders to join with other ethicists and the prime ministers, monarchs, presidents, and other top world leaders on a giant spaceship. It might sound far-fetched, but the technology is already there, and it would cost a lot less than the American "Star Wars" project. They could be put into a distant orbit around the Earth for seven days (symbolizing the seven days of creation in the Genesis story). From this perspective, and with the planetary symbol in full and awesome view, they could discuss the new global ethos and other global issues. If they were to truly ask themselves and each other, "What on Earth have we been doing?" and "What on Earth are we going to do for the well-being of all?" things on Earth would never be the same again!

Where Does God Fit In to All of This?

I had lunch recently at an exclusive club in downtown Toronto at the invitation of a fairly prominent senior politician. An eavesdropper at our table would have been surprised. While the others talked earnestly of politics or patched together business deals, at my host's request we discussed theological questions about the existence of God and whether, if there is one, He/She answers prayer or is in any way truly interested in what happens here on Earth. My host, you see, was a convinced, thoughtful atheist – with a very strong desire to believe. From his experience and perspective, he agreed with the position that humanity is facing an acute crisis and that "a power greater than ourselves" is needed to meet it. However, his question was whether or not such a Higher Power is there to answer the cry, "God help us," and, if there is, do we have any indication that He/She cares enough to respond to such an appeal.

It is important for the reader of what follows to know the underlying beliefs of the author. It is only then that the opinions and arguments expressed can be seen in their proper context, only then that true communication can be hoped for or achieved.

Like many of you, I first learned to believe in God in the parental home. Both my father and mother had been "converted" or "born again" (as evangelical Christians like to describe it) when they were in their late teens or early twenties in Belfast at evangelistic rallies held by a then-famous preacher called Billy Nicholson. They emigrated to Canada and were married in Toronto not long afterwards.

I cannot remember a time when my late father, who eventually went on to be ordained as an Anglican priest after some thirty years in business, wasn't involved in running a Sunday School, a Bible class, or youth camp. We attended church two or three times on Sunday and often midweek events as well. I was a boy chorister, then later a youth leader and a reader at Sunday services. It came as no surprise to anyone when, at nineteen, I enrolled at the University of Toronto with the declared intention of being ordained eventually at Wycliffe College.

It would be wrong to create the impression that I simply sailed along through my teens and young adulthood without a query, problem, or question about the Christian faith or its expression in the form of Anglicanism. Like many, I had a keen interest in learning and a deep desire to get a hold on things for myself rather than simply accept intellectual hand-me-downs from authority figures. Even as a choirboy I had difficulties with some of the more savage parts of the Bible and the fact that, while religion was supposed to bring people together, it seemed perpetually to drive them apart into dozens of opposing camps.

The course in Classics at the University of Toronto, with some pass courses in Oriental literature (mainly the Bible from a purely academic, historical perspective) really opened my eyes. I now had not just the urge to question but the tools and knowledge to do so in much greater depth. These four years were followed by three more spent reading ancient history and philosophy at Oriel College, Oxford. Here, one of my tutors was a quiet agnostic, the other, my philosophy don, an outspoken atheist. I was compelled to rethink everything I had held to much more rigorously than I had either expected or wished.

On taking my degree at Oxford, I was at last ready to study theology at Wycliffe College. It was here, in spite of the school's conservative ethos, that I became quite familiar with new, critical approaches to the biblical texts, especially the Gospels. Anybody who thinks you can go through nine years of intensive academic studies like that and not have your original childhood faith challenged, changed, and developed is suffering from a great lack of insight and imagination. If our spiritual life is indeed a journey, it could be said I had moved a very long way. This is not to claim that I had necessarily *advanced* a long way compared with others. I was simply quite a different kind of believer than when I'd set out.

But that was only the beginning. When I finally graduated, was ordained, and began my parish ministry, I had little idea just how much working with my parishioners and sharing in their trials, joys, and griefs would further reshape my faith. The rather rigidly held dogmas of the seminary were all right in the classroom but often of little use in the flesh-and-blood situations of real people with real needs. After seven years as a minister, I returned to Oxford for postgraduate studies in Patristics (the Early Church Fathers) and then returned to Wycliffe College, first as a lecturer and then as professor of the New Testament and Greek.

The story of how I left teaching to become a full-time journalist and broadcaster, and the various travels and other experiences that career led to, I wrote in *Always on Sunday*. Here I merely want to record that my twenty years of observing and writing about religion and ethics around the globe have had a more profound effect upon my beliefs than anything that went before. You can't see the glory of God in the face of a devout Muslim, Hindu, Sikh, or other believer and go on thinking that Christians alone hold the only answer or the only way to God. You can't see two young atheists living in crude lodgings in the heart of Calcutta at their own expense and working for no pay in Mother Teresa's hospice for the dying without challenging the idea that only believers are truly moral or compassionate. You can't witness the horrible poverty and illness that one sees in the Third World and not ask disturbing questions, not just about our own inhumanity but about God's love and justice.

I am not arguing that because I have had this particular life experience and still, in spite of it all or because of it all, believe and trust in a living, caring God today more than at any previous point in my life, therefore the reader should do so as well. What I do want to make very plain is that the faith in God behind *God Help Us* is not based upon an unexamined set of dogmas or traditional tenets of religion. The truth is that I am often in hot water with many traditionalists because of some of my views. But, when all is said and done, the hypothesis that there is a loving, wise, infinitely creative, spiritual Presence in the very warp and woof of the universe is the only one that ultimately satisfies the demands of both left-brain and right-brain thinking for me. What's more, it's not just a matter of an hypothesis, a cerebral event, or an abstract idea. Like many of you, I have tried to put this hypothesis to the test in the only crucible that is finally completely authentic for anyone – one's own life. This God makes Himself/Herself known in nature, in the lives of other people, in sacred scriptures, in other faiths, in the deepest relationships we have with intimates and friends, and, supremely, in the ministry, death, and Resurrection of Jesus of Nazareth, called Christ. It is my deepest conviction that it is only with the partnership and help of God that the spiritual leap forward I have written about here will ever come into being.

PART ONE

KEEPING FAITH

On the Right Track

I try to begin each day with a four- or five-kilometre walk. One morning – a bright, crisp November day – I came to the crest of a gravel pit about half a kilometre from our home. As I stood there for a moment, three deer suddenly came loping out of a cedar swamp to my left. They stopped on a slight rise about a hundred metres in front of me and turned to gaze intently at the dense bush they had just left.

At first, I thought they had caught my scent and were watching me. But just then the object of their real interest emerged from the trees. A small, beagle-type hunting dog, his nose glued to the ground, was in hot pursuit. He gave hysterical, ear-piercing howls at regular intervals as he ran back and forth, picking up the trail.

It was quite a study. The deer stood absolutely motionless, as if fascinated by the dog's furious exertions. Meanwhile, totally oblivious to the fact that if he had only paused to raise his head he could have caught full view of his quarry, the beagle kept circling and sniffing.

All at once he yelped in ecstasy and started off in a direction at a right angle to the deer. I thought he would vanish over the horizon on the wrong spoor. However, the dog suddenly snapped to a halt, circled back, and then made straight for the right spot. The deer – two does and a fawn – wheeled abruptly and in a few seconds, with a flash of their white tails, were lost in the woods on the other side.

The beagle never once lifted his head; he never once saw what he was after. The last I saw of him was as he, too, disappeared into the distant forest. He was destined to be a very tired and frustrated dog at the end of the day.

The incident stayed with me on my walk and for the rest of the week. It seemed to encapsulate in symbolic form a phenomenon that is a deeply rooted part of our human condition.

Our minds and hearts tell us that there must be a meaning and purpose to our existence. Our innate desire for happiness and fulfilment must, we feel, be grounded in a real possibility somehow, somewhere, of its being satisfied.

From time to time, we pick up the scent of a transcendent or larger-than-we-are experience that convinces us we are on the right track. For some, it might be music that gives the clue. For others, it is nature, or being with certain people, doing a particular kind of work, or reading great literature. But most of the time we have our noses so close to the ground of everyday living that the real object of our quest could be standing in front of us, staring us in the face, and we would never see it.

We are geniuses when it comes to finding and following false trails.

Religion purports to put us in touch with the real source and end of all our longing, the Being Who made us and for Whom we were made. Yet, strange though it may seem, religious people also can be so caught up in their religiosity that they never catch a clear sighting of what or Whom they are ultimately supposed to be dealing with.

In fact, one of things the Bible makes very obvious is that religion can and frequently does become a major obstacle to "finding life." That's why I believe it is helpful to draw a distinction between religion on the one hand and spirituality on the other.

Religion is basically about beliefs, rituals, and rules. All of these can be right and good in themselves as means to an end, but they quickly become ends in themselves. Once this happens, they block the very vision they were intended to facilitate.

The harshest words attributed to Jesus Christ were reserved for those extremely religious people who, he said, were putting burdens on other people "too grievous to be borne." They were not only failing to enter into the Kingdom of God themselves but were hindering others from going in as well. Unfortunately, the same could be said of many aspects of church life in our own time. People long for life and are given dogma or ritual or church canons (rules) instead.

Whereas religion chiefly concerns itself with externals, spirituality is an inner matter, the determination to look beyond the signs and tracks of God's presence to the vision of the Real Thing.

Don't misunderstand me. I am not a religious anarchist. I believe certain structures, rituals, and creeds can have a useful role. But they are always secondary, and where and when they get in the way of people experiencing the grace and love of God they should be scrapped or radically changed.

There is a tremendous spiritual thirst in society today. Like the beagle-hound, many are weary and worn by the hunt. Their lives seem spent chasing elusive or futile goals. They dimly sense there must be something more.

Religion's challenge is to help them look up, and then take this vision back into their daily lives.

— False Paths —

Words, as T. S. Eliot reminds us, often crack and break under the burdens we impose on them. The phrase "I love you" is but one example.

There are other problems with language. A word meaning something specific to the speaker might carry a quite different meaning to the hearer. An example I can't forget happened to me when I was sitting for my finals at Oxford.

I had ten, consecutive, three-hour papers to write. The first morning I was there early, properly attired in a dark suit, white bow-tie, and mortar-board. The results of three years' study hung in the balance.

As the doors opened and we crowded in to the exam room, a fellow student suddenly became hysterical and began screaming. There was a great commotion and an ambulance soon roared up to take him away. This was unnerving, to say the least, but I took a seat and looked at the exam. I was dimly aware of one of the dons striding up and down the aisle beside me with a student in tow, but I paid them little heed.

All at once, they stopped at my desk and the don asked, "Pardon me, sir, but are you Fitt?" Given the other student's breakdown, I thought he was asking if I was "fit." Thinking I must look quite ill, I stammered, "I feel fine, sir."

He stifled a smirk and explained that he wasn't asking after my health. There were names pasted on the corner of each desk and I had taken the one belonging to an anxious Mr. Fitt. I finally got seated in the right place, but by the time I got back to my college for lunch the news of my gaffe had gone before. There were jokes about it in the senior common room that night.

What bothers me a good deal today is the way in which the term "spirituality" is being tossed about. Like "lifestyle" it has become a sort of buzzword covering a multitude of sins.

The encouraging thing, I suppose, is that currently there is a growing interest in things of the spirit, an awareness that, however essential a reasonable amount of material prosperity may be, we do not live by bread alone.

While religious institutions are obviously in a state of decline, the number of men and women in our society who hunger for an authentic spirituality – a framework of thought, words, feelings, and actions that articulates their awareness of being more than consumers or mere ciphers – is rapidly increasing. They have seen the techno-wonderworld around us, including the enormous injustices it condones, and they rightly question whether this is all there is.

The trouble, I repeat, is that in the welter of options being offered in the name of spirituality today it is terribly easy to be led astray. That's why I want to offer a few basic principles – a sort of consumer's guide or *caveat emptor* – for determining what is right and best for you.

• In an instant society, beware of those offering instant, easy solutions to life's problems and mysteries. Spirituality and the development of one's inner life takes time and discipline. A lot of so-called spiritualities out there at present are aimed at an infantile lust for magic.

• An authentic spirituality always fosters personal growth, wholeness of outlook or worldview, and taking responsibility for one's own life. Beware of those who would be your guru or guide, taking your money while making you their spiritual dependant.

• True spirituality and awareness of one's nature as a "child of God" always lead to a keener social awareness than before. Be suspicious of any spiritual path that leads you to an otherworldliness unconcerned with the material universe or its other inhabitants. As Robert Frost said, "Earth's the right place for love [and we might add, for justice]: I don't know where it's likely to go better."

• Enhanced awareness of other dimensions of reality than those immediately apparent to our senses, and the conviction that the Spirit of the Creator is in all things and has a purpose for everyone of us, should result in a clearer ethical vision for ourselves.

There are some pseudo-spiritual teachers today who preach that morality is a matter of indifference, that each of us must live many lives so that we can experience every facet of human experience, criminal as well as altruistic. Reality in moral conduct as well as anywhere else is what we choose to make it, they insist.

This is a dangerously seductive lie. Beware of any spirituality that offers moral nihilism as its own "higher way."

Ultimately, there is an unfailing litmus test to apply. It's very ancient but I doubt it can be improved. "By their fruits you shall know them."

True spirituality bears the fruit of greater compassion, tolerance, and personal maturity. Anything offering less is a fake.

— The Perennial Philosophy —

A professor of anthropology at a British Columbia university who teaches a course on Religion and Culture wrote to me recently. He had, he said, assigned his students an essay in which they were to examine a column I had written on prayer and then answer the question: "Can this man be said to believe in the Perennial Philosophy?"

The students did the project and then asked their teacher to find out if they were correct in assuming (a) that I do in fact believe in it and (b) that I must at some time have had the kind of all-encompassing "mystical experience" described by such people as Alan Watts, author of *The Way of Zen,* or F. C. Happold, in his book *Mysticism: A Study and an Anthology.*

"Many of my students are convinced that mystical experience is part of your background, but we aren't sure if that's the case," the professor wrote.

I want to share my answer to them, not because of the personal references, but because of the importance to religion and ethics of the issues they have raised.

First of all, what is meant by the Perennial Philosophy? A good definition can be found in Aldous Huxley's introduction to *The Song of God,* or *Bhagavad-Gita,* the ancient Hindu scripture. Huxley argues that the *Bhagavad-Gita,* written more than 2,500 years ago, is the first attempt to put down the essence of what all the major world religions possess as their "Highest Common Factor." Behind all the particular dogmas and rites and tongues of the various faiths, there remains this Perennial Philosophy "in what may be called its chemically pure state."

The records of the "higher religions," in his view, make it clear that ultimately they were all trying to describe the same "essentially indescribable Fact." Accordingly, Huxley sets out four fundamental doctrines that lie at the core of this Perennial Philosophy:

- The world of matter and of our individual consciousness – the world of things and animals and human beings – is the manifestation of a Divine Ground within which all partial realities have their being and without which there would be nothing.

• Humans are capable not merely of knowing *about* the Divine Ground by inference, they can also know its existence by a direct intuition that is superior to normal reasoning. This immediate kind of knowledge unites the knower with that which is known.

• Humans have a double nature, an ordinary or "phenomonal" ego and an eternal Self, which is the inner "man," the Spirit, the spark of divinity within the soul. It is possible to identify oneself with this Spirit and therefore with the Divine Ground that shares its nature.

• Our earthly life has only one end and purpose: to identify oneself with one's eternal Self and so come to the mystical, unitive knowledge of the Divine Ground, God.

I plead guilty to accepting this overall philosophy, but, as they sometimes say in court, "with an explanation." I have no problem with Huxley's first two points. The Bible thoroughly supports both: "For in Him we live and move and have our being...."

It's when we come to the double nature and the idea of possessing an eternal or immortal Self that my difficulties arise. Perhaps it's simply a matter of semantics. I believe, however, that the Hindu or eastern concept of our possessing some Higher Self that is imperishable, that is in fact God, is quite different from the Judeo-Christian concept of a body-mind-soul unity that God alone can resurrect to a future life.

I believe we have a capacity for responding to and knowing God – we are made in God's image – but we don't "have" souls, we *are* souls! What I want to guard against is the tendency of eastern mysticism (and some forms of Christianity) to downplay the body or to create a kind of body-soul dualism in which this world and its injustices no longer matter as much as "higher things."

I do agree, however, that the spark of God's divinity, or the Spirit, moves in every human being, and that seeking to allow that to control one's life is ultimately what life is all about.

As far as having had some earth-moving, mystical experience

along the lines of those described by the great Christian, Jewish, Muslim, and Hindu mystics, I can only say that that has never been given (or should I say, visited upon?) yours truly.

On the other hand, I'm convinced we are all of us mystics to some degree. By that I mean we all have the capacity for the sort of intuitive knowledge of the Ultimate Ground of which the Perennial Philosophy speaks.

Like you, I'm not given to visions, ecstasies, or other forms of paranormal experience. But, in bad times and in good, I have never been able to escape the deep inner certainty that we are one with the cosmos, and that God is in and under and through the whole of existence. As the Psalmist says: "Even if I make my bed in hell, Thou art there also."

If that's mysticism, then, like a lot of you, I'm a mystic too.

— Belief in God —

I once shocked a congregation by saying I would rather speak to a pew full of intelligent atheists than a church full of unthinking, overly comfortable Christians.

I happen to believe that atheism – the belief that there is no God – is an erroneous faith system. But is has been my experience that most of those who hold to it have at least done some hard thinking about the implications of what it would mean to be a believer.

The polls say that roughly 90 per cent of all Canadians believe in a Supreme Being, Force, or Mind behind our universe. But I doubt whether more than a tiny minority has ever really stopped to ponder the full meaning of this for their lives – or for anything else. It remains simply the ultimate insurance policy, to be pulled out of some mental drawer whenever the going gets rough. We are all familiar with the aphorism, "There are no atheists in foxholes."

People who never give God a thought from one year's end to another can get very religious when they learn they have to have an operation or when a child is hurt! However, at a deeper level, this kind of casual or push-button, emergency faith – the God-as-perpetual-crutch syndrome – is totally illogical.

As a sincere atheist once said to me, "If indeed there were a God, this would be the single most important thing to know and grapple with in my whole life." Absolutely right. From the practical as well as the intellectual side, it makes no sense whatever to state that one "believes in God" and then go about one's business as if no such reality existed. Indeed, the proper reaction to someone's bald response that they believe in God may well be, "That's nice, but so what?" In other words, the matter can't simply be left to rest there. Two crucial questions force themselves upon us: What kind of God do we believe in, what is this God like? And, given this kind of God, what does God demand, expect, or want us as humans to be and/or do?

These are the truly existential questions for a would-be believer. They have to do with ultimate meaning – with the shape, direction, and purpose of one's total existence.

For instance, if, upon reflection, God is for us a kind of punitive, super-father figure who seems to work on the principle of "Go and see what little Johnny's doing and tell him to stop," not unnaturally we will be punitive towards ourselves and harsh in our criticisms of everybody else. Indeed, it is only in recent times that we have begun to see the devastating results of centuries of belief in a patriarchal God. It is now obvious to anyone prepared to think about it that by conceiving of God as the epitome of maleness, it has been possible to wage wars, oppress women, and rape the planet – all with God's blessing!

One of my own most profound convictions is that the Spirit of God is using the current rising consciousness of women (whatever mistakes and exaggerations the feminist movement may have made or may still be making) to lead all humanity to a fuller understanding of the divine. Only as we comprehend the way in which God includes both the male and the female principles – while transcending both – will we find the healing we need for our aggression towards others and our environment.

For Christians, the answer to the question about God's nature is believed to have been revealed by Jesus. Of course, it then becomes very important how one sees him and his ministry. Is it his maleness that is important, or is it rather his full humanness and his affirmation of the individual person without regard for gender?

When it comes to the question of what God wants of us, the Hebrew and Christian Bibles speak of many things, but they all boil down to love of God, neighbour, and one's true self. Religious rites count for nothing if they don't lead to that.

Since we have heard a lot about love of God and neighbour (this doesn't mean we've done it), let me conclude with a word about love of self.

A lot of religious people use religion as a way to delude themselves. It keeps them from self-knowledge and from thinking too much about anything in depth. The Bible, however, speaks of a God who calls us to radical honesty – and the hard, inner work this implies. One verse, common to the Jewish and Christian scriptures, says it quite succinctly: "Thou requirest truth *in the inner part*" (italics added).

All of us, especially in our culture, are so easily seduced by illusions that this demand is the last thing we want to hear. But it holds the key to wholeness, or to that other word we don't use much nowadays but which really connotes the same thing – holiness.

‑ A Crucial Crutch ‑

Being the guest on CBC Radio's "Cross-Country Check Up" recently was quite a revealing experience. During the two-hour phone show (its focus was the question: "Can we be good without God?"), many callers repeated some of the most clichéd of all arguments against faith in God.

What surprised me was not that these old canards were trotted out. It was the failure of the callers to be even slightly embarrassed by them. In some cases, they were announced with a kind of "hold page one for this item" confidence that totally belied their hoariness.

Asked why he thought belief in God is important to so many people today, an agnostic professor of philosophy said that it is because "they need a crutch."

It's so obvious as to hardly need saying that some people use religion as a crutch. But to give the "crutch" answer as an explanation for the faith of the majority of humanity really won't wash in a freshman philosophy class, or anywhere else.

In the first place, when one speaks of faith or religion as a crutch it is generally understood in a pejorative sense. But, while I have used it that way myself, it must be recognized that this metaphor need not always be negative. If you are lame and can't get around on your own, a crutch not only makes sense, it becomes essential. I once sprained an ankle playing rugger for the University of Toronto. I was grateful to have a crutch for several weeks.

We all like to think we are such independent self-starters that we don't need to lean on anyone or anything. But life has a way of breaking in on us and snapping us up short. We soon find that our assumed invincibility is an illusion. If that is the point at which we begin to recognize our dependency upon the living God, this crutch might literally be our salvation!

But there is also a sense in which the use of the term "crutch" to explain one's faith in God is not merely negative but insulting and demonstrably false. Faith in God, for Jesus, meant not a crutch but a cross. The same has been true of believers of all faiths down the ages.

Was the faith of Martin Luther King, Jr. a weakling's crutch? What about Mother Teresa in Calcutta, Archbishop Desmond Tutu in South Africa, or the late Archbishop Oscar Romero in El Salvador? Who can consider the bravery in the face of threats and martyrdom of the six Jesuit priests gunned down in November 1989 in El Salvador and say their faith in God was a crutch?

The truth is that, while many may find their faith gives them a seat in the comfortable pew, for millions all over the world today, to be a believer is to pay a price. It is costly to be a Baha'i in today's Iran, a true Christian in Beirut or Belfast, or a steadfast Jew in Syria or Iraq.

Ultimately, of course, the real question at issue is whether or not it is true that there is a God Who is the source of all goodness and meaning. To imply that because some people abuse religious faith the phenomenon of faith itself is thereby explained away is nonsense.

This applies as well to the other tired argument put forward by several callers. In essence it says religion has caused terrible divisions, wrought untold miseries, and even waged wars. Therefore faith in God is a sham. But this is a logical *non sequitur* of mammoth proportions. Tragically, it is indeed true that religion throughout history has been abused, mocked, and contradicted by its own adherents. Yet none of this either proves or disproves the central thesis of religions: that there is an ultimate reality, which most of them call God.

The abuse of political power by rulers – a historical theme even more constant than the hypocrisies of religious people – does not mean there is no such thing as political power or that there is no correct use for it. Freedom is misused by humans every moment of the day in one way or another, but nobody would argue that freedom itself is therefore a chimera of somebody's imagination.

The same is true of most of the gifts of life – our sexuality, parenthood, food, and drink. They can be the fount of great blessings or the wellspring of untold distortions and excesses. The abuse of anything is no reason for denying the reality itself. Even criminals know this. Counterfeit money would have no currency value if it were not for the fact that there is real money out there.

So too with faith in God. Yes, there are charlatans and cheats and contradictions galore. But the genuine article is there too – and always has been.

— Moral Relativism —

Late one night, while I was a student, I was walking back to my own college, Oriel, through the vast, main quadrangle of Christ Church College, Oxford. (It's called Tom Quad, after the great bell that hangs above the main gates.)

The quadrangle was utterly deserted except for myself and one other undergraduate, who was dressed in formal attire and quite obviously intoxicated.

That in itself was nothing out of the ordinary. What was odd was that, with his bow-tie sadly askew and his hair looking as though it hadn't seen a brush or comb in a week, he was walking teeteringly around the balustrade of the fountain in the middle of the lawn, repeating something over and over to himself.

As I passed by, I could make out what it was in spite of his slurring. He was intoning: "After all, everything is purely relative." I was tempted to wait until the inevitable happened and he fell in, but instead I headed off to bed with his words of dubious wisdom echoing in my wake.

Drunk or not, the youth was voicing a philosophy or ethical stance that has come to enjoy enormous popularity in recent times. The average person might never even have heard of moral relativism, let alone be able to give an account of it or recognize that it is really the proper name for his or her outlook on conduct. But it is the prevailing doctrine in the majority of so-called developed countries today.

Put at its simplest, the doctrine that "everything is purely relative" means that there are no absolutes where right or wrong are concerned. All morality is conditioned and conditional. What is right for you might be wrong for me. It all depends on our own preferences, background, situation, or what have you.

As societies become ever more pluralistic, and as the traditional influence of established religions continues to decline, relativism means that there is a decreasing ability to find a moral consensus on anything. Private conduct, as long as no law is broken, becomes totally "a law unto itself." This outlook is encapsulated in such expressions as "whatever turns your crank," "whatever gets you through the night," or "if it feels good, do it."

One of the prime casualties of such a belief, of course, is the younger generation. It is well-nigh impossible to inculcate a meaningful value system in children when the unspoken but underlying assumption is that all moralities are equally provisional

and equally good. This might be frightfully democratic and en-
lightened, but surely youth can be forgiven for being confused!

Faced with this tide of moral relativism, the temptation for
authoritarian institutions and for fundamentalist individuals of
every camp is to trot out the old, long lists of moral absolutes and
shout that until all of them are observed once more the world will
continue to go to hell in the proverbial handcart.

This is a singularly unhelpful tack to take. We have long passed
the stage where the majority of people are prepared to make
choices solely on the basis of the "thou shalts" and "thou shalt
nots" of a particular book, a particular ecclesiastical person, or a
particular creed. We don't want to act on the dictates of some
external, moral authority, in blind obedience. We want to act out
of our own deepest convictions. If there are moral absolutes, we
want to be persuaded, not forced to accept their existence.

What's more, we know instinctively that some of these "absolutes" are more absolute than others. Lying (false witness) is
absolutely forbidden by the Ninth Commandment. But, for
example, Christians and others lied to the Nazis while hiding Jews
during World War II. Most of us would agree that, while such lying
was not a good thing in itself, it was, as the far lesser of two evils,
the right thing to do.

Similarly, the Eighth Commandment quite categorically for-
bids stealing. Nevertheless, faced with the prospect of either
seeing one's child die of hunger or stealing a loaf of bread, who
would not agree that such stealing, while not a good, is nonethe-
less right?

Both Jewish and Christian morality teach that, when all is said
and done, there are really only two moral absolutes: love of God
and love of neighbour as oneself.

St. Augustine's pithy condensation of it all was, "Love God
and do what you will [to do]." In the so-called Golden Rule, "Do
unto others what you would have them do unto you," the duty to
neighbour is summed up.

This, of course, was not original with Jesus. The version given
by Confucius (551-479 B.C.) puts it in the negative form: "What

you do not want done to yourself, do not do to others." In some
ways this is preferable. The saying, "Do not do unto others what
you want them to do unto you; their tastes may not be the same"
also has a lot of merit in it!

The nub of the matter, however, is the avoidance of causing
pain to others by word or deed. Such a "law" is written in the
human heart and conscience, no matter how deeply covered over
by selfish impulse.

This is why adultery is wrong, why slander and racism are
wrong. They are a denial of genuine love. Everything is not "purely
relative" after all.

— Good Without God? —

Late in 1979, shortly after Mother Teresa received the Nobel
Peace Prize, I had the privilege, together with a photographer, of
spending time with her at the mother house of her Missionaries of
Charity in Calcutta. We visited the orphanage with her, watched
the feeding of hundreds of hungry street people, and then went
with some of her workers to the hospice she runs for the destitute
and dying.

I have written elsewhere about Nirmal Hriday, the hospice set
in a wing of the temple of Kalighat, as indeed have others, most
notably Malcolm Muggeridge. What I want to recall here, though,
is the deep impression made upon me at the time of my visit by two
young Canadians who were helping care for the desperately poor,
diseased folk who were lying there waiting to die.

They were not only donating their time; they were paying their
own living expenses as well. Where most people would have
wanted the publicity of having their names and photos published
(since they were obviously "doing good"), this pair preferred to
remain anonymous. Asked for their religious affiliation, they said
they were atheists. They did not share Mother Teresa's faith, but
they counted it an honour to be part of her service to humanity.

This encounter moved me because there's a curious notion

floating in many religious circles that secular humanists, agnostics, and atheists are incapable of being "good." According to this view, true ethical and moral values are the sole property of those who believe in God. Thus, the argument runs, when you remove religious instruction from the classrooms of the nation, for example, you are inevitably leaving the children either with no ethical principles at all or, worse, with false principles espoused only by the enemies of faith.

The problem with this kind of thinking is that – to quote from the old musical *Porgy and Bess* – "it ain't necessarily so." In fact, there is a major, harmful error at work here. No denomination, church, sect, "ism," or set of beliefs has a corner on ethical behaviour, on choosing and doing the right over the wrong. Those who fanatically cling to the dogma that their particular tradition or religion has a monopoly on goodness are self-deceived.

It would not be so bad if those so deceived were the only ones to suffer the consequences. Tragically, however, the ramifications are global. There can never be global solutions to our urgent problems until there is an ongoing and serious dialogue between believers and non-believers of every variety. We urgently need a global ethic, one to which every citizen of Earth can give assent and allegiance.

One of the biggest stumbling blocks to the elaboration and declaration of this universal ethic is the arrogant exclusivity of those who refuse even to think about such a dialogue on the grounds that they alone already know and practise all that can be discovered about ethical truth. They believe God has told them to stand apart and avoid all fellowship with "sinners."

Since the dominant culture here is (nominally) Christian, it makes sense to inquire whether or not this kind of ethical isolationism or self-righteousness has the blessing of the founder of the faith. My conviction, after study and reflection, is that it profoundly does not.

The Gospel teaching is full of paradoxes. Those who think they are first will be last. Sinners and publicans "go into the Kingdom of Heaven" ahead of those who are convinced they have cornered the market on righteousness. It is not those who have gone around saying "Lord, Lord" who are promised the Kingdom but those who have done "the will of the Father."

In the famous Last Judgement parable in Matthew, chapter 25, the righteous are extremely surprised that the criteria for receiving eternal blessing are not a matter of right beliefs, extensive prayers, or the fulfilment of rituals. Instead, the question is whether or not the sick and the prisoners were visited, the hungry fed, the naked clothed, and the homeless given shelter.

When, on one occasion, the disciples became very upset because someone who was not a follower of Christ was doing good works, their master rebuked them sharply. The rebuke is followed by a verse that I have yet to hear used as a sermon text by any preacher: "He that is not against us is on our side."

I do not conclude from any of this that belief in God is not a matter of enormous importance. The point being made is that today, as never before, humanity needs to find and take its stand on as large a piece of common ground as possible if it is to have any hope at all of meeting the vast problems facing the species. We can't solve global crises, from poverty and hunger to almost total environmental degradation, without enlisting the help of all men and women of goodwill, regardless of their creed or lack of one.

Recognizing that others don't have to share your faith to be truly concerned about restoring health to the Earth and justice and peace to the nations is a freeing experience. It's also the only way we're ever going to make a pluralistic future work.

— Heart and Mind —

Suppose you were a minister, priest, or rabbi and a person came to you for counselling. Say they were depressed, in grief, or had a marital problem. There are two approaches you could take.

You could be very cerebral and detached, analysing their situation, flipping through your mental computer for the correct label to apply to their dilemma, and finally sending them off with some books to read or a referral to a psychiatrist. Or, you could take a much more intuitive, emotional approach, becoming so involved in their difficulties and feelings that by the end of the session the two of you might be in tears together in an orgy of shared self-pity.

Obviously, neither tactic would be of much help to the man or woman in need. What is called for in most instances is a method that holds a balance between mind and heart. Some detachment is essential if you are to be able to see the person's problem objectively; some empathy and feeling is necessary too, however, if you are to enter into their suffering sufficiently to communicate a true sense of caring and of renewed hope.

It is popular today to speak of a left-brain or right-brain approach. I prefer, however, to use the terms from Greek mythology taught by my Philosophy of Religion professor when I was in the seminary. He liked to speak of the Apollonian and the Dionysian response to any given reality.

The Apollonian approach takes its name from the Greek god Apollo, the god of learning, emotional distance, order, and control. This is the way of logic, analysis, objectivity, and linear thinking. It is rational, cool, and uninvolved. It is marked by remoteness rather than immediacy.

By contrast, the Dionysian approach, so called after the Greek god Dionysus, the god of wine and of the dance, is the way of intuition, emotion, spontaneity, warmth, and of the body rather than of the mind. It is marked by the instinctual rather than the intellectual, by feeling rather than thought. Its keynote is subjectivity.

While all of us share in both, it is possible to see some people as clearly much more Dionysian than Apollonian, and vice versa. Zorba the Greek was Dionysian; the young man he called "Boss" was the opposite.

These categories can be of help in making sense of much around us that otherwise seems unconnected. Applied to music, for example, Bach is obviously Apollonian while Tchaikovsky is Dionysian. This is not to say that there is no intuitive warmth or "heart" in Bach, nor any mental activity in Tchaikovsky, but the predominant characteristic of each, in these terms, is as I have said. Taking classical music as a whole, however, and contrasting it with country or rock music, it is clear that you would lump Tchaikovsky with Bach in your Apollonian list while the others would be labelled Dionysian.

When applied to religion, this kind of analysis can be illuminating. The Anglican Church, to which I belong, is on the Apollonian side of the scale – often too much so. The criticism that Anglicans are "God's frozen people" is not without some basis in fact.

Anglican worship is stately and orderly. It holds reason and intellect in high esteem. But if you watch an average congregation of Anglicans singing the regular canticle "O be joyful in the Lord" some Sunday morning, you could be forgiven for supposing that somebody important had just died! Members who can be very Dionysian at a party or when watching an NHL hockey game on TV suddenly become extremely Apollonian when their knees hit a pew-kneeler.

Fundamentalists, particularly Pentecostals, on the other hand, veer strongly towards the Dionysian. Their emphasis on emotion and religious experience gives an enviable warmth and enthusiasm to their life and worship. However, the failure to pay as much heed to Jesus' words about loving God with "all your mind" as they do to other Bible verses has exacted a high price. The intellectual or Apollonian underpinning is weak. Thus, for example, you have a situation in which many of them are arguing for a "young Earth" – created some ten thousand years ago – when the entire body of science refutes this motion as ridiculous.

All religions today face an enormous challenge: how to communicate a living faith that makes sense intellectually in the modern world while at the same time heeding the growing thirst of untold millions for an authentic, inner experience of God.

The only ultimately satisfying spiritual commitment is one that flows from a balanced blending of both the Dionysian and the Apollonian approach. That's why the great commandment is to love God with all our *heart* and with all our *mind* and with all our *strength* – and our neighbour as ourselves.

— The Power of Prayer, I —

There is a passage in Mark Twain's *The Adventures of Tom Sawyer* in which Tom and Huckleberry Finn have a discussion about prayer. The boys conclude that there can't be too much in it, despite what they've been taught and what the preacher says. Otherwise, how can they explain the fact that they never get the new fishing rods and hooks or any of the other things they pray for so ardently? And how is it that the teacher, skinny Miss Watson, doesn't "fat up"?

It's amazing how many people never get past this childish view of prayer as some kind of blank cheque issued by God to those who toady up sufficiently. Often those who consider themselves quite sophisticated in most areas of life hold a view of prayer that boils down to the belief that if one can succeed in twisting God's "arm" correctly the desired results should be assured. But this is by definition magic and not prayer. Magic consists of saying the right formula or doing the proper rituals in the belief that whatever powers there be are *compelled* to respond positively.

I believe that the often-quoted words of Tennyson, "More things are wrought by prayer than this world dreams of," happen to be true. But I am also convinced that there is no other aspect of the spiritual life that is more misunderstood. At its heart, prayer is not about asking for anything. It's about making contact with the Source and very Ground of our Being; it's a matter of holding oneself still in the presence of that light that is beyond light and that energy that is beyond energy. As the ancient wisdom puts it: "Be still, and know that I am God."

I have heard preachers say that the fact that human beings are "praying animals" is one of the marks distinguishing us from other creatures. They imply that our need to pray elevates us above the other species. The truth is the reverse of this. Animals live in the constant awareness that they are part of the cosmic flow, that they are "in God." That's one of the reasons they are so healing just to have around. They just are. They relax us because they are so at home with themselves, so at home in the universe, so completely themselves.

Paul, in a moving speech recorded in Acts, once reminded the Athenians that we are all "God's offspring," that in Him we "live and move and have our being." The problem is that, unlike the rest of creation, we forget or ignore this in the midst of all our distractions. The true function of prayer is to re-establish this vital linkage. So, rather than thinking of prayer as a kind of endless whining and pleading, coming to God with an endless shopping list of wants, we can see it as taking time to let the assurance of the Presence flood over us once more.

There is no essential need for a special place, special words, or holding the right images in our minds. Instead, prayer is a relaxed letting-go of everything and of claiming what has been already given. Some mystics in all faiths pray a short prayer before simply waiting in silence. It goes something like this: "God, I put myself in your presence. I pray to you not as I think or imagine you to be, but as you know yourself to be." You can think of it as a little like fine-tuning a TV or radio. We know the signal is there. It's a matter of getting the frequency for proper reception. Yet even that metaphor is not quite apt, since it lays too much emphasis upon getting something right. Rather, prayer is a bit more like sitting on a beach and letting the warm surf roll over you.

This is not to say one should never pray in the sense of asking – either for oneself or for others. But we have to be careful. You can't blame sceptics for wondering about the morality of a deity who would play favourites by doling out his bounty to a select few. Jesus rejected that nonsense when he noted that God sends the rain upon both the just and the unjust equally.

I believe prayer operates more scientifically than that. In other words, I'm convinced that power is generated when one is in contact with the Source of All Power, just as surely as an appliance comes to life when it's plugged in. To pray for oneself or others is to release spiritual energy. Just because science can't measure it doesn't mean it isn't there. It doesn't guarantee success, wealth, or anything like that, but it does supply the courage and grace to be and to become what we are meant for.

It's presumptuous to pray for certain things for other people. Their own needs and wishes, not to mention God's will for them, might be quite different from what we arrogantly suppose! Far better simply to "hold" them in the light and ask that they be able to receive all that God wants to give them. That is the kind of prayer that flows from love. And, as Coleridge once said: "He prayeth best who loveth best...."

— The Power of Prayer, II —

A colleague of mine used to reply to the usual, banal question "How's it going?" or "How are you today?" in a manner all his own. With a twinkle in his eye, he'd say: "Ah well, I cannot but complain."

Since nobody likes a complainer – and when you say hello you're not necessarily looking for a speech or a long-term relationship anyway – the startled greeters would usually slip away mumbling to themselves. My friend could get on with his writing.

Complaints, however, are not always something negative. For example, child-rearing experts tell us that it's a good sign when an adopted child begins to complain. It shows he or she now feels sufficiently accepted and at home to take a risk. They no longer feel compelled to please at any cost.

It might come as a surprise to many that complaining has a vital role to play in one's inner, spiritual odyssey. To miss the truth of this is to stunt one's growth and to lend an air of unreality and hollowness to the quest for deeper knowledge and experience of God.

In counselling, during my seventeen years as a professional cleric, I realized that the last thing people expected to be told was that they needed to give themselves permission to be angry at God. But often this is the very thing that the person who has suddenly lost someone, or who is facing illness, marriage breakup, or other severe difficulties and tensions, needs to do most.

When, for whatever reason – be it depression, anxiety, loss of direction, or the temptation to quit your post in life – you feel "God-forsaken" and that the "heavens are as brass" when you pray, your greatest need might be to complain. Loud and long. Perhaps for the first time in your life, your most honest feelings about the ultimate reality we call God need to be spilled forth.

It isn't easy. Years of pious traditions and attitudes have left us feeling that to be angry with God is to invite being struck down from above. Christianity hasn't done a good job of helping people deal with anger in general. But when it comes to anger at the Ground of All Being, it's been of no help at all.

Yet this needn't have been so. In fact, there are ample grounds for this kind of radical honesty, both in Scripture and in the lives of the heroes of faith.

What has always appealed to me about the collection of poems on the spiritual life that we call the Psalms is the way the various authors aren't afraid to speak out. They had such a robust confidence and sense of acceptance that they could tell God exactly how they felt on any topic – about Him/Her, about life, about others, about injustice. Compared with their tumultuous outpourings, most of our prayers seem anaemic, utterly superficial.

If they think God has given them a raw deal, they say so in no uncertain terms. If God seems to be "hiding His face" from them, they complain bitterly. When they are depressed, they therapeutically list all their symptoms – the aches and pains, the sleeplessness, the inability to eat or to face other people, the diarrhoea, the sense that it has always been like this and it always will be, the overwhelming sense of dread and hopelessness.

It is no accident that one of these Psalms, 22, a detailed description of the symptoms of depression, is the one Christ is said to have recited to himself as he hung upon the cross. It begins, "My God, my God, why hast thou forsaken me? Why art thou so far from helping me, and from the words of my roaring?"

This haunting cry, recorded only by Mark and Matthew and left out by Luke and John for pious reasons, is an intense complaint. But the fact that it is uttered in the face of an abyss of suffering, weakness, and apparent defeat is also a ground for hope. It is precisely because of Jesus' total trust in a God of infinite compassion that he struggles to express his sense of betrayal. It is because he has known a heavenly "Father" that his dark night of God-forsakenness wrings forth such a protest.

The Psalm he was repeating does not end in despair. It closes with a statement of faith that "the kingdom is the Lord's," meaning that even in the pit of the worst horror we humans can face, God is still present and in control.

God does not want or need endlessly repeated human flatteries and praises. God does, however, look for a little truth sometimes in our walk with Him. It really is quite safe to express your anger. He's big enough to take it, and to love you just the same.

⟞ The Power of Prayer, III ⟝

The response to my columns on prayer was remarkable. What this says is that there is much more interest in spiritual matters among readers than many experts suppose.

On the surface, the media are about news, commentary, and entertainment. But probing more deeply reveals that behind almost every "story" – whether of tragedy, achievement, crime, or punishment – an enormous amount of praying has gone on.

While I'm convinced that the urge to pray is so much a part of us as to be justly called an instinct, the truth remains that this is a crucial area of our inner life about which we need to keep learning more. A fledgling might have an instinct to fly, but it needs to be encouraged and shown how.

Experience plus reflection have made me aware of three major, erroneous assumptions about praying that hinder a good many people from making real progress.

• *The I-talk-you-listen syndrome:* We all have acquaintances or relatives who, in the words of a familiar hymn, are "friends who give us pain." These are the non-stop talkers who give mental assent to the idea that conversation is a two-way street but ignore it completely when it comes to the crunch of face-to-face encounters.

The majority of prayers are like that – even, or one might say especially, in church. God gets a real earful at 11 a.m. Sunday mornings, but the thought of allowing some silence for God to speak scares most preachers half to death. If you want to get much more out of prayer than you ever have before, spend most, if not all, of your private praying time in a relaxed silence. Listen to the voice of God within. It is in the inner stillness – walking, sitting on the subway, driving the car, by a quiet lake – that we learn to hear God's side of the dialogue.

• *The emergency or crisis-only syndrome*. One of the things we value most about friendships is that people are there for us in moments of sudden need. We're rightly suspicious, however, of those who only seem to discover our existence when calamity of some kind strikes them or hangs like the sword of Damocles over their heads.

The headline given to my first piece on prayer when it was originally published (columnists don't write their own headlines) read: "Human instinct to pray takes over in times of crisis." That's true, but if that's the only kind of prayer you know, you're really a "user" type of person. We might like to be able to do it, but ultimately any attempt to reduce the God of the universe to the stature of an automatic emergency button we push in times of panic is an insult. On the other hand, if praying is something you learn to do both in good times and in bad, then you're on your way to developing the friendship with God that prayer is all about.

• *The I-have-to-use-polite-or-pious-language syndrome*. During the seventeen years I spent as a priest under obedience to a bishop, I became aware that many people think of praying as "something only nice people do and only in nice language." This is manifestly untrue, and nothing cripples praying like waiting until we are "good enough" or can find the correct churchy phrases to use.

The Psalms have always been the classic school of prayer for both Judaism and Christianity. There's something in them for every human situation – for times of grief, of anger, of depression and despair, of deep anxiety or of great rejoicing. But what always impresses me is their utter integrity. If the Psalmist is fed up or frustrated by the way he/she feels God is treating him/her, there isn't the slightest hesitation in blurting it out.

This might be a good time to read the Psalms all over again. The verve, the nerve, and the freedom of these conversations with the Ground of all Being will startle or perhaps even shock you if you haven't read them before, or have read them simply in that mind-numbing way we all experienced when we were young. These are prayers that wrench up the deepest feelings of the soul and hurl them out for God to deal with. Such direct prayer from the depths is the most valid prayer of all.

— God and Science —

There's bad news for atheists these days, from – of all places – the world of science.

It's not just that the further science pushes back the barrier of our ignorance about the universe the more the mysteries multiply – though this fact in itself must not be glossed over. Old, mechanistic theories that left room only for energy and matter – leading to a purely materialistic view of reality and making all morality a mere code of convenience – have had to be given up. We have come to realize that the naive pictures of the universe that prevailed in the 1930s – simply structured atoms in motion – have vanished before a scenario that is incredibly more complex.

As scientist-philosopher Shimon Bakon has said: "It is increasingly understood that the picture we have of what is going on … is merely *a mathematical construct* of relationships obtaining between the various building blocks and energies. We know they exist without grasping their true nature" (italics added).

He goes on to point out that new theories of the Big Bang (15 billion years ago) and the expanding universe that followed have put the old assumptions about limitless space and limitless time into question. If we have a rapidly yet symmetrically expanding universe, we have to think of a point in time when it all began. What happened then is far beyond scientific understanding. New discoveries of quasars, black holes and other "singularities" have only increased the mystery, Bakon adds.

The result of the loss of former "certainties" has led to increasing modesty on the part of scientists, on the one hand, and to a sense of wonder that spills over into faith, on the other.

What intrigues me is the way the "super-scientists" today are talking about a "mind" or God in and behind the cosmos. Intriguing, too, is the way they are using language that borders on the mystical to discuss ultimate reality. In fact, reading modern physicists today, one might be astonished at their new-found interest in eastern and western forms of mysticism, and at their willingness to speculate about metaphysics (that which lies beyond the physical). This was once considered to be territory reserved for theologians alone – and therefore highly suspect!

A story currently going the rounds makes the point in a powerful way. Picture the scientists and physicists climbing an awesome mountain peak in their quest for the summit: a final insight into the mysteries of the universe. At last they reach the top, only to find a group of mystics and theologians having tea and saying, "So, here you are at last. We thought you'd never make it!"

The freshest account of the extraordinary phenomenon of how science is "finding God" is the cover story of the April 1988 issue of *The Atlantic*. Over a colour photo of a butterfly runs the caption: "Did the Universe Just Happen?" The subhead reads: "Controversial scientist Edward Fredkin says no – the universe is a computer and was built for a purpose."

The lengthy, at times difficult article deals with the thinking of one of the most remarkable, seminal thinkers of our time. Fredkin, a self-made millionaire among other things, works at what the jargon now calls "the interface of science and computer wizardry."

Simplified to the limit, Fredkin's theory is that, while matter and energy are basic components of the universe, there is one more factor that is even more pervasive and primary – information. Just as every cell of our body is programmed according to the information coded in the DNA, so every particle in the universe has its built-in code – the law of its being and energy. He makes the daring assertion that the universe is like – in fact *is* – a vast computer processing this almost infinite mass of information. What's more, he posits the theory that this cosmic computer is in actuality working out some cosmic problem.

Obviously, this raises the question: Who or what set this computer in motion? Where is it, in some fifth or sixth dimension within the universe or in some meta-universe beyond?

Fredkin holds it is in the latter realm. In other words, he looks beyond the world of the senses to the world of metaphysics, or God. In fact, as the author of the article, Robert Wright, suggests, "The best physics, Fredkin seems to believe, is metaphysics."

One of the striking things about this theory, it seems to me, is the way it tackles the old conundrum of *creatio ex nihilo* – creation of matter and energy out of nothing. If information is the primary substratum of our world, the problem is ingeniously solved. Matter may be made up of information, but what is information made of?

My answer, and if I understand him rightly, Fredkin's answer, would be: "It flows from the Mind of God."

— The Evolution of a Belief —

Science arose out of the human sense of curiosity. Religion, which was much earlier on the scene, began with our sense of wonder. As primitive human beings experienced the world, there were phenomena that caused awe and wonder on every side – the fury of the storm, the ferocity of a volcano, the miracle of a bubbling spring, the mysteries of death.

The earliest stage of religion the world over is expressed in what is called "animism." In essence, this was the belief that every object that had energy or activity enough to affect humans in any way was animated by a life and will of its own. The tree moving and rustling in the wind, the leaping waterfall, the mountains, even stones of unusual shape or position – all were held to be the abode of supernatural spirits.

That animism was the common religion underlying the background of the people of the Old Testament is witnessed to a hundred ways in the Bible. There are all kinds of references to sacred springs and wells, holy mountains and groves. There were, of course, evil spirits or demons as well as good ones. It paid to know which you were dealing with.

The next stage we find is that of polytheism, or many gods and goddesses. At this point the spirits become personified – supernatural beings thought of as being in human form and tied to specific places or regions. These deities could be harmful or friendly, but they had no ethical attributes such as a love of justice or mercy. Small wonder the intellectuals of classical antiquity were so scathing in their criticisms of the wild escapades of the divinities on Mount Olympus!

It was the world-shaking achievement of Moses, as a result of his encounter with God, to bring us the understanding of monotheism – one God over all, a God of righteousness and grace. What we have in the rest of the Hebrew Bible is the unfolding of the full nature and implications of Moses' discovery. Through the history, and especially through the prophets, of the Jews comes an emerging picture of God as Lord of the entire cosmos. A God of justice and of love, not just for Israel or for a particular age, but for all nations for all time.

Unlike the image presented by the Greek philosophers, the Bible's picture of God is intensely personal. Whereas the philosophers thought of God as "the unmoved mover" or the abstract, first principle of being, the Hebrew-Christian vision is one of a God who seeks out every one of us in loving encounter. He/She is not only Creator of the universe but the very Ground and Source of our own personhood: "In Him we live, and move, and have our being."

Such a faith, however, poses an acute problem, one that the unbeliever doesn't have to face: If there truly is a loving, almighty, spiritual Being behind and through the cosmos, why is there so much suffering and pain? Above all, why do the innocent so often suffer while the wicked seem to flourish?

What has always appealed most to me about the Bible is that it meets this awesome dilemma head on. Indeed, much of the Bible will make no sense at all unless you realize how deeply this intellectual and emotional puzzle tears at the hearts and minds of its authors. It lies behind the often angry cries of the Psalmist. It is the central theme of Job. It is at the heart of Isaiah. It explains the (to us) more bizarre passages and books dealing with the so-called "last days." In these, the attempt to justify God's ways towards us results in a lurid picture of a final reckoning, when all wrongs will be righted and the wicked will be punished forever.

No easy answers are given. To tackle a problem head-on does not automatically produce a neat or satisfactory solution. Even when the Bible closes, with the promise that all things will be made new, the difficulty remains.

But we are not left without important clues. The kind of God revealed to Moses, the prophets, and through Jesus can be trusted, even in and beyond the valley of the shadow of death.

— The Problem of Evil, I —

Recently I received a note. It read: "News item from Grimshaw, Alberta; the body of a 3-year old boy who was lost in the bush was found yesterday. Christopher Cochrane had wandered away from his parents on Sunday at Lac Cardinal Provincial Park, just west of Peace River." To this the writer had appended: "God sees the little sparrow fall.... But he does nothing about it! Some love; some God!"

I have other readers who, unlike this man, never sign their name but regularly send me similar items cut from newspapers and accompanied by sarcastic remarks about the kind of God who would "let" such things happen. Though I see anonymous letters as evidence of cowardice, I recognize the legitimacy of the question posed.

The atheist or the agnostic can get off scot-free on this one. If you deny there is a God or say you can't be sure, there's no necessity to explain evil and pain. If the cosmos (contrary to what the root of this word implies) has no Shaper or Creator, if everything from a Mozart piano concerto to a baby's toes is the result of a primitive, random collision of molecules, then it makes no sense to yelp "Why?" when the innocent suffer.

For the believer, however, the difficulty is acute. How can we read the grotesque litany of wrongs and disasters in our newspapers and still say we believe in a loving "heavenly Parent"? How can we watch unexpected ills strike down "the dearest and the best," or hear grim medical news ourselves, and still trust?

In the tight space of a column it is nearly impossible to attempt an answer. But the nettle must be grasped. First, though, let me say how surprised I am that some of these letters assume that this is a conundrum I have never thought about before. The writers have so little knowledge of religious thought or of my own writing that they actually think they're the first to have spotted and raised such an issue.

The question of "theodicy," as it is technically known – how to justify God's ways towards humanity – is at least as old as the Book of Job. This question has been in the forefront of my own spiritual quest ever since I was old enough to reflect for myself on the implications of faith.

You can't be close to people in trouble the way I was as a minister, or see as much of the Third World as I have since I became a journalist, and pretend there is no problem. Indeed, the one thing that puts unbelievers (rightly) off faith in God more than anything else is the preacher or lay believer who treats this question lightly or shrugs it off with some pious banality: "Ours is not to reason why ..."

On the other hand, I am equally disturbed by anyone professing to have the complete, magic answer. You can't start throwing Bible texts or religion at someone caught in the toils of a blatant evil. Even after all our wrestling, some element of the "mystery of evil" remains.

But several things are clear:

• It makes no sense to blame God for evils resulting from our own actions or those of others. *Yet this goes on all the time.* Freedom is one of our greatest treasures, but you can't be a free or moral being unless you can choose. And choices mean being responsible for consequences.

If we deplete the ozone layer and skin cancer kills innocent youngsters, it's ludicrous to blame God. If the slopes of the Himalayas are denuded of trees for firewood and then floods destroy thousands on the plains, this is hardly the fault of the Deity. The same is true when nations spend millions on guns while children are left to starve or rot with disease.

The New Testament word for sin means "to miss the target." As long as our choices miss the mark, as long as we make mistakes, suffering will result.

• But this does not mean that God "sends" tragedy as a punishment, despite what some religious leaders teach or have taught. Disease, accidents, or death are not divine retribution. That certainly would contradict God's compassion. Nor are they "sent" for our moral improvement. Yes, how we cope with them might well lead us to new insight, maturity, or creativity – Beethoven with his deafness – but it is folly and cruelty to tell sufferers, "It's God's plan."

• If this is not to be an utterly chaotic, *ad hoc* kind of world, we know that basic natural laws must prevail. Gravity is a blessing; it can also kill. The energy latent in a hydrogen bomb is the same energy that fires the sun and stars. The car we use for travel can kill a child.

But great evils still lie unexplained: the pain of animals in a natural order "red in tooth and claw," catastrophic earthquakes, the scourge of pestilence, drought and famine; and why do the evil often seem to prosper while the good get pushed to the wall?

— The Problem of Evil, II —

No thinking person can reflect upon the suffering in the world without wondering how a loving Creator could permit or condone it.

For some, the difficulty is so acute they find belief in a loving God impossible. Many, because they are too bright to believe this mysterious and incredibly beautiful universe happened just by chance, opt for a rather curious dodge. They push the God of Judaism, Christianity, or Islam rudely out the front door and hurry around to the back door to sneak in a cold, sterile deity whom they call "The Force" (courtesy of the film *Star Wars*), "The Prime Mover," "The Ultimate Intelligence," or what have you. There is an intellectual dishonesty involved in this solution, and I reject it out of hand.

The real problem of theodicy is to hold to both sides of the dilemma: the divine compassion and the reality of suffering.

I have a very eloquent friend who professes to be an agnostic precisely because of pain and evil. He is particularly articulate about the problem of animal suffering and the way all nature seems to be "red in tooth and claw." How, he asks, can a loving God have made the world this way?

He raises a serious point. Unless you see nature only through the sanitized lens of a Walt Disney camera, you know that a great cry of agony goes up from the animal kingdom night and day. It seems to be a case of eat or be eaten. The feet of a helpless frog sticking from the jaws of the swollen snake make a point we could establish in a host of different ways.

However, in his justifiable concern, my friend always exaggerates and overstates his case. A more balanced view would take into account the following:

• It is erroneous to suppose that all creatures are in a relationship of predator and prey. Thousands of species live in a mutually helpful, symbiotic way. Some of the largest, most majestic of animals live wholly at peace with the rest.

• The most horrific, needless pain to animals and birds is caused by us. If the animal rights activists have done nothing else, they have helped raise our consciousness here. We can't blame God for the invidious notion that we are the centre of the universe and the rest of creation is ours to torture and exploit at will.

• Physical pain is an essential survival mechanism for all sentient beings and is the price we pay for being alive. A miraculous nervous system, without which pleasure or awareness of living would be impossible for any creature, brings with it the corollary of an ability to discern and avoid what is unpleasant or harmful. This renders us all liable to suffering.

• Without the checks and balances of predators, certain species would quickly overrun the planet and eventually bring about total desolation. (Humans are now threatening to do precisely this.)

• It is unfair to go on about animal suffering without acknowledging the wonder of watching the soaring of the great birds of prey or the stealthy grandeur of the tiger "burning bright in the forests of the night." In fact (to echo the words of poet William Blake), it is the very awe one feels in seeing the agility, design, and grace of the beasts of prey that constitutes part of our intuition that, in the raw presence of nature, we are close to a wise and loving Presence we call God.

In the end, of course, some mystery remains. That's why the great prophets and mystics have always used imagery of a world or a dimension to come when there will be a "new creation." The lion "will eat straw like the ox" or lie down with the lamb, and all killing will end.

In the final resort, whenever I ponder the overall question of pain and evil, I am struck forcibly by the fact that the greatest spiritual geniuses have looked directly into the face of this reality as they have affirmed their commitment to a loving God. None of them, from Moses to Jesus Christ, from Muhammad to the founder of the Baha'is, has lived aloof from or ignorant of this brute fact.

I find it odd indeed when agnostics tell me they think Jesus was the most important ethical teacher the world has ever known and then completely pass over in silence the fact that he believed wholly in a loving God *in spite of* his own experience of injustice and pain. You can't honestly say you respect someone as the wisest and best human being ever to have lived and then turn around and deny the most fundamental tenet of that person's teaching and outlook! If Jesus and the others were wrong about God, they were wrong about everything important.

Finally, however, it doesn't matter so much what we *think* about the problem of pain and suffering. It's what we're *doing* about it that counts.

The Problem of Evil, III

A reader once wrote to say: "I never miss your column but I can't believe that a person who is intelligent … can actually believe there is a loving God. Nine weeks ago my adored, darling daughter died very suddenly leaving two small children. She was the light of my life. I now have nothing to live for. I'm a senior citizen in poor health and a widow.... She was only 36 years old. It's no use telling me others have gone through similar griefs since their pain can't possibly ease mine. I hurt so badly I couldn't describe it. She was always such a good girl and so kind to all who knew her. Why would God (who doesn't exist) do this? I was born Jewish. I no longer have any religion and if there is some God or whatever I hate him."

Anyone, believer or not, who hears this woman's pain and can't identify with her bewilderment and her anger against "God or whatever" lacks all feeling. Her cry epitomizes the problem of reconciling belief in a loving God with this "vale of tears."

It's foolish to blame God for human error or malice. We can debate whether or not God should have given us free will, but, once given, such freedom means the power to choose evil. Even so monstrous an evil as the Holocaust of six million Jews and others by the Nazis sprang from human decisions.

It can be argued, indeed, that the so-called "silence" of God during the Holocaust or other human horrors indicates the total seriousness with which the Creator views this gift of freedom. It is so important that God has limited His or Her own power to act because of it. Our freedom means that God is no longer absolutely omnipotent. Furthermore, once you have an ordered world, God can't be always intervening capriciously to flout His or Her own laws. Once the trigger has been pulled, not even God can stop the bullet speeding towards the innocent.

But, in the case of this young mother who died, none of this really applies. She is needed by her children, her husband, and her widowed mother, yet she dies. Meanwhile, others, who are perhaps wicked, or who have no responsibilities and have wanted to die for a long time, continue to flourish. According to Billy Graham (followed by many others), while we can't fully understand why God permits evil, it must be stressed that it is humanity and not God that bears the guilt for it. Adam's original disobedience is the reason the world is not the way it was originally meant to be. Death, like everything else that is bad, is ultimately "our fault."

Frankly, this won't do, however convenient it might seem. It makes no sense to me, and I'm very sure it would make no sense to this widow. It uses biblical mythology inappropriately, mistaking important imagery for historical facts. In his book *The Problem of Pain*, C. S. Lewis argued that "pain plants the flag of truth in the fortress of a rebel heart"; that is, God sends or allows suffering to teach us a lesson or convert us. Many Christians follow this line, but again it raises far more difficulties than it solves. God becomes a sadistic monster. The divine end, we are being told, justifies the means. We expect humans to be more moral than that! It clearly is immoral to do or cause an evil in order that good may come.

The same critique applies to those who try the "pain is God's punishment" tack. The Bible itself rejects this view in the Book of Job and in the sayings of Jesus about natural blessings and disasters coming alike upon the just and the unjust. Thus it is both unbiblical and horrifyingly unjust to go around preaching, for example, that AIDS is God's judgement upon homosexuals or others.

What about those who try to explain evil by saying it only seems to be bad from our very limited point of view, but that from an eternal point of view it either doesn't exist or is really good? This is playing word games. It satisfies neither the heart nor the intellect. To tell someone in the depths of their pain that their experience is illusory or really "a good thing" is an ultimate cruelty.

Traditionally, Christians have argued that in the cross of Jesus we see God entering into our suffering and drinking our cup of pain. God becomes a fellow sufferer, or, as Dorothy Sayers put it, "takes His own medicine." There is much comfort for many believers in this, but it doesn't explain why evil is there in the first place.

I agree with Rabbi Harold Kushner (author of *When Bad Things Happen to Good People*) that part of the answer lies in the fact that there is such a thing as chance or luck in the universe, and that perhaps there are "corners of chaos" still in this world waiting to be aligned into an ordered cosmos. There are some things over which God might not yet have full control. We need to rethink the orthodox concepts of God as almighty or omnipotent. Indeed, as I wrote in *Harpur's Heaven and Hell*, I believe the "process" theologians might be right. God too might be in process or evolving; God too might have a "night" or a "shadow" side of which He/She is struggling to be free. We are co-workers in this cosmic struggle as we work and pray for the coming of the Kingdom of God on earth.

Nevertheless, I am convinced that God knows and feels this woman's agony. God accepts her hate. God is with her as she extracts meaning from her loss and finds the courage to live again.

— Am I a Christian? —

Over the years I have had the interesting experience of being on a number of radio phone-in shows in distant cities such as Calgary and Edmonton while sitting in my study at home. Once, I debated with a succession of callers from the Okanagan Valley on a show called "Talk-Back," hosted by the owner of Radio CJIB in Vernon, B.C.

While most of the callers wanted to talk about their experiences of near-death or their reasons for either belief or disbelief in a future life, there were also the inevitable true believers who wanted to grill me on the matter of my Christian orthodoxy – or lack thereof.

One Vernon participant led off with the question, "Are you a Christian?" I have learned over the years that this seemingly limpid, ingenuous query usually cloaks a devious agenda. What is sought is not an assurance that the one being questioned belongs to a Christian Church, espouses the historic creeds, or is trying to be a follower of Jesus. What the questioner is really asking is whether or not you've had an experience (being "born again" or "saved") or are prepared to make certain affirmations ("I have accepted Christ as my Saviour," or some such similar formula).

In other words, they are demanding to know if you fit the definition of being a Christian that the particular group they belong to endorses and accepts. The question thus should actually be, "Are you the kind of Christian I am?" The inference clearly is that if you're not you're outside the pale of proper Christianity altogether.

This uncharitable and quite unbiblical attempt to make you jump through certain experiential or verbal hoops in order to establish your current religious status and eventual eternal destiny is to my mind one of the least attractive habits of those who are certain they alone have the truth.

Inasmuch as my work involves attempting to think in fresh ways about long-held values and venerable religious beliefs, it is inescapable that it is often controversial. As I said in the introduction, you can't walk an inch in the territory that most interests me without treading on somebody's sacred toes.

What I have noticed most in more than twenty years of covering and commenting on moral and religious issues in the media is that religious people seem to feel very uncomfortable with anyone who doesn't agree with them – until they can find the right label to apply. Once they have decided that x is a liberal or that y is a humanist, a secularist, an agnostic, or a lapsed-this-or-that, they tend to feel they can disregard the actual truth of anything x or y might say or write. It certainly saves a lot of time, as well as any need for reading or thought!

In trying to pin a label on this writer, the religious critics (mostly, but not all, from the right) have a rather difficult task. They feel shocked from time to time by the things I write, but they are bound to admit that, nevertheless, I am a believer. A man who mixes a lot with conservative Christians recently wrote a letter in which he said the most frequent criticism he has heard from them is that "Harpur thinks too much."

Their view of being a Christian, apparently, involves having a metaphorical frontal lobotomy and blindly accepting whatever this church or that book tells them. Surely, however, the ancient Jewish teaching, adopted by Jesus, of loving God with all your mind as well as with all your heart and soul and strength commands a prior obedience.

I really dislike religious labels. But since many are quite keen on them, and since they are having difficulty coming up with an adequate one for me themselves, I'd like to make a suggestion. I used (when compelled to) to describe myself as "an uncomfortable Christian," but a fuller, more accurate description today would be: "A radical-liberal-conservative-evangelical-Christian-humanist."

This needs an explanation. By "radical" I mean concerned with the roots (from the Latin *radix*) or fundamentals of any given spiritual or religious question. By "liberal" I refer to a commitment to openness and to the use of reason wherever appropriate and possible. By "conservative" I mean concerned to preserve and maintain the essential truths of the Judeo-Christian inheritance. By "evangelical" I mean the conviction that there is indeed Good News to be shared and made known. By "Christian" I mean committed to following the teachings of Christ. Finally, by using the word "humanist" I want to assert my belief that any true religion worthy of the name has as its highest aim the celebration and the enhancement of what it truly means to be a human being in God's world.

As St. Irenaeus put it: "The glory of God is man [humanity] fully alive."

Jesus reportedly put it even better: "I came that they [humanity] might have life, and that they might have it more abundantly."

— PART TWO —

GROWING SPIRITUALLY

⤙ The Miraculous Child ⤚

An old professor of mine, Dr. Ramsay Armitage, had some sage advice for young ministers faced with doting parents and their infants. It was suitable for baptisms or any other occasion when one was expected to comment on the surpassing charms of what, to the casual outsider, might seem like a very unremarkable – not to say nondescript – new arrival on the human scene.

Holding an imaginary baby in his arms, he would beam his warmest, most beatific smile and say, "My, that *is* a baby, that certainly *is* a baby!"

Beneath his humorous, gentle approach, Armitage held an awareness of a fundamental truth. The extraordinary conviction of most parents that their offspring is the nonpareil of any child ever born anywhere springs from deep, essentially religious stirrings.

All religions and myths from earliest times have stressed the theme of the miraculous child. It abounds in the classical Greek myths. It appears with Moses in the Old Testament and with John the Baptist and Jesus in the New Testament. The universal truth behind such myths is that our unconscious mind knows we have a divine origin, all of us. The myth of the miraculous child is a way of openly acknowledging that every newborn is potentially a saviour figure, a fresh beginning on behalf of the world.

That, admittedly, is a controversial position to take. What cannot, it seems to me, be denied is that every newborn is a potential spiritual genius. All the required gifts are there: a boundless sense of wonder, an incredible trust, an amazing simplicity and guilelessness, an open-mindedness linked with an enormous capacity for the sheer joy of life.

As Wordsworth puts it in his ode, "Intimations of Immortality From Recollections of Early Childhood":

> Not in entire forgetfulness,
> And not in utter nakedness,
> But trailing clouds of glory do we come
> From God, who is our home:
> Heaven lies about us in our infancy!
> Shades of the prison-house begin to close
> Upon the growing boy"

But, whereas if we had a child who showed early aptitude for some sport, for the dance, for art, or for music we would spare no expense and effort to see this talent developed, when it comes to spiritual gifts we ignore them and blithely allow the "prison-house" to eclipse them entirely.

Is it any wonder, then, that so many of today's youth, in spite of all that is showered upon them, feel hollow at the core, devoid of meaning, and frustrated by a culture that appears to hold out "bread" but is actually offering them "stones" instead? What are street gangs, substance abuse, or mindless sex other than expressions of attempts to fill a spiritual void? Not all young people are deceived by such things, of course, but even among those who have never been tempted by violence, drugs, or promiscuity there is a widespread sense of alienation and of angst: "What is the point of it all?"

This, to my mind, faces us with a crisis much greater than our apparently all-consuming fears over the constitutional future of the country.

Significantly, there are growing signs that parents and educators are aware of the problem and are becoming more and more concerned. The single topic of greatest interest to parents' or teachers' groups that invite me to speak these days is a variant on the theme, "How do we impart spiritual values to our children in the midst of a materialistic culture?"

Separate or independent religiously oriented schools are the answer for some; church school, or Sunday School as we used to call it, is the approach taken by others (a rapidly decreasing number, one must add); some parents are combining with others and experimenting with informal classes in their own homes. But, in spite of their worries, the majority are still doing little or nothing.

It's a little like the situation over the environment. Polls show this is the number-one concern of Canadians. But they show as well that we are not really prepared to endure any hardships or changes in our lifestyles to do anything serious about it.

Like it or not, anyone who truly cares about the spiritual and moral welfare of their children must be ready to pay the price. There is a radical challenge involved.

In a word, you simply cannot impart that which you haven't got yourself. You can't hope to see your youngsters acquire desirable ethical and spiritual values unless these are not only professed but lived out by you yourself in your own home. No hypocrisy is more transparent than the "don't do as I do but as I say" syndrome.

The initial responsibility, thus, is ours as adults. If we haven't got a meaningful worldview and a set of spiritual values that works for us, it's time we did.

— Fathers —

Many men today, if the immense popularity of books and seminars on the subject is any indication, are feeling some confusion over their masculinity. In part, men are reacting to the challenges felt to be presented by feminism. In part, there seems to be a nostalgia or longing for the ideal father, a wise, primitive embodiment of maleness – a cross between Tarzan and Merlin the magician.

Any weekend, across North America, groups of middle-class,

well-educated men can be found at woodsy retreat centres listening to lectures on how to recover the "hairy man" within, getting in touch with their inner grief and other emotions – frequently with open crying sessions – having their dreams explained, exchanging their life stories, or beating on jungle-style drums for soul-therapy.

One of the most constant themes at such workshops is that of the lack of authentic myths and rites of initiation into manhood for modern, western males. Another is the blame laid upon the collective fathers of the men who attend, and who are now, for the most part, fathers themselves.

Since, in my view, self-knowledge is a primary ethical imperative, I am loath to say anything that would rain on the parade of those committed to these various manifestations of a nascent "men's movement." Men are in many ways (apart from economics) just as much in need of true liberation as women.

Nevertheless, I have some misgivings. From my pastoral counselling as a minister, as well as elsewhere, I know how easy it is, and how damaging, for both men and women to get hung up on the alleged inadequacies of their parents. Certainly it is essential to try to understand one's childhood and the inner dynamics of the personalities and home life that were the matrix for one's early outlook and development. It's of great importance to see one's father and mother as clearly and as objectively as possible. This means recognizing and admitting their shortcomings and their mistakes.

But it's just as serious for one's mental health to remain mired in bitterness and blame over these faults as it is to lack the courage to face up to them honestly. The blunt truth is that, apart perhaps from Jesus Christ, not a single human in history has ever had perfect parenting. Our maturity takes a long step forward on the day we truly realize this, accept the fact that we alone are responsible now for who we are and what we are becoming, and determine henceforward to focus on what was good in our past rather than the opposite.

Nothing is more of a waste of time, effort, and potential happiness than looking back either in grief or in anger to childhood as we judge our parents according to some utterly unrealistic and imaginary ideal. I have particular worries about many young fathers today who, chagrined or disillusioned because their own father never was the kind of pal or soulmate they now fancy they would have liked, are resolved to make it up to their sons by being "the best pal a kid ever had."

It's my observation that for every boy who is neglected by his father in our society there are hundreds who are being spoiled and kept as emotional dwarves by overly protective, overly indulgent kid-pleasers who are confusing catering to every whim and want with genuine love. All a youngster has to do today to send one or both parents into a tailspin or turning cartwheels is to mutter aloud a few times the magical incantation, "I'm bored" or "I want…"

Personally, I'm convinced that the majority of children in North America today suffer from too much attention, too much sycophancy on the part of adults in general. As American family psychologist John Rosemond of Gastonia, N.C., said to a group in Winnipeg last year, Victorian parents were probably right after all. Children should be seen and not heard quite so much. The distance once imposed between them and adults was actually most beneficial – for everybody. As Rosemond pointed out – and I strongly agree – the best thing you can do for your child is to "help that child get out of your life and into a life of his or her own." The more a boy or girl is given responsibility, left to stand on his or her own feet, and offered the blessing of benign neglect, the sooner, in my view, they will gain the maturity they'll need to cope.

Anybody who has been in an elementary or secondary school lately knows that nothing has done more to undermine discipline and a respect for adults than the pervasive myth that children are simply tiny people and the natural equals, or "pals," of parents and teachers alike.

I think of my own father with great fondness, though still seeing him warts and all. I could never accuse him of trying to be a pal to me. Growing up as a boy, I can thankfully say he probably never knew where I was or what I was doing at least 50 per cent of the time. If I became bored, it was my problem. A lot of reading and a lot of creativity followed.

My father did a great deal for me. But I think he did most when he did nothing at all. On Father's Day, I feel I can say, "Thanks for nothing, Dad" and know he'll understand.

— God the Father —

I have respect for the Jewish tradition of not mentioning the name of God and of using indirect expressions instead. The reluctance to speak directly of God came from the commandment not to take the name of God in vain. But it flowed also from the awareness that God is the ultimate mystery, and that all one can do is to speak of this mystery by means of metaphors, similes, and other images.

When Jesus spoke of God as Father, he was using this kind of symbolic language. That it is imperfect can be seen simply by pushing it to its limits.

The word "father" connotes not just gender – conveying the false and horrendously damaging myth that God is therefore male – but a set of relationships that might be fine in the ideal sense but can be profoundly misleading in the real world of our humanity. To press the imagery of fatherhood too far can do enormous psychological damage to those whose experience of their earthly father was much less than healthy.

Take the case of the number of people who experienced their own father as a domineering, punitive tyrant. What of the many victims of child abuse at the hands of their male parent? It is virtually impossible for them to form a concept of a heavenly father devoid of cruelty, violence, and guilt.

Those who only knew their father as absent, whether physically or emotionally, often tend to experience God as absent or indifferent. Whatever their head tells them they should believe, their gut gives a different message.

Speaking symbolically, there is a "God-shaped space" in every one of us that aches and yearns until it is filled. It is of incredible consequence, however, just how this "space" is occupied and with what. We become like the God Whom we worship, the God with Whom we long to unite, just as surely as lovers grow similar over the years.

The importance of this bedrock truth can be illustrated in many ways. For example, the feminist theologians are right in their contention that the dominance of an overly male concept of God down the centuries has had an overwhelmingly negative impact on the female psyche, has led to an easier acceptance of war, and has had a sad effect upon our relationship with our planet.

Probably the most frightening example of what I'm talking about focuses on the traditional, religious concept of hell. If you believe in and worship a God Who is capable – for whatever reasons – of condemning billions of people to a place or state of eternal torture, you risk becoming like Him!

Queen Mary I (1516-1558) won the nickname "Bloody Mary" by torturing and burning "heretics." Her justification was that "as the souls of heretics are to be hereafter eternally burning in hell, there can be nothing more proper for me than to imitate the divine vengeance by burning them on earth." Few ideas in human history have had more inhumanity and misery flood from them than this one. It carries an understanding of God and of Christ that the majority of rational folk can see is immoral and sadistic in the extreme.

True, sayings purported to be those of Jesus that portray hell as a place of fiery torment appear in the Gospels, but, it is Matthew who is darkly obsessed by this theme. It occurs only once in the earliest Gospel, Mark, once in Luke, and not at all in John. In other words, it barely appears in the most primitive tradition of Jesus' teachings, and even there has to be understood – as all religious language must – in a symbolic way.

In Mark, we know Jesus is talking symbolically, since he says: "If your hand offends you, cut it off...." "If your eye offends you, pluck it out...." He is plainly not talking about self-mutilation! He goes on to speak not of "hell" but of Gehenna, which was the garbage dump for Jerusalem, where a perpetual fire was kept burning. He is saying, in a graphic way, your life can become garbage if you simply seek your own will and defy God.

Some will ask if there is no place of punishment after death, what difference does it make whether one is a Hitler or a saint in this life? In other words, is there a divine justice?

It would take a book to answer, but let me say this. We will one day "see" the full implications of all our thoughts and acts. To *know* that, even as we are known, will be judgement and "hell" enough.

Thankfully, that is but the first step. Heaven is not about sitting around; it's about growing and moving on into fullness of Being, by God's grace.

⟶ True Friendships ⟶

I interviewed an expert on suicide the other day for a program on Canada's religion and human affairs network, Vision/TV.

A lot of what he said made quite an impact. I was surprised, for example, to learn that, on a per capita basis, Canadians resort to suicide more frequently than do Americans.

Is this because we're more reserved – we express our emotions less freely? Is it because we live in a northerly clime and spend more time indoors alone? Is it because we get fewer hours of sunshine? At the moment, we need more research to enable us to answer such questions with accuracy.

I was struck also by the fact that, in North America today, three times as many men take their lives as do women.

Here the reasons are more obvious. As my guest noted, women are much readier to ask for help than men in our society. In spite of some progress, we still live by the code of machismo. Men are very loath to admit to any weakness – especially to other men.

Rev. Gordon Winch, who trains volunteers for distress centres, says that because women are much more likely to have a close friend with whom they can share their deepest concerns, they are much less likely to become so desperate that suicide seems the "only way out."

Many men, perhaps even the majority, do not have real friends. They have acquaintances and "pals" but that's not the same. The hearty *bonhomie* that pervades TV's painfully boring beer commercials indicates a kind of comradeship that looks like friendship but is, of course, mostly a cover-up. Unfortunately, it mirrors much that passes itself off as friendship among males today.

There is also an underlying competitiveness among men, and such a deep need to project an image of coping that honesty in relationships with other males is almost impossible.

Many husbands take pride in the statement: "My wife is my best friend." But, as Winch pointed out, "God help the woman whose husband says this. You have to realize what a heavy burden she's carrying!"

The fact that suicide occurs with greater frequency (per capita) in rural areas or in places such as the Northwest Territories is further evidence that excessive individualism and a lack of support systems figure largely in this tragedy.

What all of this underlined for me was the way in which we seem increasingly so disconnected from one another in our culture. Behind not just the more dramatic signs of malaise, like suicide, but also such tragedies as runaway teens, broken homes, wife-battering, and alcoholism lies a pervasive inability to forge and sustain meaningful personal relationships. For many, the art of making and keeping genuine friends has become as mysterious as the secret of the Pyramids.

With this in mind, here are four habits which are essential for getting beyond superficiality in relationships:

• It is obvious; it is repeated again and again; yet so very few really practise it. I'm speaking of the art of listening. Everybody seems to believe in listening as long as it's the other person who's doing it! Just sit back and watch what happens at lunch at work or when a group is out for dinner. One of the reasons so much of it so often seems such a waste of time is that nobody is really listening to anybody else.

• Allied to listening is the increasingly rare skill of giving the other person one's total attention. Our minds are so distracted by the myriad things going on around us and inside us that most of the time we give our kids, our spouses, our "friends" less than 10 per cent of ourselves. The people who have meant most to me in life have always been those who, when they are with you, are with you 100 per cent.

• Never was there a greater need than now for the wisdom of the Jewish philosopher Martin Buber. Buber said there were two basic rules for interpersonal relationships: (1) Be direct, that is, avoid all game-playing, pretense, or hypocrisy; and (2) develop an "I-Thou" relationship with others rather than an "I-It." By this he meant, always treat the other person *as a person,* and not as an object to be manipulated, dominated, used, or possessed. And insist on the same for yourself. There is a dangerous tendency today to "thingify" other people in order to exploit them – sexually, financially, or politically.

• Finally, there's caring. I believe true caring is what Jesus meant when he said to love one another. There is nothing mushy or sentimental about this. It has little to do with fancy talk. It means simply wanting the very best for the other person and acting accordingly.

— His-story —

A student of mine, who was clearly fated to be almost anything but a scholar, once complained about trouble with his history studies. "History," he wailed, "seems to be just one damn thing after another."

Well, yes. History, at first glance, seems to be just the recounting of dates and events from the past. In this view, the ideal history of a nation or an era would be the total record of everything that was said and done by everybody at every moment for the entire period.

But this kind of "objectivity" is neither possible nor desirable. All history writing consists of judgements about what facts to include and what to omit. How this selection (which amounts to a subjective interpretation) is made depends on the historian's criteria of what is important.

There is justification for the view that all history is contemporary history, as choices about what was or was not important in the past depend largely on what your (or your culture's) current interests and values are. We know how communists, for example, have written or rewritten history to fit their particular dogmas. We know too that most history is written by the victors. It reads quite differently when written by the losing side!

Where this has enormous relevance for the whole of humanity, however, is that 99.9 per cent of the history of any part of the world at any time has been written by men.

History quite literally is "his-story," the story of male-inspired victories and disasters told from an exclusively male point of view. The entire account of where we have been and what we have done *and its evaluation* has been from a masculine perspective. The distortion in human self-understanding this has led to is part of the reason we are in the mess we are in today.

I have written much trying to clarify an even more fatal, yet similar distortion in religion. Only future generations will fully know how terribly warped our ideas of God are because of centuries of male-dominated writing and thinking about Him/Her.

The founders of the world's great religions were male; their sacred scriptures were written by men; interpreting theology has been a male preserve for centuries; religion remains the last and strongest obstacle to acceptance of the equal humanity of women. The present struggle to deny women power over their reproductive lives is rooted in a visceral awareness by male hierarchs that to surrender control here is to lose it completely.

Thankfully, this situation is changing. Women are being ordained; they're teaching and writing books about theology; they're participating in making decisions in religion instead of just dishing out ham and scalloped potatoes to the clergy or baking pies to sell to each other at church bazaars.

The truth is, we need a more balanced conception of God because the macho, aggressive, competitive "idol" we men have made in our image has blessed war and planetary destruction for too many centuries already.

If you care for neither history nor theology, you could give some thought to the extraordinary domination of science by males and male-inspired myths.

In an article in the April 1988 issue of *The New Internationalist* magazine, psychologist Judy Gahagan argues that men are attracted to and lord it over science, not out of a creative search for knowledge but from a deep need to control. Contrary to the theory that women are gripped by "penis envy," she says that men are the ones obsessed by envy. They feel excluded from the primal, creative process of giving birth. The resulting insecurity and resentment can only be assuaged by "creating secrets and miracles for himself or by exerting total control over women."

When the American scientist Edward Teller sent a telegram announcing his pride and joy – the first successful detonation of a hydrogen bomb – the message read: "It's a boy!"

For Gahagan, Teller's choice of image was fitting, "a telling hint of what makes mad, male science tick." Even the mushroom cloud of the bomb was phallic in its symbolism. The whole of the scientific rush to be the first in a particular field has less to do with love of knowing than with a competitive "rush to paternity," she says.

Science has a hierarchy in which the "hard" sciences are those that "penetrate" the mysteries of the universe while the "soft" sciences are those dealing with relationships, behaviour, and the like.

Rape and exploitation of the earth, as opposed to nurturing it and co-operating with it, are the natural expressions of this lust for control. Violence against women assumes a near-cosmic dimension.

Without a recovery of the feminine side of our humanity, we are certain to repeat the errors of the past, to worship false gods, and, ultimately, to destroy ourselves.

— Jacob's Dream —

In all the years I spent training to be an Anglican priest, nobody ever said a word about dreams.

As a student and later a professor of Scripture, I knew that the Bible was full of accounts of various people and their dreams. But knowing that and taking dreams seriously were two different matters.

Today, I am convinced you can't fully understand either the biblical stories or the meaning of your own life without coming to grips with dreams and their significance for inner transformation. Dreams are not just idle phantasms of the night or the product of the mind doing some useless knitting. To use Sigmund Freud's phrase, they are the "royal road" to the unconscious, to that unknown well within us from which the most powerful forces flow to shape our lives.

Unfortunately, most of us forget or pay little heed to our dreams. Some of us have such an obsession with control and with left-brain thinking that the idea of heeding dreams is one we instantly repress. Others, perhaps a majority, regard dreams as rather amusing but ultimately meaningless, because they seem to speak a foreign language.

From my reading, particularly the books of Carl Jung, and from interviews with various dream analysts as a broadcaster, it has become clear to me that the reason we can't fathom our dreams is because we have estranged ourselves so far from nature, from our bodies, and from symbolic ways of communicating ideas. If you come to your dreams demanding that they answer to some literalistic, linear-type of reasoning, you are doomed to be disappointed.

The language of dreams – as of poetry, myth, or religion – is that of symbolism and imagery. It is primitive, but not in a pejorative sense. When it comes to the communication of the most profound thoughts, our basic or instinctual mode seems to be metaphorical.

The other fascinating thing about dreams is that they never tell us the obvious. Their role is to put us in touch with some aspect of our selves or our lives of which we are currently unconscious.

They may warn us, as some dreams of dying undoubtedly do, that we are living too superficially and not heeding the fact of our own mortality. They may reveal to us some part of our "shadow," some as-yet-unlived facet of our larger self that is crying out for expression or development.

Their function, it seems, is to assist us in the process of inner transformation, the realization of our true individuality and creative fulfilment.

When you begin to pay attention to your dreams, a funny thing happens. They gradually become much clearer and easier to remember. Not always, but every once in a while their symbolic meaning breaks in upon you, and you are amazed at the incredible wisdom they bring to bear on your life.

Rather than say more, let's consider briefly one of the most famous dreams in literature, that of Jacob at a place he called Bethel.

To understand this dream – and the same is true of our own – we first have to know the context of the dreamer, his life situation.

Jacob was, in contrast to his twin brother, Esau, a homebody and a "momma's boy." What's more, at the time of the dream, he was on the run. He had twice cheated his brother and had worked a blatant deception on their blind, aged father as well. He finds himself out in the wilderness. Night is falling and he has no place to sleep. Filled with fear and depressed by the loneliness of the spot, he finally falls asleep with his head on a stone for his pillow.

Then, he dreams. There is a ladder set up on the earth with the top reaching to heaven; there are angels going up and down the ladder. Suddenly, it seems to him that God is at the top and is speaking to him. The Lord promises him that the land he is lying on will one day be his, and that he and his descendants will be a blessing to all humanity.

On awakening, the symbolism of the dream strikes Jacob like a lightning bolt. The ladder, with its angel-like beings going up and down, has shown him that there is a communion going on between his soul and higher range of consciousness. He is aware of having been in touch with a level of transcendence "above" which reveals itself as divine. At the moment he least expected it, he gets assurance that his life is filled with promise and that there is an awesome future before him: "For I will not leave thee...."

Bereft at leaving his mother's house, he has suddenly discovered the truth that he is and always will be in "God's house." Small wonder he says out loud: "Surely the Lord is in this place; and I knew it not.... This is none other but the house of God, and this is the gate of heaven!"

Universalized, the truth of Jacob's dream applies to our inner journey, too. Often the very moment when we feel Godforsaken or afraid can be the opportunity for a higher consciousness to break through.

If we are aware and open to it, we can find ourselves saying with Jacob: "Surely God *is* in this place, and I never knew it."

— A Spiritual Tonic —

Few of us got through our school days without having to debate or write an essay on the topic: "Resolved: that the pen is mightier than the sword."

Today's students probably see this in an updated form: "Resolved: that the word processor is mightier than the bomb." But, as Winston Churchill said when he was taken against his will to see Niagara Falls for the second time, "the principle of the thing remains very much the same."

Personally, I never felt there was much contest about the truth of this proposition. The superior might of ideas and thought over any force has never seemed to me to be in doubt. Mental activity is the precursor to every meaningful human endeavour – from baking a pie to writing a concerto, from planning peace to putting people on the moon. Long before I write a column, long before any author creates a book, there is the idea or mental image of that which is coming into being. That's where the power resides.

One of the most potent rediscoveries of contemporary thought is the immense energy latent in the images we carry about of ourselves and of what it is we want to do with our lives. Some of these ideas or images are so deeply hidden in our unconscious that they only surface in dreams or at rare moments of self-examination. They might be the products of childhood experiences now repressed. They might have been created by our parents, early religious training, or other forces. They exert great influence, both positive and negative.

But it is not only unconscious or subconscious ideas that control our destinies. Much depends on the thoughts, patterns, models, or goals we consciously hold in our minds. No spiritual law is more sharply etched into the fabric of human reality than the one that says that the brain will try its best to realize or bring to pass that which the mind holds before it.

As the school of positive thinking is fond of pointing out, the Bible itself declares: "As a man [person] thinketh in his heart, so is he." Think failure and we fulfil our own prophecy. Similarly with the reverse.

The place where this truth is being reapplied most creatively today is in the key area of healing. Doctors, as well as non-medical healers, are finding that "imaging" wellness, meditating upon pictures or ideas of health and wholeness, can profoundly affect physical and emotional well-being. They are becoming ever more aware that modern medicine, with all its wizardry, too often focuses on illness and encourages negative self-images. The thought then becomes parent to the disease – or at any rate to its recalcitrance.

A note of caution is needed, however. We must beware of those who understand this in a too-simplistic manner and proceed to lay burdens of guilt and/or failure on those who are ill. One of the most tragic things about fraudulent faith healers – and well-meaning but shallow proponents of the "every day in every way I'm getting better and better" outlook – is the way they imply that if you are sick it's your own fault. Illness is a much more complex reality than that.

This caveat aside, though, it is the wise person who develops the practice of using regular meditation or some other form of storing the mind with images of renewed strength, peace, and wholeness.

As St. Paul reminds us: "Whatsoever things are just ... pure ... lovely.... Think on these things."

Reading parts of the Bible or other inspired scriptures can help enormously. Here is another of my favourites, from Isaiah: "They that wait upon the Lord shall renew their strength; they shall mount up with wings as eagles; they shall run, and not be weary; and they shall walk, and not faint."

Try this. Picture yourself as a soaring eagle – not with frantically beating wings but with wings spread, soaring, as a column of warm air (a thermal) lifts you effortlessly. You soar higher yet your body remains motionless, a "still point in a turning world." Relax and "soar" for several minutes.

Then change the image to that of the long-distance runner. You are running easily with no trace of weariness. You feel a surge of joy and well-being.

Finally, in your mind's eye you are walking over some familiar, loved terrain. You cover mile after mile. You see yourself walking without a trace of fatigue.

In some ways that's the most powerful image of all. Most of us can rally strength for life's big moments. It's the daily grind, the unglamorous "walking," that can get us down!

This, in brief, is a prescription for a spiritual tonic. Take daily before breakfast or at bedtime. No drug plan needed. Available everywhere, for all ages. Side effects – wonderful!

— Michelangelo's Slaves —

Two rival archaeologists discovered a skeleton near an ancient battlefield in the Holy Land. One, examining the remains, immediately announced the find's date as the period of the Philistine conquests. He pointed to the man's weapons and amulets as proof.

The other bent over the bones, pried something from the clenched fingers, and, after a moment's scrutiny, replied: "I can do better than that. I can tell you the year, month, and day he died, and the cause of death as well. He died of a massive heart attack on the day David killed Goliath."

When the first scholar expressed total scorn and disbelief at this kind of precision dating, the second showed him the clay "ticket" he had retrieved from the dead Philistine's fist. Translated, it said: "A thousand to one on Goliath."

The best-known sculpture of David is the larger-than-life, marble masterpiece by Michelangelo in a gallery in Florence. With true idealism, the superbly muscled, naked form shows David just seconds before the actual combat. He carries his sling with the stone in place. Yet, apart from the intense look of concentration on his brow, the sculpture embodies an overwhelming sense of calm. It's the typical moment of reflective serenity before action that marks the best art of classical Greece. It stands in marked contrast to Bernini's David (in the Borghese Gallery, Rome), which portrays him life-size in the strenuous act of throwing.

What makes Michelangelo's David so moving, however, apart from its own innate beauty and commanding strength, is the approach. You come to the towering figure down a long corridor lined on either side with a row of half-finished sculptures called simply "The Slaves." The faces are sightless, the features but roughly chiselled, the torso and limbs at times obscure. The strongest impression is of mighty beings struggling to free themselves from the drag and weight of the huge marble blocks and emerge as fully human.

When I first saw all this some years ago, I was reminded of the saying of the classical Greek sculptor who is reported to have stated that he didn't *create* a statue: "It's already there. I merely set it free from the stone." In any case, the symbolism of the juxtaposition of Michelangelo's Slaves and his idealized David had a potent spiritual impact that has stayed with me ever since. It has seemed a parable or myth of what our human journey is ultimately all about.

Most people believe that life is about happiness. But those who strive for happiness, or who are constantly plagued by self-examination as to whether or not they're as happy as they think they deserve to be, often become frustrated and then immobilized. It's a little like the centipede who was asked which leg he moved first when walking. He became so self-absorbed and confused that he finally couldn't move at all.

Life, according to the essential message of both ethics and religion, is not primarily about pleasure or happiness. It's about personal transformation. It's about growing awareness or consciousness of who we are, what we're really doing, and where our lives are going. In short, it's about a process of becoming what and who we were intended and designed to be.

To put it in the mythical mode, we're like the Slaves of Michelangelo. We're struggling to cast off or shed the rock from which we are being hewn so that we may become fully human and alive. Just as the sculptor uses hammer and chisel to "free" the form within, so, too, we are being molded and shaped by life, or, as I prefer, by the hammer of the Spirit of God. Changing this analogy, Paul says we are being metamorphosized (like the metamorphosis of the caterpillar into the butterfly) "from glory unto glory." For Paul, the ideal on which the divine sculptor has his eye as he works on us is Christ himself.

But, like all analogies, neither sculpture nor biological metamorphoses can be pressed too far. The missing factor is the passivity of the emerging statue and of the butterfly chrysalis. In our transformation, it is not just a matter of what life or God permits or does to us as objects. We are autonomous subjects. We are actively engaged as partners in the process. It matters supremely what we do with and how we react to the hammer blows and opportunities of life in this world. To put it in biblical terms, there comes a time (or times) when we have to "wrestle" with the "angel" of God.

Those who passively sit back and parrot phrases about everything being "in the Lord's hands," or who claim to have moment by moment, clear-cut guidance as to what they should do on each and every occasion, are stunting their own development by using their religion to avoid the tough responsibility of authentic living. They risk ending up as spiritual midgets.

The business of ethics is about making difficult decisions. It's focused on bearing the angst and struggle oneself. It is, for believers, a partnership with God. But, as the old preacher once said: "You gotta pray and believe as though it all rested on God and live and act as though it all depended on you."

— The Creative Spirit —

There's a fundamental ethical imperative that gets scant, if any, attention in the media, and that is the ongoing responsibility to "become what you are." This sort of maxim appears riddling, enigmatic, even paradoxical at first sight, but it expresses a life-changing idea.

We don't all begin with the same talents, opportunities, health, or physical appearance. Indeed, life, as John F. Kennedy (and many others) said, is unfair in many ways. Yet we are all created in the *imago Dei*, the image of God. No matter what the external differences might be, we are equal in essence, in our basic humanity, as "God's offspring."

To become what we are means to realize to the fullest extent possible the spiritual inheritance given to every human being by virtue of being human, created in God's likeness. Being "like God" means having the power to choose, to make moral decisions; it means having the capacity for self-reflective thought; above all, it means the gift of creativity.

However, our culture fosters a kind of élitist view of creativity. Poets, writers, musicians, filmmakers and the like are held to be creative; the rest, the masses, are not. I, for one, don't accept that. We all have creative potential as part of the human condition. The only truth behind the view that some are creative while most are not lies in the way some people let their creative juices course through them while others let theirs remain dormant, blocked, or denied.

Basically, becoming creative involves finding ways to get in touch with our innermost selves and the God-given sources of energy within. This is not a complex process, and one doesn't need to spend a fortune on "how to" books or self-improvement seminars to begin it.

If we want to hear what our inner voice or vision would say to us and through us, it's obvious we have to value ourselves enough to make the time to listen or tune in. There's nothing magical or esoteric about this. One doesn't have to be a guru, mystic, or saint. But it does require some self-discipline, and it can't happen without regular times of solitude. For a generation that has to have taped music even while jogging alone – not to mention the habit of switching on the TV or radio the moment we find ourselves alone – true solitude is a rare commodity indeed. We avoid it like the plague.

Manifestly, we are not all meant to be great artists, composers, inventors, or playwrights. But the same creative spirit that moved in Michelangelo, Mozart, and Shakespeare moves and breathes through the whole of creation – and so in each of us. We can all draw from that same well in whatever station or role we find ourselves. To the extent that we do so, we are becoming what we are, creators like the Being Who made us.

One secret is not to worry about others' achievements or success but to be true to whatever allurements and glimpses we discern in ourselves. We can't help but be original in whatever we do or create – however humble it might be – if we are faithful to what is at the core of our being.

When young people cry, "How can I be original when it's all been done before?" the answer is: "By being fully yourself." Since each of us is unique, the reality we know and express will inevitably have its own unique quality or "slant."

Next to listening and to solitude, one needs to acquire the habit of eccentricity. I don't mean by this the deliberate attempt to be odd or "off the wall." That's not creativity, it's downright tiresomeness. However, in its root meaning, to be eccentric means to be out-of-the-centre.

Think of yourself as standing on a hill and the horizon you see around you as a circle. It's obvious that everyone standing where you are will have the same view or viewpoint. To get a different perspective, you have only to climb to a different height or vantage spot. When you move out of the "centre" where the mob stands – with its herd view of success, trends, and values – you immediately see a fresh horizon.

If you can define this vantage point and compare and contrast it with what the majority hold to be the only valid or normal view, you can't help but be creative. This applies not just to painters or prophets but to business executives, house-husbands, and secretaries as well.

Finally, learn to think holistically. The greatest bane of western civilization, though it has achieved so much, has been our obsession to dissect, analyse, and divide up reality into smaller and smaller categories and specialties. This can be seen in our great modern hospitals, with their infinite array of specialty gadgets and their at times appalling inability to give either patient or family a whole view of what's going on.

The truly creative thrust today lies with those prepared to put things back together again and look at them in the round – to see where they fit into the seamless robe of the total cosmos. Fusion, not fission, is the paradigm of the future.

⟶ Family Ties ⟶

Bertrand Russell once pointed out that there is no bishop anywhere who would dare to preach what the Gospels say Jesus taught about the family.

This is worth thinking about. To hear most clergy and evangelists going on about either the nuclear or the extended family, you would think Christ regarded them as holding an absolute value akin to that of God. However, he manifestly held no such comfortable view.

As with many other things Jesus is reported to have said, the Church has conveniently ignored his words on family relationships, or changed them around to suit its own needs and traditions.

Christ's attitude to family ties was profoundly radical: they are never to take the place of one's loyalty and devotion to the ultimate Source of all Being, the One he called Father. Anything or anybody that takes the place of God is an idol. Nobody can serve two masters.

Consider: the churches with the greatest claims to catholicity (universality) have always treated the Mother of Jesus with a reverence that has come at times very close to worship. Jesus himself had a very different attitude. On several occasions he is barely civil with regard to her.

For example, Mark tells us that once, when Jesus was surrounded by a crowd, his mother and his brothers came and had word passed up to the front that they wanted to speak with him. When he was told about this family delegation, he looked around at the throng and said: "These are my mother and my brothers! For whoever does the will of God, the same is my brother, and my sister, and my mother."

Clearly he wants to create a new definition of family, one not based upon the old ties of blood but on the much wider kinship of all those who seek the new humanity.

Once, John's Gospel says, when Jesus' mother wanted him to intervene in an embarrassing situation where the host at a wedding had run out of wine, Jesus spoke to her quite sharply: "Woman, what have I to do with you?" (A better translation is, "Woman, what has this got to do with you and me?")

While obviously Jesus upholds the commandment to honour one's parents, it is clear that, as with all other aspects of morality, he was concerned to understand this at a deeper level. Truly honouring one's parents can never involve choosing their will for one's life over the will of the Heavenly Father. No prompting or coercion by natural parents is ever to take the place of duty to love one's true, inner self or to obey the voice within.

That is why, for example, when Jesus talks about marriage, and the fact that "for this cause shall a man leave his father and mother and cleave to his wife," the emphasis is upon the operative word "leave."

Most clergy and other counsellors are well acquainted with the devastation wrought in marriages in which one or the other of the two partners has never truly cut the emotional umbilical cord between themselves and a particular parent. It is only too possible to be of adult age, married or single, and to be dominated still by parents – even when one or both may be dead. They are carried within one's own psyche. Jesus' command is "Leave!" – accept adult responsibility for yourself, your feelings, your motives.

In all my years of being around organized religion I can honestly say I have never once heard or read an intelligent exposition of Matthew 10:35: "For I am come to set a man at variance against his father, and the daughter against her mother, and the daughter-in-law against her mother-in-law."

This text can be explained in a number of ways. What you can't make it do is fit cosily into any of the usual clichés about family life.

Commenting on the verse that follows – "And a man's foes shall be they of his own household. He that loveth father or mother more than me is not worthy of me." – Bertrand Russell says: "This means the breaking up of the biological family tie for the sake of creed – an attitude that had a great deal to do with the intolerance that came into the world with … Christianity."

We could debate that. But my reason for raising this whole issue is to make people aware that there are real risks in trying to solve family problems today by simplistic appeals to "traditional Bible values."

Indeed, one of the worst family ills of our time, wife-beating, has often been made worse and not better by religious teachings that make an idol of the family and make the woman feel only terrible guilt if she does what she often desperately needs to do – get out and run for her life.

— Salt of the Earth —

According to a piece of rural wisdom – one quite familiar in churchy circles – clergy are a bit like manure. Gathered together in a pile, they raise quite a stink and are next to useless; spread out across the land, there's no telling how much good they can do.

Although fairly brusque and earthy, this imagery is not without its biblical parallels. In the Sermon on the Mount, which is the traditional basis for much of western ethical thought (if not practice), those who wish to be followers of Christ are told they are "the salt of the earth."

As the text points out, salt that has lost its flavour or saltiness is only fit to be thrown out and trampled under foot. It is equally true, however, that salt that remains in its box or in a saltcellar is impotent. The power of the metaphor lies in the fact that salt has to be spread out, stirred in, or widely sprinkled in order to be effectual.

All of this touches upon an extremely weighty matter, namely, how is any society to be transformed into a more caring, more just, more human community? How is the global family to be preserved from anarchy and enabled to progress towards greater wholeness, unity, and self-fulfilment?

Revolutions and conquests simply beget more violence and oppression. Politics alone will never accomplish it. Ideological slogans are of no avail.

The miracle of social transformation is ultimately an affair of the heart or the inner life of every individual on the face of the Earth. Like the action of salt – or of yeast, or of light, the other great biblical images for the same phenomenon – its work is largely unseen and silent, yet its presence is always and immediately known by its results.

All the spiritual geniuses down the centuries have taught that what happens in the inner life of each individual is a microcosm of what is projected onto the "screen" of the world. While this conveys a warning, I find it at the same time a source of great hope. It is so easy to become discouraged by constant news of world crises, of massive calamities, horrible crimes, or other social evils. Many wonder at times whether we are making any moral advances at all, or, worse still, whether progress is even possible.

The challenge to be the salt of the world is a recognition that each of our individual lives makes a tremendous difference. If we remain steadfast, if we strive to maintain our own integrity and to grow morally and spiritually, we inevitably influence the macrocosm.

As Sophia, the sharp-tongued, elder member of the "Golden Girls" foursome would say: "Picture this." The readers of my column come from every possible walk of life. The penetration of our society they represent is truly extraordinary. They are "stirred in" thoroughly to the total mix of daily work and leisure. What they think, say, and do makes a profound difference.

As salt that retains its savour, their stand for the highest values and their witness to compassion and justice for all combine with that of others to permeate the whole social order.

If we take a deeper look at the meaning implicit in the salt metaphor, we can see how this actually works. In the hot climate of the Middle East, centuries before modern refrigeration, salt acted as a preservative. It cut decay and kept things from going bad. That is how all people of goodwill are to function in the moral order – as a brake or an antidote to corruption and chaos.

But there is a second, much more positive intention involved here as well. Anyone on a low-sodium diet knows full well that salt is valued (in antiquity as now) because it brings out the taste of food. It adds a zing or spice to even so bland a dish as oatmeal porridge. (My father always made the porridge in our home when I was a child, and I still remember vividly the mornings when, in the general rush of things, he forgot to add the salt!)

The last thing anyone concerned with ethical behaviour wants to do is to end up seeming to be "preachy-preachy, teachy-teachy" or the like. Even less attractive is the role of the moral heavy, the killjoy who rains on every party. That's why it's so important to emphasize the fact that trying to live on the side of the highest possible ethical standards is to identify with the forces and energies that bring out the "full taste" of what it means to be a human being.

That's why the *truly* religious or spiritual person, contrary to the stereotype or caricature we have of him or her, always seems more alive, more sensitive, more in tune with reality than others. Every religious tradition can point to hundreds of examples.

Jesus himself was criticized not because he was a "goody-goody" but because he enjoyed life too much.

— Longing for Wholeness —

You can't determine ethical conduct – the right or wrong decision in any set of circumstances – without some grasp of the larger picture. No human choice or action takes place in a vacuum.

Accordingly, any philosopher, theologian, or other scholar who thinks about ethics and ethical principles has an obligation to wrestle constantly to make sense of major trends or changes at work in the world. For particular courses of action to be right, it's necessary to have an understanding of what their consequences will be – not just locally but in global terms, as well.

What I want to describe here is a way of looking at our contemporary world that brings together a number of key movements or developments that might seem, at first sight, to be quite unrelated. There is, I believe, a highly significant convergence of thought going on behind what many perceive as the sheer chaos of the daily news in the press or on radio and television.

Let's begin by listing some of the paramount themes that provide a focus of interest or dedicated commitment for large, growing segments of North American society: the "New Age" phenomenon, feminism, the men's movement, holistic medicine, the peace movement, the recovery movement (from alcoholism, child abuse, wife-battering, and so on), and the "green" or environmental movement.

The next step is to pose the question: Have all of these anything in common? Could it be that there is some underlying or overriding psychic thrust at work here that unites these apparently disparate groupings and knits them more comprehensibly into the fabric of our universal quest as human beings?

My own conviction is that the more deeply one reflects on what is going on in all of these movements, the more certain it becomes that the answer must be in the affirmative. The core, unifying stratum is that of healing, a restoration of wholeness or health.

Here's why. Whatever one thinks of the New Age phenomenon, it's clear that its central energy or motivation stems from a longing to find a new and wider wholeness of mind and body. There's a radical discontent with materialism, technology, and traditional religion as modes of understanding oneself. There's a conviction that reality is much wider than the tenets of "scientism" (a false worship of science and the insistence that the only possible truth is that brokered to us by scientists). Whether it's by channeling, the search for alleged past lives, or the use of crystals, runes, and tarot cards to bring physical health or peace of mind, New Age enthusiasts are seeking to be made whole.

At a profound level, the same urge lies behind the massive struggle of women in our time for liberation and empowerment. Similarly, anyone who takes the trouble to investigate the new men's movement will quickly find that many men today feel wounded, somehow robbed of their full masculinity, and in need of emotional, mental, and physical renewal.

In the case of the widespread and growing recovery movement, the search for healing from abuse or various addictions (from food to alcohol, drugs, and sex) is even more obvious and needs no further elaboration. The same can be said of the booming interest in holistic or alternative medicine.

Nobody knows how the mess in what used to be the Soviet Union is going to resolve itself, and meanwhile, the United States, which has never yet signed a test-ban treaty, is continuing to test and produce new nuclear weapons daily. The peace movement, aimed at healing the world of the curse of ever greater armaments and the pervasive addiction to war, is needed more at this juncture than perhaps ever before.

The word "ecology" comes from the classical Greek word for a house or home. The underlying thought in the ecology or environmental movement is that this planet is home, not just to humans but to every living thing. If one part of the home or of its occupants suffer, all suffer with it. When you study the flood of books and witness the mushrooming of advocacy groups, you can see one concern at the heart of this unprecedented awakening – the healing of the Earth. That's why cultural philosopher Fr. Thomas Berry says we have entered a new era in planetary history, the "Ecozoic Age."

I urge readers to follow this new paradigm of healing in their own thinking, since there isn't room here to develop it as I would like. Let me, however, add one concluding thought; it's one that is pregnant with meaning for all religious institutions in our time, particularly the Christian Church.

Basically, all religions, properly understood, are about healing –

the healing of the rift between humans and Ultimate Reality, or God; the healing of relationships with others; and the healing of the individual himself. The key terms of Judeo-Christian religion – "salvation" and "holiness" – come from root words meaning "wholeness" or "health."

Unfortunately, the major faiths have yet to realize either what it is that today's world is really longing for or what it is that religion itself is about and could offer to the world. As a result, the gap of alienation from religion gets wider just when it could be bridged.

— Perfection —

Our cat, Percy, when he's not curled up on one of our best chairs, snoozing, likes to stalk and pounce on his various toy mice. The other day, though, when I was reading by the lake, he escaped the house and took his hunting outdoors.

Out of the corner of my eye I noticed that Percy had assumed his gunslinger mode and was intent on "making a kill." On the shore, two metres from the cat, was a big beaver munching on a stick while cocking a sceptical eye at Percy.

You could tell the cat's thoughts; this was the rodent of his wildest dreams, larger than life and right on his own doorstep! Fortunately, my approach saved Percy the surprise (not to mention the worst licking) of his life. But somehow the sight of the size and power of the beaver as he plunged into the water and vanished depressed him. Percy sulked for the rest of the day.

I was tempted to quote Browning to him. You know the lines, "Ah but a man's reach should exceed his grasp, or what's a heaven for?" But, aware in this case that an excessive grasp could have produced not heaven but the opposite, I reflected that, while it might be noble to have high ambitions, these can and often do lead to unnecessary suffering when they have little or no base in reality.

In fact, one cause of the commonest of all mental and emotional maladies, depression, is the gap between what we or others expect and demand of ourselves – our goals or standards of performance – and what we are either suited or empowered to achieve. The greater the unreality of these expectations and demands, and the more out of sync they are with our basic natures, talents, or opportunities, the deeper the depression.

This happens frequently with young people whose parents exert unrealistic pressures, whether it be in sports, career choices, or in marriage partners. The suicide of a young student in the sensitive film *The Dead Poets Society* resulted from this sort of despair and throws light on some of the tragic teen suicides we see today.

I have a particular concern for the way this same principle works in Christian circles. Anxiety and depression figure much more than most people imagine amongst those who are either devout churchgoers or who have had a strict religious upbringing. From counselling as a priest, I know there are countless thousands of church members who go around laden with guilts and glooms caused by the gulf between what they feel their religion demands and their own lives.

Nothing has contributed more to this sad state of affairs than the false teaching that to be a Christian means one has always to be perfect. This can result either in a constant attempt to run from one's flaws, to repress them instead of dealing with them – a sure route to despondency – or to spending most of one's life in a futile struggle to be something we're not.

The chief source of the perfectionist delusion is the belief that, since a Christian is one who follows Christ, he or she must struggle to be like him, that is, perfect. But Jesus never claimed to be perfect. Indeed, as I argue in my book *For Christ's Sake*, there is evidence in the Gospels that he, too, was fallible, knew anger, was ignorant of some things, and so on.

To be like Christ is not to be perfect but to do as he did. That is, to follow one's own vision of God and of life no matter where it might lead. It means daring to defy all convention, all family or public opinion, all institutional opposition *that would weaken one's hold on what he called the Kingdom of God.*

That's a much more demanding, yet much more realistic challenge than that of a moralistic, perfectionist mirage.

Yes, there is a verse in the Sermon on the Mount that the King James Version translates: "Be ye therefore perfect even as your Father which is in heaven is perfect." But, with respect, the translation is faulty. The Greek word here translated "perfect" is *teleios*. It can denote perfection, but in the sense not of ethical perfection but of a thing becoming or being what it was intended to be, like a fully mature tree or a truly "liony" lion. Aristotle, who began as a biologist, uses the word to describe any organism that achieves its true purpose.

A better translation thus would be: "Become a complete or fully realized person, just as your heavenly Father is fully God."

We need to realize our *own*, real potential – not somebody else's idea of what it should be.

— The God of Jacob —

Life is difficult. So say all the great religions, as Dr. Scott Peck reminds us in his popular book *The Road Less Traveled*. Many people are finding this to be particularly true for them at this moment – whether because of stress at work, the stress of not having a job at all, family problems, the need to make career choices, or the sheer pressures of life in general. Many have written recently to ask about ways to "tap into" sources of spiritual strength. Others have noted that, in my writing, I have said it's not necessary to use eastern methods in order to meditate. They have asked for specific alternatives.

Obviously, there are no magical formulas, no easy panaceas. As I have said elsewhere in this book, part of what is wrong with our culture is the simplistic idea that there must be a push-button answer for everything. But there are tried and tested ways of finding courage and other resources essential to problem-solving and personal growth.

I would like to suggest several verses or "mantras" (meditative prayers) that can be highly effective. They are used as "mind-conditioners" or "spiritual affirmations" by people in all walks of life, from business executives to homemakers, teachers, and airline pilots. They happen to come from the Judeo-Christian tradition, but other religions have similar meditative tools. You don't have to be fervently pious to use any of them. I suggest they be repeated throughout the day. This way they can eventually become a natural part of one's inner life.

Probably the most helpful method is to pick the one that appeals most and stick with it. These come from the King James Version of the Bible because it is probably still the most familiar. It certainly has the finest language.

• "God is our refuge and strength, a very present help in trouble. Therefore we will not fear." (Psalm 46:1-2)

• "The eternal God is thy refuge, and underneath are the everlasting arms." (Deuteronomy 33:27)

• "Be strong and of a good courage; be not afraid, neither be thou dismayed: for the Lord thy God is with thee whithersoever thou goest." (Joshua 1:9)

• "The Lord shall preserve thee from all evil: he shall preserve thy soul." (Psalm 121:7)

• "They that wait upon the Lord shall renew their strength; they shall mount up with wings as eagles; they shall run, and not be weary; and they shall walk, and not faint." (Isaiah 40:31)

• "I can do all things through Christ which strengtheneth me." (Philippians 4:13)

• "With God all things are possible." (Mark 10:27)

• "The Lord of hosts is with us; the God of Jacob is our refuge." (Psalm 46:11)

For those who like the idea of using one or more of these – or some other passage – but whose eyes tend to glaze over whenever they hear biblical terms, I'd like, without sermonizing, to illustrate just how much power and relevance they can have for one's life.

Take the last one: "The Lord of hosts is with us; the God of Jacob is our refuge." This is a simply astonishing affirmation of faith, based on the author's own personal experience.

In the phrase "the Lord of hosts," the author is thinking of God or Divine Intelligence as the Creator and Sustainer of the whole universe. This is the Divine Spirit in all His/Her majesty, might, wisdom, and power – the Maker of the spiralling galaxies and of the human eye or brain. This Being, he says, *is with us*. The more science probes the wonders of the heavens, and the more we understand of the mysteries of the origins of life, the more potent such trust and faith becomes.

But there is more. It is the style of Hebrew poetry always to balance the first half of a verse with a second, which either repeats or develops the original point further. So, he goes on, "the God of Jacob is our refuge." To see why many regard this statement as even more encouraging in a way than the first, you have to understand a little of who and what Jacob was, according to the biblical account.

Jacob was human, anything but saintly or perfect. In fact, the record makes it quite apparent that he was a momma's boy, a bit of a coward, and a trickster as well. The name Jacob (later changed to Israel) means "a supplanter," "a deceiver." You might remember (perhaps from Sunday School) how, with his mother's help, he tricked his blind father, Isaac, into giving him the birthright that belonged to his brother, Esau. Esau himself was tricked into complying with this for a "mess of potage" served up by Jacob. If you read the story in Genesis for yourself, you can readily see what a real wheeler-dealer Jacob was before he finally learned his lesson and shaped up.

What this says, then, is that we can affirm the presence with us of "the Lord of Hosts" – God thought of as the Ultimate Energy and mover of the cosmos. But we can also lay claim to the presence of the One who loved fallible Jacob and Who also loves us. In spite of and through everything. Even beyond the grave.

— Twelve Steps —

On one gorgeous, late-summer day I was sitting in a downtown hotel room with about 150 other people. While outside the crowds were rushing to see the Blue Jays play the New York Yankees, the earnest souls inside – each of whom had paid more than $300 to be there – were engaged in a marathon self-help course. It had begun at 6 p.m. on the Thursday evening and would end at about 8 p.m. on the Sunday night.

Interestingly, these people, a cross-section of ordinary folk, were willing to pay that kind of money and put in that much time when I knew for certain that most of them would have felt really hard done by if they'd been asked to spend an hour or so in church and to toss five dollars into the collection plate.

Something highly significant is going on. *Newsweek* has reported that the number of self-help organizations in the U.S. quadrupled between 1981-91. According to the Roman Catholic monthly *St. Anthony's Messenger*, 15 million Americans attend 500,000 group meetings of one kind or another in a single week! Canadians are following suit in proportional numbers.

The unifying thread in all of these groups is the theme of self-help or recovery. In addition to general self-improvement, people today are looking for healing for all sorts of problems, from chronic addictions to the trauma of childhood sexual abuse. They are finding in the process that it's not enough to get rid of one's personal demons – low self-esteem, guilt, repressed rage, alcohol, drugs, gambling, compulsive sex, phobias of every description. The great need is to replace them with something much more potent. In short, the quest is ultimately a spiritual one.

This being so, it's not surprising that the American National Self-Help Clearinghouse reports that the fastest-growing category of self-help groups today is made up of those known as "12-Step programs." In fact, an estimated 200 recovery or self-help programs so far have been "spun-off" from the original 12-Steps concept of the founders of Alcoholics Anonymous (A.A.).

Bill Wilson and Bob Smith, who founded A.A. in 1935, had

both been members of the influential Oxford Group Movement, which aimed at spiritual renewal through an emphasis on key Christian teachings. These included the experience of God's Spirit in daily life, regular meditation and prayer, sharing one's weaknesses and one's faith in group sessions, and "witnessing" to others. In other words, their approach to an addiction to alcohol or "spirits" was profoundly spiritual. The closer the new 12-Step programs for various problems stick to the basic tenets of A.A. – and some do so much more than others – the more spiritual they are. And the more successful they are, as well.

Indeed, surveying the whole phenomenon of the appeal of such groups today from the stance of an observer of social and religious trends, I have become convinced that the churches have an enormous amount to learn from the 12-Step Program of A.A. Put more strongly, I believe that if what is happening at A.A. meetings in church basements were happening upstairs in the main sanctuary with the Sunday congregation, the churches would not be in the urgent state of crisis that now grips them.

Upstairs, parsons *talk* about God, about personal transformation and Christian values, while downstairs at the A.A. meeting people are *experiencing* all this. Worshippers sing and pray about forgiveness, humility, repentance, and new life. Former drunks who find sobriety know what these words mean in the present.

The very first time I was invited, as rector of the parish, to sit in on an A.A. meeting in a bare crypt many years ago, I recognized what that group had that most church services I had been in up to that point lacked:

• Some real, basic honesty. Nobody could con anybody else for long with phoney sanctity, social or religious superiority, or ersatz success.

• A deep sense of tolerance, unshockability, and fellow-feeling towards every member of the group.

• A common bond uniting them because of a common experience of failure and powerlessness.

• A realistic, everyday language that everybody could understand.

• A moving sense of utter dependency upon God "as we

understand Him" or a "Power greater than ourselves" to lift them out of their weakness and restore them to sanity.

It is, to my mind, a searing indictment of the churches that to find these powerful, undeniably Christian values being truly lived and experienced one should have to move beneath, beyond, or outside the churches altogether. The self-help groups blossom and flourish, while the institution proclaiming itself the sole purveyor of the Gospel or "Good News" increasingly finds itself a kind of chaplain to an ever-shrinking, ageing remnant.

I want to stress that the final message in all of this is one of hope. Today there is an unparalleled opportunity for the churches to be born again. Re-examining the 12-Step Program's principles could bring about the kind of recovery or healing the churches themselves must experience, or they will perish.

They'll find as they do so that what is basic to A.A. now was basic to believers in the earliest days of Christianity. It succeeded then and it can again today.

— The Value of Guilt —

Just after murdering the king, Macbeth imagines he hears a voice cry, "Sleep no more! Macbeth doth murder sleep."

Then follow the beautiful, oft-quoted lines:

Sleep that knits up the ravell'd sleeve of care,
The death of each day's life, sore labour's bath,
Balm of hurt minds.

Macbeth is tortured by the horror of his deed. But his wife, Lady Macbeth, mocks him and tells him he's a coward: "A little water clears us of this deed; How easy is it then!" Only as the plot develops does the full significance of what she has connived at begin to sink in. In the famous sleep-walking scene, she keeps wringing her hands as if washing them. She imagines she can still see blood on them – "Out, damned spot! out, I say!" – and then she exclaims: "Here's the smell of the blood still: all the perfumes of Arabia will not sweeten this little hand. Oh, oh, oh!"

In this play, Shakespeare has given us a classic study of a human emotion that is basic to any kind of thinking about ethics and right conduct, yet at the same time an emotion that is alarmingly out of vogue today – guilt.

Like it or not, our capacity to feel remorse or deep grief over something we have done is partly what distinguishes our species from the non-human. An inability to have such feelings when we have brought harm to others is the mark of serious psychopathology of some kind.

Guilt merits a great deal more attention today in terms of its positive potential for human advancement precisely because it has been given such bad press ever since the dawn of modern psychology and psychiatry. Indeed, I would contend that there is a direct correlation between the increase in certain kinds of crimes – for example, the recently released statistics on crimes of violence by young people in Canada, or crimes against women and children – and the way in which guilt has become a taboo emotion to be avoided at any cost.

Don't get me wrong. Humanity owes a debt of gratitude to Freud, and to all those who have explored the enormous amount of damage and suffering caused to people down the years by the corrosive, soul-destroying effects of false guilt or of guilt left unresolved. What's more, one of the more healing insights of the present era has been the awareness of the ways in which bad religion can manipulate its followers through the inculcation of guilty feelings. The amount of unnecessary agony caused in this manner defies description. People have had needless guilt-trips laid on them "too grievous to be borne," and all in the name of Christ, who came to reveal a more abundant life!

But it's one thing to recognize that our human ability to feel guilt can be exploited, abused, or perverted. It's another to disparage guilt, or treat both the word and the reality as the ultimate in bad taste. That way lies moral disaster.

There is a deep sense in which guilt is to our moral nature, to conscience, what pain is to our physical being. No sane person seeks pain, but pain has an extremely important function. It lets us know when something is threatening our health. So, too, guilt is a psychic or inner messenger signalling spiritual unease. It is ignored or repressed to our own hurt.

As the doctor summoned by Macbeth for his wife expresses it, guilt lies beyond the power of medicine to cure:

> More needs she the divine than the physician,
> God, God, forgive us all!

When Macbeth, a couple of scenes later, begs the doctor to cure her, he pleads:

> Canst thou not minister to a mind diseased,
> Pluck out from the memory a rooted sorrow,
> Raze out the written troubles of the brain,
> And with some sweet oblivious antidote
> Cleanse the stuff'd bosom of that perilous stuff
> Which weighs upon the heart?

The doctor then sagely replies: "Therein the patient must minister to himself."

The good physician has it right. Guilt over moral lapses, harm brought on others, things done that we ought not to have done, and things left undone that we ought to have done calls out both for the forgiveness of God and for the act of then forgiving oneself.

The worst thing you can do for someone is to tell them not to feel guilty when it is apparent to them and to others that they have good reason to do so. By offering excuses or "cheap grace," one simply short-circuits genuine healing and stunts any true moral development. There are times when all of us need to feel the pangs of guilt and to seek genuine repentance, that is, a reversal of direction. It's obviously true of the alcoholic or the wife-beater, but, it's true of the rest of us as well.

Forgiveness is the divine last word on human error, not guilt. But the reason more people don't glow with a sense of forgiveness today is that current standards tell them they've never done anything really wrong. Ethically speaking: no real moral convictions, no guilt; no guilt, no gain. Only slow descent back to the jungle.

— Forgiveness —

Socrates went about trying to make people think and was put to death by the state for his pains. His alleged offence? Corrupting the youth of Athens in the fifth century B.C. and showing "impiety" towards "the gods."

Socrates was fond of two metaphors to describe his role. He said he was a kind of midwife, one who helped the youth cut through all the bafflegab that passed for knowledge to bring to birth the truths that lay within them.

He also liked to think of himself as a gadfly, stinging people out of their complacency or ignorance and propelling them towards new insights. He was devoutly spiritual in his own, unique way.

Not everyone is likely to be pleased by what follows. But it must be said all the same. I intend to look at what is unique, if anything, about Christian ethics.

If you were to ask a group of conservative Christians what they thought was new or unique about the Christian ethic, the response would most likely be one of surprise. The traditional view has been that the whole thing is something original, a completely new revelation. But scholars have been aware for decades now that the ethical teachings of Jesus, for example, can be found already in the teachings of Judaism as recorded in the Talmud, an ancient compilation of Jewish oral teaching.

Most of the material in the Sermon on the Mount, as found in Matthew's Gospel, has its earlier parallels in this Talmudic tradition. Not only that, the study of comparative religion has shown that many of the central teachings of all the major faiths are common to all. Thus, the Golden Rule of treating others as we ourselves wish to be treated exists, as we have already seen, in various forms in most religious codes.

However, there is one teaching of Jesus that does stand out as totally original and unique. Paradoxically, it is the one most neglected down the ages by Christians themselves. I'm referring, of course, to his words about loving your enemy:

Ye have heard that it hath been said, Thou shalt love thy neighbour, and hate thine enemy. But I say unto you, Love your enemies, bless them that curse you, do good to them that hate you, and pray for them which despitefully use you, and persecute you; that ye may be the children of your Father which is in heaven: for he maketh his sun to rise on the evil and on the good.

There is absolutely nothing I know of in any other ethical tradition to compare with this for radical originality. It contravenes our every instinct. If ever it were to be practised on a global scale, it would transform the shaping of the human story. For example, war would be impossible. Personal resentments and hostilities that rob so many of joy or zest in living would all but disappear.

Before anyone can love an enemy, he or she must be willing to forgive them. But, as a reader wrote to me recently, "forgiving is the most difficult thing in the world."

I believe she's right. She must be, or so many people wouldn't hold to their grudges and grievance against others for so long – sometimes souring an entire lifetime and taking an incalculable toll on their own health and happiness in the process.

There is no magical answer. Forgiveness, I believe, has to be learned like any other skill. You find it by doing it. But whatever secret there is to it lies chiefly in this: You have to realize more and more deeply how much you have been forgiven yourself. Only then does the compassion come to release others from the bond of your hatred or dislike.

To love (not like!) one's enemy is the next step beyond forgiveness. It takes both the grace of God and a heroic effort of will, but the rewards are ultimately enormous.

Jesus realized, among other things, that our enemy is a very special person. Your enemy is the one who dares tell you the truth your best friends shy away from. Your enemy is the one who shows you your back, the part of yourself you never see. Your enemy points up the aspects of your own life or personality that you secretly can't stand. It is better, much better, to have a noble enemy than a faithless, pusillanimous friend.

— Life After Death, I —

The afternoon of December 23, 1990, was cold and bright in southern Ontario. As Brenda Perks, a vivacious young woman who planned to announce her engagement on Christmas Day, drove north on Highway 404 at about 3 p.m., her car suddenly hit an invisible patch of black ice.

She pulled hard on the wheel to counter a skid. The car careened dangerously, swerved on to the ice-slicked grass of the median, then slid sideways into the southbound lanes. There was a terrible crash as an oncoming car hit her, smashing her vehicle and leaving her with critical head and other injuries.

Airlifted by helicopter to Sunnybrook Health Science Centre, Brenda hovered close to death for just over twenty-four hours. She died at 5.30 p.m. on Christmas Eve.

A few days later, I received a phone call from her father, Brian Perks, a former newspaperman and now publisher of several trade journals. Perks, who was a stranger to me (someone had told him I had written a book on life after death), told me briefly about how his daughter had died and asked for a chance to talk to me about some strange experiences he had on December 25, the day after her death. We met in my study, and here, condensed, is what he had to say.

On Christmas Day, he was at the home of Cindy, Brenda's married sister. Full of grief, at about 11 a.m. he went down to the recreation room in the basement. He said aloud: "Oh Brenda, Brenda, Brenda."

Then "an astonishing thing" happened. Perks distinctly heard Brenda's voice, as if behind him "at about shoulder height," saying, "It's okay." The words, full of emotion, (Brenda was a "theatrical, happy type") had the same nuance as if she had said, "There's no sweat, no problem."

Perks paced the length of the room, turned to come back and suddenly "saw" his daughter. Striving for strictest objectivity, he said that the seeing was not with his eyes but "with my brain." But this was not some ordinary act of recall or imagination: "It was a positive seeing process. There was a light behind her head, some distance back. It looked like a ball of light and it illumined the sides of her long hair, leaving her face in deep shadow. I couldn't make out her features, yet I discerned she was talking to me. It was like TV without the sound on."

Perks felt distressed and said aloud, "Brenda, I'm sorry but I can't hear you." The vision, or whatever it was, vanished, and he suddenly felt very cold. Perks then ran upstairs, got a sweater and rushed back down.

He sat on a sofa. Time, perhaps an hour or so, passed uneventfully. Then, as before, he heard her voice saying calmly, "You mustn't hate."

Perks was even more startled and surprised than ever. He wasn't aware of being angry (although most people in grief have a lot of unrecognized rage) and his reaction was, "What on earth is that supposed to mean?"

He sat, stunned and confused, wondering whether or not it had really been Brenda – since he was a self-defined "hardnosed bugger" who didn't believe such things were possible anyway – when the final experience came as a kind of "proof."

Perks says he suddenly felt something take over his whole body. Beginning in the pit of his stomach, it "whooshed" up through his frame so powerfully that he expected it "to come out my mouth." Instead, this weird presence, which was "both physical and mental," went up to the top of his skull where it exploded in a single, agonizing cry: "Joey."

Brenda, he explained, was devoted to her pet cat, Joey, and he immediately knew she was worried about its fate, left alone in her apartment. "It was like another's pain and anguish experienced inside yourself as an alien presence. It was a most extraordinary experience."

Perks, who had never so much as given the possibility of a hereafter or the survival of human personality beyond the grave a moment's thought prior to these strange encounters, has been profoundly shaken up by all of this.

He hasn't had a sudden, religious conversion, and he's not an evangelist for immortality. But all his previous assumptions and attitudes to the big questions of existence and meaning have been shattered. He is now adamantly convinced that "the human spirit can exist after death – at least for the length of time between Brenda's death and her encounters with me the next day."

He told me: "I now am convinced there is a spirit within us, and also that my daughter is happy and not in any kind of pain."

Today Perks will tell you that at first he thought his experiences were a comfort and a "gift." Now he's aware that they are also an enormous intellectual and moral challenge. "I'm having to rethink everything I believed and valued before."

As I point out in my book *Life After Death*, millions of people who once kept silence for fear they'd be thought crazy are now coming forward with stories startlingly similar to Perks'. Millions of others have had a near-death experience.

One of my research findings has been that, like Perks, many of these people were agnostics or atheists. They have come to belief in an afterlife only *after* their paranormal experience. It seems that those who have long argued that belief in life after death is just wish-fulfillment may all have some serious rethinking to do.

‒ Life After Death, II ‒

The Buddha's enlightenment came with the realization that we live on illusion. Our normal, day-to-day ego battens itself on illusions about the nature of reality and about the aims and purposes of living.

As one reflects upon North American society, one illusion leaps out as more potent and endemic than any other – the illusion that each of us is somehow going to live forever.

At the root of most of what passes for entertainment, at the heart of our obsessions with lifestyle, personal appearance, health, success, and that great bugaboo, security, lies a feverish denial of our own inevitable mortality. Almost all advertising, particularly on television, is vitiated by the baseless, unexamined assumption that death is nowhere on the horizon for anybody. The same premise lies beneath the surface of the highly commercialized fitness craze – jogging oneself silly, "pumping iron" until you're blue in the face, or playing squash at an age when one ought to be smelling the roses.

The last thing we want to hear is the sentiment so aptly put by the late British psychiatrist R. D. Laing. He said we frantically try to ignore the fact that we are all infected with "a sexually transmitted disease [life] with a 100 per cent mortality rate." This fear and denial of death, which permeates our great medical institutions as palpably as it does the glossy fashion magazines – and our present funeral practices – has some extraordinary consequences. It accounts for, among other things, the shallowness and general lacklustre quality of life as it is lived today by millions.

If there is one thing the great philosophers and religious thinkers of the past have agreed upon it is this: coming to terms with one's mortality is the *sine qua non* of living intensely, in depth, in the here and now. Never to give death a thought is to live the life of the fattened steer that grazes on, oblivious of its destiny.

One of the things I observed firsthand when I was a parish minister was the way in which those who have had a heart attack, or some other "nudge" that has reminded them of how precarious a hold we have on life, suddenly change their values and attitudes. The same phenomenon has been widely reported by Dr. Raymond Moody and many other experts who have been researching the effects of having a near-death experience while undergoing surgery, suffering cardiac arrest, or during some other "clinical death" trauma. In almost every instance, the patient's sense of what is truly important in life is profoundly altered – for the better.

So far from being morbid or anti-life, the frank facing of the truth that from the moment of birth we are committed to a process that ineluctably ends in death underscores the miracle of nature, of friends and loved ones, of the fact that we are here at all. It lends meaning and clarity to our experiences of beauty; it heightens all pleasures, whether of body, mind, or soul.

Interestingly, dream analysts such as Carl Jung and Dr. Marie-Louise von Franz, his disciple and collaborator, have shown that when people refuse to take their mortality seriously, their unconscious mind often forces them to wake up to it. When a person in their prime suddenly dreams of his or her own death, they argue, it doesn't mean that death is imminent. What is happening is that the unconscious is saying: "You're trying to live too superficially, pretending you're forever young. It's time to cut the nonsense and think more deeply about where your life is going, about what's really important."

Once the hard reality of death breaks into one's consciousness, the avoidance of all the truly big questions is no longer a luxury one can afford. To face death squarely is to bring into sharpest possible focus the meaning of your own life. What is the point of it all? Is there a God before Whom one is responsible? Is death indeed the end of everything, or is it some kind of birth into an entirely new beginning?

These are the truly existential questions – and ultimately, the only ones that matter. Traditionally, religion has been the place where one would begin to look for the answers. And, if we understand religion in the widest possible sense of the word, I would maintain that it is still the proper place to start.

Unfortunately, the communication gap between religious institutions and the majority of citizens today is so wide that the normative answers can no longer be heard or understood. This means that if our churches, temples, and synagogues want to recover their vital role in these twilight days of the second millennium A.D., some quite revolutionary changes must take place.

It's not sufficient to tinker with prayer books or to introduce quirky gimmicks into services. It's not even a matter of finding new words for old dogmas. What's needed is a drastic re-examination of the underlying concepts in the light of the new ways in which ancient questions are now being asked.

The faiths can get excited about fund-raising. I wish they were more excited about this.

— Your Epitaph —

Robert Frost wrote a poem in 1942 in which he mused about the kind of epitaph he would choose.

I would have written of me on my stone:
I had a lover's quarrel with the world.

One of the most moving – and often funniest – experiences one can have is to walk through an English churchyard and read the inscriptions. One I heard of said: "At 40 miles drove Willy Smidder; his axle broke and his wife's a widder." In the churchyard at my first parish, St. Margaret's-in-the-Pines, West Hill, Ontario, one old motto on a woman's gravestone said: "She hath done what she could."

I particularly like the simple epitaph on the grave of Charles Williams. Williams, an important and yet little-known novelist of our century (*War In Heaven, All Hallow's Eve, Descent Into Hell*) lies buried in a tiny churchyard in the heart of Oxford. After the dates of his birth and death, the stone reads: "Under the Mercy."

It may seem a sombre subject, but I wonder how many people ever do what Frost did and imagine what their epitaph might be.

This can be a surprisingly helpful, even therapeutic thing to do. It is not only a kind of *memento mori*, or reminder of one's own mortality; it acts as a kind of focusing meditation for one's life. In other words, it's by thinking of how we would like our life one day to be summed up that we can clarify our goals more sharply. Another way to do it would be simply to ask ourselves what will have to happen for our lives to be pronounced a success *from our own point of view*.

Failure to give at least some thought to what it is that we ulti-mately care about, what it is that lies behind or ahead of all our other motives and busyness, leads to an underlying sense of angst or depression.

I remember how, when I was at college, the coxswain for our

racing "eight" became ill one day and an inexperienced replacement was dragged along to steer.

We set off all right, but suddenly there was a huge bump that nearly pitched the entire crew into the Thames. We had run up on the bank and were stuck fast – much to the indignation of some nesting swans and the embarrassment of our coach.

We eventually got loose and set off again with a crisp crunch of oars sweeping the water. All at once there was an agonized cry of warning from the coach, who was cycling along the towpath. Too late! We rammed the Oxford University crew's training boat, *The Leander*, right in midships and nearly capsized both it and ourselves. The air was filled with impolite language that could be distinctly heard across Christ Church meadows and is said to have startled many tourists.

When we finally limped back to the boathouse, the new cox was grilled as to what in the world he thought he was doing. It turned out that the poor fellow was exceedingly shortsighted but had left his glasses back at his college for fear of dropping them overboard.

The moral is obvious. If you have little idea of where you're going, you risk either shipwreck or the haunting pain of feeling that you are going nowhere in particular. That's precisely where millions of people in western society are just now. No goal, no sense of purpose that is ultimately satisfying, and thus no meaning to their lives.

True, many get by with an acceptance of some or all of the goals flaunted seductively by the culture – having the right image, "making it" both financially and in all other ways, knowing the "right" people, foods, wines, films, and places to go, or, in a word, being "successful." The trouble is that you don't have to reflect very much at all on the contemporary scene in North America to realize that this whole smorgasbord of delights can leave one with a terribly hollow feeling in the pit of the stomach. Deep in our innermost being, we feel a tremendous sense of dissatisfaction because the very instincts encoded in the cells, not just of our brains but of our whole bodies, tell us we were intended to be so much more.

Life is not about having but about being. It is not about arriving but about growing. It is not about external achievements but about inner maturation. Ultimately, it's about the often-painful journey towards ever greater wholeness as a full, human being.

If, as I believe, it is our capacity for the life of the spirit that makes us uniquely human, then growth towards maturity will mean the integration of our physical, mental, and spiritual aspects into an ever-deeper unity.

Since death is not the end but a new beginning, this process, transformed, will still go on. That's why I think I'd like my own epitaph to be: "To be continued."

— Your Life's Work —

Thousands of young people each year launch out on what they expect will be a lifetime of earning a living. How do they decide what line of work they should be going after?

Tens of thousands of Canadian workers are totally bored, frustrated, and trapped by their jobs. They can find no meaning in them. Often the pent-up psychic energy from being caught in this rut takes its toll in illness, alcoholism, and other forms of escapism. Is there any way to avoid sweating at some completely unfulfilling task for the best years of one's life, wishing the present away while waiting for retirement?

Across the country, close to one million Canadians are unemployed. This includes former executives and others in middle age who have been "terminated." Many of these are so discouraged they scarcely know any longer where to begin.

Timothy Elliott, a friend of mine who is an Anglican priest, has just completed some research on the "dynamics of work and vocation" and has come up with a plan of attack that speaks to all of the situations I've just listed. With his permission, and because it fits so closely with some of my own experience and reflection, I want to set his formula out as simply as possible. It's a "recipe" that anyone can adapt to his or her own life situation.

To use it properly, you will need to set aside some regular time for a while. To act on it, you will need a large amount of that toughest of virtues – courage.

There are five aspects or parts. First, you need to analyse your own personality. Elliott used some sophisticated techniques with his control group for this, but they're not essential.

Take a sheet of paper and make two lists – one with your strengths on it – the things you're good at, the things you're equipped to do – and another with your weaknesses. Do you like working with facts, for example, or are your gifts more with people-related activities?

It helps to have a friend check this with you. Often we overlook abilities we take for granted; sometimes we deny weaknesses that are glaringly obvious to others. You need the fullest possible picture of yourself.

Second, get to know your own life story. It's surprising how many people have never looked at their own life in terms of what its main themes have been. Often, even vocational decisions that seem sharply at odds with anything we've done before are really in tune with deeper, underlying themes. For example, I became a journalist after being a pastor and a professor. But journalism is at its best a form of teaching, and so the deeper continuity is there after all.

The simplest way to look at your story is to get a large piece of paper and draw a line across it. Then, put a series of dots on it for every major event, crisis, or change and write briefly the significance of each above or below. Any job change you make will most likely be in keeping with themes already latent in your life to date.

Third, you have to take time to analyse your present circumstances. Any decisions you make now must be responsible, and this means taking full account of current commitments, whether to relationships, banks, or whatever. There is little use deciding you are cut out to be a brain surgeon if you have large debts, six kids, and no formal education. It's not impossible, just highly unlikely.

Fourth, and to me the most important element in this exercise, is discovering and setting down on paper your deepest passion or allurement. In other words, what – all other things being equal – do you most enjoy doing in life? What do you feel most gladness doing? What really, to use a clichéd phrase, turns you on?

The happiest people I know have this one thing in common: they are all doing for a living what they would be doing anyway, even if they had all the money in the world. They sometimes find it hard to believe they're being paid for doing what wild horses couldn't pull them away from doing in any case.

I believe that by listening to the innermost promptings of our deepest likes and dislikes we are discerning the divine Spirit's voice – God's call or vocation for our lives.

If one assesses his or her personality, life story, circumstances, and deepest drives, a picture will begin to emerge of the kind of work one should pursue.

Only the fifth ingredient remains – some planning on specific, immediate steps to be taken towards such a goal. This process requires great effort. But, as an old Latin teacher used to tell us: "*Nulla palma sine pulvere;*" "No victory without first the dust of the arena."

PART THREE

A MATTER OF ETHICS

Lost in Information

At the raucous party that opens the 1960s film *The Graduate*, Dustin Hoffman is advised by a drunken friend of his father's to get into plastics as a career. The advice wasn't bad – at that time. Today it would have all the relevance of an Edsel.

A youth in a comparable situation now might well be told to "get into information." We live, after all, in what is spoken of with some reverence as "The Information Age." The reasons for this hardly need to be elaborated.

Sometimes, though, we become so infatuated with our technological wizardry that we are just as oblivious to the downside of the information explosion as an older generation was to the negative side to plastics.

You can have a glut of information. Your receptors can be assaulted by so many different messages that they become jammed. We all drown at times in an ocean of images and slogans. The mind becomes numb and switches off, or loses its ability to discern truth anywhere. We can even speak of the brain's problem in ridding itself of "toxic waste."

T. S. Eliot spoke prophetically of this dilemma years ago when he wrote in "Choruses from 'The Rock'":

Where is the wisdom we have lost in knowledge?
Where is the knowledge we have lost in information?

The cycles of heaven in twenty centuries
Bring us farther from God and nearer to the Dust.

What Eliot saw so vividly was that you can have information running out of your ears — on everything from art or wine to baseball
trivia — and still lack wisdom. We can split the atom, create com-
puters that simulate thinking, or send space probes to explore the
solar system — and yet remain fools.

That there is a very good chance of our doing so is signalled to us
in myriad ways. Take a good look at the kind of values uppermost
in the information bombardment all of us daily endure. Most of it
is obsessed with a narcissistic concern for the body — its adorn-
ment, hygiene, pleasures, fantasies, or ailments. Much of the rest
of advertising focuses on the extensions of our bodies — our homes,
cars, tools, toys, and other status symbols.

Small wonder young people are often confused and feel so
alienated. The messages are so mixed. For example, the entire
culture screams the lie that you aren't normal unless you're sexually active and that this is the greatest good known to humans,
while parents and/or others try to sound a note of caution.

We wish them to be wise about so many matters, but in all the
information of our day, where is wisdom praised as a prize beyond
all others? Good looks, athletic skills, academic prowess, success of
any kind — all these are highly touted. But there is no gold medal,
Olympic or other, for the gift that alone knows how to use these
well.

You can't get the wisdom Eliot speaks about from video stores or
newspapers. It doesn't come with diplomas or degrees. It has no
relationship to the size of one's paycheque or to one's niche in the
corporate edifice.

Wordsworth once said that poetry comes from "emotion recol-
lected in tranquillity." Wisdom comes from experience reflected
upon in tranquillity. Our culture exalts action. Reflection is the
moment of inaction that alone makes action meaningful and
targetted upon the Good.

Reflection — or if you like, meditation — carries none of the kudos or glamour of strutting and tearing about in pursuit of material success. But without it we are like the fattened steer waiting all unaware for the final axe to fall.

Wisdom comes from not resting until we wrestle a meaning for our lives, as the Viennese psychiatrist Viktor Frankl puts it; someone outside ourselves to love and live for, or some task still waiting to be done.

Wisdom comes from learning to listen to the wisdom of our own innermost being – the voice of the divine mystery within. It comes, too, from hearing this same voice wherever it speaks.

Increasingly, as one grows older – especially in this "Ecozoic Age" – it speaks aloud in all creation. There is a wisdom of the Earth itself, a wisdom in running water, in mountains and woodlands, in the wind's caress of a field of shining corn, in the flight of the peregrine falcon or the shimmer of a darting trout.

The hills are alive, indeed, with a sound of music, or with what the Psalmist calls a kind of heavenly speech. Even the starry heaven itself, he says, "utters language" as it praises the wisdom of its Maker.

It is unwise to claim to have wisdom. But not to desire it, to work for it, and pray for it is the greatest unwisdom of all.

— Advertising Values —

There's one great gift of technology that stands head and shoulders above the rest. It's the muting button on the remote control of our TV set. Were it not for that, television, apart from one or two ad-free channels, would be even more of an affliction than it generally is.

I particularly hate beer commercials, though I have nothing against beer itself in its proper place. I also dislike the commercials for hundreds of other products: toilet-bowl cleansers, furniture on the never-never plan, aids to feminine hygiene, weight-loss schemes, you name it.

Following Gilbert and Sullivan's admirable advice about

making the punishment fit the crime, it's my belief that, just as TV evangelists should be forced to watch reruns of their old programs for all eternity, our ad and marketing strategists should be locked in a room and made to view their inane creations *ad infinitum*.

But it's not just the nuisance factor, or the way 95 per cent of all advertising grossly insults our sensibilities and intelligence. There are much more dangerous forces at work.

I recognize that there are *some* ethical advertisers, and there is a place for making known a particular product's function or merits in a sane, inoffensive way. But, in one form or another, the majority of advertising in the western world is wittingly or unwittingly engaged in the propagation of lies.

Much of current marketing research is involved in the sophisticated exploration of where it is that people (always degradingly called "consumers") feel an itch. The challenge then is to come up with cleverly packaged and marketed products to scratch that itch. The temptation here to pander and pimp on behalf of every weakness – from covetousness or envy to insecurity about one's personal image or fears about one's health – has been just too seductive to resist.

But there's a more malignant twist as well. In addition to sniffing out more existing itches, like ferrets in a rabbit warren, there is a vast, high-powered endeavour aimed at constantly creating new itches hitherto unfelt and unknown – undreamed of, in fact. They thus beget false needs (wants) and then trumpet the glad news that their client just happens to have the product to satisfy them.

Bluntly put, this is immoral. It not only ensures that our wasteful consumption of planetary resources – no matter how many "green" slogans we are sold – will keep growing apace, it also flies directly in the face of the basic laws of human happiness and fulfilment.

The modern marketing message is: The more you buy, possess, consume, or enjoy, the happier you'll be.

Compare that with a more ancient wisdom. Henry Thoreau found that a basic rule for happiness was "simplify, simplify" in every way you can. Every possession complicates your life to some degree and distracts your mind.

Jesus, in the Gnostic Gospel of Thomas, is reported to have told his disciples to "become passers-by." I believe the saying is authentic. If so, nothing could be more totally at odds with the underlying message of our ad culture. What it means is: You are on a trek; if you want to enter into Life, travel light; sit loose to material things; realize your true, spiritual nature and pass by anything that would hold you back.

But the message of the advertisers promotes a second perversion – that is, that any kind of pain, suffering, inconvenience, defect, or block to our personal pleasure is a terrible evil and an injustice not to be tolerated by any decent human being. They thus falsify our view of life and trivialize the power of self-discipline and/or suffering to change our lives in a positive way.

When we suffer, we are not being singled out for punishment by some "fickle finger of fate." We are sharing in the life process of the universe itself. To live is to suffer – so say all the sages and prophets. To be told to expect otherwise is to be led down the paths of fools.

While nobody in his or her senses would willingly seek out suffering (though we bring a good deal of it upon ourselves), it can be what Jung called "a creative illness," an ordeal, whether physical or emotional, that forges inner growth and harmony. Most of our deepest insights and soul-enlargements come not when everything is bright and beautiful but when we have passed through some valley of shadow.

That's the kind of reality that Madison Avenue can't stand.

— So What? —

We are living in the age of the great "So what?" Millions of ordinary people in North American society would, if they were candid, admit that these two words could one day form a fitting epitaph on their grave. The phrase hangs unspoken in the air in the buses, subway trains, and cars as they head home at day's end. It hovers in the houses of the rich and famous as age creeps on and the glittering toys no longer amuse.

Nowhere, however, is it more bitingly relevant than in what passes for entertainment today. Beneath the hype and glitz there's a chasm of yawning emptiness. The bulk of television entertainment is merely "chewing gum for the eye." Hollywood films, still the main dish at major festivals and at movie houses here and abroad, are, with rare exceptions, largely frenzy or froth – or both. The more they pretend to deal with serious themes, the more superficial they become. Even though the critics and reviewers vie to surpass each other in their showering of clichéd superlatives and contorted, behind-the-scenes-type insights, the fact is that 90 to 95 per cent of movies hailed as blockbusters are shallow, manipulative disappointments.

They are often well-acted. They shimmer with special effects. They (nearly all now) have the obligatory nudity, the steamy, *de rigueur* faking of various sex acts, and, of course, graphically depicted violence. The Elizabethan four-letter word for sexual congress now occurs so frequently and in such a wide range of grammatical forms that you wonder how movie characters were ever able to communicate at all in the great films of yesterday.

But when you have seen and heard all this yet one more time, when the final credits roll and the house lights go back on, the question rises to a near-deafening roar: "So what?" Our senses have been assaulted, played with, even seduced, but what has there been for mind or soul? What real deepening of our understanding of or our compassion for the human condition has transpired? Have we had our hearts fired by fresh glimpses of the heights as well as the depths of the workings of the human spirit? To what extent have our minds been stretched, our ideals challenged or reinforced, our sense of excellence honed ever sharper than before?

Some will respond with the mindless argument: "I don't watch TV or go to the movies to be edified, instructed, challenged or too deeply moved. I just go to be entertained." There are several problems with that. The most important is the hidden assumption that entertainment is a kind of neutral activity totally void of values, ideology, or the potential to shape either the individual or the society. The opposite is true. A work of creativity, however great or however common, can only come into being in and with a certain moral or value-laden framework. Otherwise, it would be utterly meaningless, and formless as well.

One may well not agree with Plato's remedies for what he saw as the dangers to society posed by the purveyors of arts-and-entertainment in his time, but no one knew better than he the enormous power of imaginative creations to affect an audience for good or ill. Like it or not, everything we give our undivided attention to enters our consciousness and is stored or dealt with in some way. It plays a part in shaping who or what we are, even though we might be rejecting it with one part of our mind.

The fact that something is viewed as entertainment, according to Plato, renders it just that much more insidious. The audience or the reader is lulled into feeling that nothing of any ultimate importance is going on; it's simply a matter of receiving pleasure. The more technically skilful the production, the greater the risk of unknowingly swallowing the hidden message or values. If this message or these values cheapen or erode our sense of excellence, if they promote a coarsening of our taste and a vulgarization of manners, language, and thought, we need to take a hard look at what is really taking place.

It is, to my mind, no mystery that life appears void of meaning to so many when their leisure hours are spent feeding mind and heart with what is vacuous or mean. It's a spiritual diet utterly bereft of either vitamins or calories fit for sustaining a purposeful, in-depth existence. You watch the TV show, read the pulp novel, or go to the movies, and at the end of it all none of it really matters. It has simply "killed" time, the most precious gift we have.

What's the alternative? Well, one solution is to turn the set off (Canadian children spend more hours watching TV than they do in school!), avoid seeing films that insult one's intelligence or demean one's humanity, and leave the shallow novels on the shelf. Nothing is as sensitive to what the public will pay for and swallow as the commercial media of every stripe. They will only respond with higher quality if the public demands it by hitting them where they hurt – in the cash register.

What would accomplish most both for individuals and society, however, would be a massive return to the great classics of music, art, literature, and film. The greatest blessing of today is that all of these are so available and cheap. They deal with eternal themes. They elevate and inspire. They help us as humans to know we can be better. Life glows with meaning just because they're there.

— Euthanasia, I —

There's a familiar, apocryphal story that tells of the stranger who meets an attractive woman in a bar. He asks her if she would be willing to sleep with him for a million dollars. When she replies in the affirmative, he asks her whether she would be prepared to do so for fifty dollars.

"Of course not," she retorts indignantly. "What kind of a woman do you think I am?"

He replies: "We've already established that. We just haven't agreed on a price."

This anecdote illustrates an important principle, one with a wider application than appears at first glance.

The basic fallback position of those who would shirk entirely the awesome decisions facing us as a result of the miracles of current medical technology is to piously affirm: "We mustn't play God."

But, as in the fictional meeting in the bar, we're no longer discussing whether or not to "play God." That decision has already been taken. Anybody who thinks otherwise would do well to spend a few hours visiting in an intensive-care unit, or for that matter in the other wards of any hospital.

For better or for worse, our species now has the capability of directly interfering in a whole range of processes once thought to be sacrosanct, irreversible, the private concern of the Creator. Indeed, as the Bible itself maintains, our ultimate calling is to be co-creators or "fellow workers" with the very Ground and Author of the cosmos. We're doing that now as never before.

The real question, as we approach the crucial issues of life and death today, is not whether or not to "play God" – that's already been established – but, what kind of God are we going to be?

For example, having taken the power to save and prolong people's lives far past the point where nature or God would once have snuffed them out, how is this God-like intervention to be consummated? Put quite baldly, is it a proper use of our new "divine" mastery to continue a person's physical life long past the point where it has any meaning, dignity, or value to them?

What kind of God would deliberately and by artificial means prolong the dying of someone who has reached "a vegetative state"? Or someone terminally ill whose pain can not be sedated by even the most powerful drug? Or someone facing the total disintegration of all their mental and physical capacities?

Few of us could stand by passively and watch our dearest pet – or indeed any animal – suffering in a terminal agony and not feel compelled to act mercifully. Yet when it comes to what is generally called euthanasia, nearly everybody panics and wants to back off from dealing with it openly and frankly.

Certainly only a fool at this moment of history would dare to try to state categorically what ought or ought not to be done in each and every case. But unless we in Canada are prepared to begin an informed, thorough, public debate, we will continue to condone a situation in which modern medical advances often cause a more intense form of human suffering than the maladies they are aimed at healing.

More and more people today who, when they were of sound mind and in reasonable vigour, were deeply opposed to ending their days in an artificially prolonged, tortured form of seemingly endless dying are finding themselves in precisely that calamitous state. In spite of "living wills," in spite of everything, they cannot live and they cannot die. They plead with friends and loved ones, they beg their doctors, but nobody will give them the euthanasia (the word means, literally, "a good death") they so desperately seek.

In the worst scenario of all, many are reduced by strokes, accidents, Alzheimer's disease, or other calamities to a state where they are mentally unable even to ask for final relief. Anyone who thinks this is exaggerated has very little experience of the real world of hospitals, nursing homes, or chronic-care facilities.

It is a fact, though one not willingly discussed by most doctors, that direct or so-called "active euthanasia" is practised already in some cases where the patient, the family, and the physician agree. But, while merciful and just, in my view, the secretiveness and the *ad hoc* nature of such decisions – as well as the great legal risks – mean that the matter cannot be left there.

— Euthanasia, II —

Is it ever right for a doctor to assist in procuring "a good death" (euthanasia) for a patient in extremis *or facing a painful future without hope of recovery?*

This was the question I posed to readers of my weekly column. The responses, more than 200 letters (many quite lengthy and detailed), constituted one of the most moving experiences in my journalistic career.

People opened their hearts and shared things they said they had rarely discussed with anybody else. They told stories of great heroism, of love beyond measure, of great pain and an infinitude of tears.

While obviously not a scientific study, I believe this sampling of responsible, intelligent, and articulate citizens from every walk of life illustrates where most Canadians stand on this complex moral question today.

Here, in brief, is what I discovered:

• There is a remarkably deep concern in society over this matter – far greater than any of the media coverage or public discussion to date has shown.

• It's not death that people fear; they're frightened of a prolonged dying hooked up to a medical wonderworld, of a total loss of dignity and meaning, and of causing endless agony for their loved ones.

• Because of this, there is virtually unanimous support for doctors allowing the moribund or the hopelessly brain-damaged patient to "go." People do not want "heroic measures" taken to resuscitate or sustain them when all hope for at least a minimal quality of life is gone. They argue almost unanimously for so-called "passive euthanasia," that is, any approach to letting the dying or hopelessly comatose have a good death short of intervening with a needle.

• But, in addition, *about 90 per cent of respondents said* "Yes, under certain circumstances, there is a time and a place for active euthanasia."

• There was concern about the possibility of abuse and the need to establish guidelines. Many argued that we should all make our wishes about euthanasia for ourselves known well in advance. "Living wills," they said, should be given full legal status.

• Many said they wouldn't want to be artificially kept alive while others needed care, but very few argued for euthanasia because of the costs of current practices.

The Reverend Gordon Winch, a director of the Distress Centre, Toronto, expressed opposition. Noting that his main concern is with suicide prevention, Winch says that "growth in approval for those who choose to end a life of suffering creates some problems for those who, facing similar circumstances, choose to live. They are made to feel guilty they have chosen life.

"A related problem is found in the high cost of the last six months of life in medical services.... Spiralling health costs seem to put pressure on families and patients who are terminally ill to choose some form of shortening the length of life."

He adds: "Many people fear a future full of unbearable pain. I'm told at the Pain Clinic at Toronto General that most pain can be relieved and that rarely is there severe pain where no easement is possible. We have not been able to make this widely known or believed."

Karen Rawlings, head of a right-to-life group, wrote: "The euthanasia debate is the pro-life issue of the 90s. My answer to your question is a resounding 'no!' A doctor's sworn oath is to heal not to kill...."

Two or three argued that pain and suffering are really good for you and part of God's plan. "It's not Christian," they said, "to take your own life or anybody else's – even if they ask for it."

Typical was the man who wrote: "It's a poor comparison to say we would put a pet out of its pain.... God is letting it all happen to see how we handle it and to let us know how hopeless it is without him.... He works in mysterious ways."

On the majority side, there were simply dozens of stories like this·one: "My friend is 83, alone, with advanced Alzheimer's disease for four years. She tried suicide twice last year but failed. Hospitalized with double pneumonia in January, she made a living will, got rid of everything and then stopped all the medications she had been taking for 12 years. She expected to die but did not. She had always loved life.... On April 5 she stopped eating. Still she did not die. She is now getting blood transfusions so she will be strong enough to ship to a nursing home. She's terrified. She is being kept alive against her will for a life she does not want. Her terror is not to die, it is in being kept alive. She has made a choice that society will not accept. Now she faces a future that can be only more physical and mental pain."

I wish this was the most pathetic of the cases revealed. Far from it. Space prevents me from repeating the worst. Horrific things are happening today in the name of medicine and respect for life. That's why this debate must go on.

⁓ Euthanasia, III ⁓

Controversy over the right to die and euthanasia is now set before us as a major ethical debate for the 1990s.

Any ethicist, columnist, doctor, or cleric who thinks he or she has the final, definitive right and wrong of this matter is suffering from a serious delusion and needs to stop and reflect. It will be a great tragedy if people simply line up into rigid, opposing camps and begin hurling insults and one-sided pronouncements at one another, as in the abortion debate.

I want to try to clarify here some aspects of the discussion so far that trouble me and, in my view, obstruct the quest for answers.

• There seems to be no shortage of those who want to end all useful discussion by arguing that "we mustn't play God." The Roman Catholic bishops of Oregon and Washington recently issued a joint pastoral letter called "Living and Dying Well: A Pastoral Letter about the End of Life." Commenting at a press conference later, Bishop Thomas Connolly of Baker, Oregon, said: "We want all power in our hands and every choice available given to us. It sounds like we are trying to make ourselves God – instead of being His servants."

Bringing in God in this way is enough to stop many good folk from thinking any further for themselves. It's (no doubt unconsciously) a form of theological blackmail. What's more, it's neither logical nor compassionate to "make ourselves God" at every step in modern medicine by massive, high-tech interventions, and then piously draw back and refuse to make responsible decisions when the patient wants a merciful end or it's obvious that further care would simply prolong dying.

Surely it's the opposite of what the healing profession is all about if, having defied nature's way at every point by its technowizardry, at the end it abandons the patient to an existence like that of a fly impaled on a pin – unable to live, unable to die.

For better or worse, a humanity that, to use the German theologian Dietrich Bonhoeffer's phrase, has "come of age" – has become a co-Creator with God through technology – must assume all the awesome responsibilities that go with this, from a right use of nuclear fission to a sane decision about when enough is enough in the attempt to keep people alive.

• A great deal is said by some about "passive" euthanasia as opposed to "active" euthanasia. The first, which is approved of by most authorities, including most medical associations and religious institutions (even the Vatican), refers to allowing a terminally ill patient to die without taking "heroic" measures to prevent it.

Active euthanasia, on the other hand, which is prohibited by the Criminal Code of Canada, denotes the taking of some specific action – for example, administering a lethal drug dose, which brings death quickly and without pain.

The problem, however, as anyone familiar with this issue knows, is that the incredible complexity of high-tech medicine today has blurred the lines between these two to the point where it is more a game of semantics than true ethical reasoning to differentiate between them. For example, if you take someone off a respirator at their request when you know that to do so will kill them, is that really less "active" than giving a patient dying in agony a lethal injection of morphine? Is it truly more ethical and less active to let an impossibly deformed infant (for example, one technically described as a "monster") die by slow starvation with the sign over its crib "NPO," an abbreviation of the Latin for "nothing by mouth," rather than to give it a quick, merciful death?

• It is pointless trying to carry on a meaningful debate without being quite realistic about the current situation. There is absolutely no question that so-called active euthanasia is being performed by many doctors in Canada right now. In private, some doctors are forthright about the fact that they have obeyed the wishes of a patient and/or family when there was no hope whatever of recovery, and have given a lethal dose. Their own rationalization is that the injection is to relieve pain, even though they're aware that in the amount administered the morphine or other drug will precipitate a peaceful end.

I believe they are correct in doing so, and that they are fulfilling their total responsibility towards the patient's well-being. However, under the law, they are liable to criminal prosecution. It's time this situation was talked about more openly, and that doctors were given more protection than they now have.

• Perhaps the worst fallacy vitiating a clear ethical discussion of this entire dilemma is an underlying assumption that death is the greatest of all possible evils, a horrific medical failure, and something that must not and will not ever happen to any of us. Our death-denying culture has bewitched us so that our mortality, our most obvious common attribute, is treated as though it were the ultimate enemy.

From my own experience as a priest, I can say there are times when death comes to a patient as the ultimate healer and as a friend.

— Euthanasia, IV —

She was a dignified, elderly lady when I first met her ten years ago. Then, a few years later, she had a debilitating stroke. Her first wish was to die.

"Why doesn't somebody give me a needle or hit me over the head with a shovel?" she would stammer with the greatest difficulty and in the midst of bitter tears. "I can't go on like this."

In time, though, she recovered enough to use a walker. Some days, she would proudly stand at attention to show how she could manage without props. Occasionally she even gave us a military-style salute.

But, while she learned to cope with a nursing home, her memory was so bad that she'd forget the end of a sentence before she had really begun it. She had the will, but, to her deep frustration, little ability to communicate. Having known her before, it tugged at us to see her wave good-bye from her window – a tiny, frail, white-haired figure, like a ghost from the past.

At ninety-three, after four years of living surrounded by the incontinent, the senile, and the demented, she had another stroke. She was rushed to hospital and placed in intensive care. Stabilized, though she never regained consciousness, she was moved to a regular room. She was fed intravenously and, when she got pneumonia, antibiotics were added to her other medications.

In the end, after about five weeks, the tubes were removed and she was allowed to do what she had so desperately wanted to do ever since her first stroke – to die more or less in peace.

The vision of her after her second stroke, lying there week after week, will stay with me a long time. She was obviously dying, and she had always – even before any of her illness – made it clear that she never wanted to go to a nursing home, never mind be kept living by artificial means once her active life was over. Yet there she was, suspended between living and dying, at the mercy of forces over which it seems nobody had any control.

I thought it was wrong then. I still do. After the second stroke, she shouldn't have been sent anywhere. The humane and moral thing would have been to have given her the best possible care where she was and to have allowed her to die naturally. It was a mockery of the healing art and an injury to her human dignity to try to keep alive by pills and tubes a ninety-three-year-old woman who was brain-damaged and unconscious as well.

Yet this is not an isolated incident. It goes on all the time. What's more, it's not easy to stop.

At times it's simply because of human error. For example, an Ohio man is making legal history by suing a Cincinnati hospital *for saving his life*.

Edward Winter, eighty-four, had made it known that he never wanted to be revived if he were close to death. He knew from experience what a curse it can be for elderly people to be resuscitated. His own wife had suffered a lengthy, painful death after medical intervention (electrical shock) had left her brain-damaged.

So, when he had chest pains and collapsed in 1988, a doctor at the hospital agreed to enter a "Do Not Resuscitate" order on his chart. But the doctor forgot to put it on the bedside monitor. Thus, when Winter had another heart attack and sudden death threatened, his nurse took the usual emergency action.

Applying the electrodes, she revived him. Two days later, he had a stroke. This left him in a nursing home, partially paralyzed, unable to speak without tears, and angry at having to live out such an existence against his will. Doctors say he won't improve and that he could live for many years. A prolonged, living death! His medical bills total about $100,000 (U.S.). His savings have gone.

But it's more than a matter of such errors. Medical technology today has produced a mind-set that too easily takes over. Death is regarded as the ultimate insult, an unacceptable failure. Death must be kept at bay no matter what the other costs – loss of dignity, loss of freedom, loss of everything that makes life worth living. Our chronic-care nursing homes are full of the evidence of what happens when the medical wizardry goes awry.

At times it is the family and relatives who are the problem. Many doctors tell me that often when, in their judgement, an elderly person ought to be permitted to die as comfortably and as quickly as possible, they are subjected to intense family pressure to keep intervening. The risk of being sued if they don't comply makes it difficult, even impossible, always to follow their conscience.

Frequently, it is the doctors' own fear of death that complicates the picture. Part of the unwillingness to let anyone die is rooted in the medical staff's denial of their own mortality.

― The Gulf War, I ―

The following six columns were originally published after the invasion of Kuwait by Saddam Hussein's Iraqi forces in 1990. The United Nations Security Council, with support from Canada, had imposed an embargo against Iraq and against occupied Kuwait. A January 15, 1991, deadline was declared, authorizing the use of force to drive Iraq from Kuwait if no peaceful withdrawal had occurred by that time. American and British troops had been stationed in Saudi Arabia since August, and were later joined by a multinational force representing France, Italy, Japan, and others; Canada sent three warships with 800 sailors, and eighteen CF-18 fighter jets with 450 personnel to provide air cover.

Operation Desert Storm was begun on January 16. Iraq launched Scud missiles against Israel and Saudi Arabia. Hundreds of thousands of Iraqi troops and civilians were killed, wounded, or captured in the largest air attack in world history. Hussein ordered his forces to withdraw from Kuwait on February 23, 1991.

The point of view given here was a decidedly minority voice during the Gulf War, both in Canada and in the U.S.A.

Riding the euphoria that has marked the international scene since the recent, head-spinning changes in East-West relations – the end of the Cold War, the breaching of the Berlin Wall, the reunification of Germany – there are those who see the huge, multilateral blockade of Iraq as the harbinger of a new global morality. We will no longer tolerate aggression by one state against a weaker one. All right-thinking nations will rise in a new, God-endorsed righteousness to stop evil dead in its tracks. We are on our way to an end to war and a millennium of peace.

I would love to think so, but the signs at the moment, the fall of 1990, point in exactly the opposite direction. In fact, given the nature of Saddam Hussein and the awesome armaments massing against him, the world is now hurtling towards a conflagration worse than anything we have seen since the Second World War.

Some aspects of the present crisis lead me to believe that, far from seeing the dawn of an age of peace, we are in mortal danger of an unequalled onslaught of darkness. Instead of newness and originality of thinking in the approach to the outrages of Hussein, we are in the grip of the same tired, clichéd – and extremely deadly – thinking that has shed the blood of millions down the ages.

Make no mistake, the United States is clearly signalling to all with the eyes to see and the ears to hear that it intends to destroy "Hussein, his family, his mistress," his military threat, no matter who or what gets in the way. Force is going to be met by greater force once more.

There is a façade of diplomacy, but the arms build-up is where the real thrust is. Once enough troops, sophisticated weaponry, and logistical support are in place, the timely provocation or pretext will easily be found to justify all-out war.

The economic blockade requires a patience, a will, and a cost that the American people simply will not endure for any lengthy period. They want a quick fix, and George Bush feels he must somehow give it or lose face both at home and abroad.

There are some alarming elements here for all who see this as a moral crusade:

• Neither Kuwait nor Saudi Arabia is a democracy in any sense of the word.

• The U.S. itself tolerates the grossest kinds of human-rights abuses abroad when it suits its own interests, for example, in China, Central America, and so on. It has its own way of crushing small nations that thwart its will.

• With the Cold War over, the U.S. military machine desperately needs "enemies." How convenient to find one who "is not like us," who looks different, who has a different religion, and who can (by much straining) be compared to Hitler!

• Bush is in big trouble at home over the budget and other matters. Students of history know that nothing diverts a people from domestic troubles like a foreign military adventure. Significantly, Margaret Thatcher, whose political stock rose during the Falklands War but is now bottoming, is egging Bush on and sounding more bellicose daily.

This war, if (God forbid) it happens, will not be moral. It will not be a "just war" or a sign of a new world order. With its inevitable piles of corpses, its total ruin of the environment, and its legacy of even greater hatreds, it will be one more horrible testament to human folly. As the Bible says, we will have returned like a dog to its own vomit.

Speaking of the Bible, the politicians and all those now calling or preparing for a "hit" on Hussein should ponder well what is meant by "the Samson solution."

You will remember that when Samson was captured by the Philistines and was blinded, they brought him into a great amphitheatre to mock him. Samson asked to be led to where the two main pillars that supported the edifice were standing. Then, bracing himself between them, he heaved outwards and brought the entire structure down in ruins on top of him. Thus, he killed more in his death than in any battle he had fought.

There are Israeli strategists who have spoken of a "Samson solution" – the unleashing of a nuclear response – should Israel's survival ever be threatened. It easily could be, if Hussein seeks to bring the Arab world back to his side by wiping out Tel Aviv or another city.

Or Hussein himself could decide to take everyone with him rather than go down to defeat. He might have a nuclear bomb, despite what the Americans believe. Certainly he reportedly has incredibly powerful new explosives, chemical and biological warheads, and the rocketry to turn the entire Middle East, including the oilfields, into his funeral pyre.

Only a global outcry from ordinary folk like you and me can stop the drift towards war – a policy that is not just unethical but an insane "descent into hell."

— The Gulf War, II —

"Thou art weighed in the balances, and art found wanting." (Daniel 5:27)

I remember sitting as a small boy in Sunday School, in a church basement in the east end of Toronto, listening round-eyed with wonder as the teacher told us the Bible story of the fall of Babylon in 538 B.C. None of us ever dreamed then that we would one day see the entire world gripped by the throat and shaken by events set in motion by and from Babylon – or Baghdad, as it now is called.

Here is the story, in brief:

Belshazzar, who had succeeded to the throne of his father, King Nebuchadnezzar, threw a great feast. As he, his wives and concubines, and all the dignitaries wined and dined, Belshazzar called on his slaves to bring out gold and silver cups and other artefacts his father had stolen from the temple when he had sacked Jerusalem.

But, as they ate and drank from these, celebrating the victory their idols had given them over the God of the Jews, suddenly the king's "countenance was changed" and he began to quake with fear.

"In the same hour came forth fingers of a man's hand, and they wrote ... upon the plaster of the wall of the king's palace: and the king saw the part of the hand that wrote."

Belshazzar at once summoned his astrologers and wise men. He demanded to know what the writing said and what the vision meant. When they proved unable to tell him, his wife remembered the Hebrew captive, Daniel, and urged that he be consulted.

Daniel told the trembling king that the writing said: "MENE, MENE, TEKEL, UPHARSIN." (I recall our delight when one of the boys in our class paraphrased this as "Minnie Minnie tickled the parson.")

Daniel then gave the interpretation in words that have come ringing down the ages ever since: "God hath numbered thy kingdom, and finished it. Thou art weighed in the balances, and art found wanting. Thy kingdom is divided, and given to the Medes and Persians."

That night, King Darius swept through Babylon with his hordes and Belshazzar was put to death. The Babylonian empire was no more.

At this fateful moment of history, some 2,500 years after the destruction of Babylon, we realize sadly what a very little way we have come as a species since that time. If anything, the message declared to Belshazzar all those centuries ago in Babylon/Baghdad has more relevance today than ever before.

Weighed in the balances – and found wanting. That's what this present, tragic crisis is saying to us right now.

History – many would say God through history – inevitably and constantly sifts and judges all nations, cultures, and empires. We are at such a point of judgement at the moment.

The United Nations has been weighed and found wanting. It has been deceived into setting arbitrary and artificial deadlines; into so-called negotiations, which were the equivalent of holding a gun to the head of Saddam Hussein and ordering him to do our bidding or else; and into resorting to a measure of force out of all proportion to the force used in the original act of aggression against Kuwait.

The United States and its allies, including Canada, are being judged and found lacking because of hypocritical double standards where international aggression and injustice are concerned. We have not pursued justice for all parties in the Middle East, particularly the Palestinians, with the same vigour we now so eagerly are devoting to war with Iraq.

Our whole western lifestyle is being judged as we show just how far we are prepared to go in the sacrifice of innocent lives and our own moral values to fight for oil and the preservation of greedy consumerism.

Saddam Hussein also has come to a point of judgement and of sifting. His callous disregard for basic decencies and the rule of law, his failure to beat swords into ploughshares for the safety and betterment of his own people – this (and much more) is now reaping the hellish harvest of war.

What leaps out most cogently as one surveys the events of the past months, and especially of these past few days, is that the verdict of being weighed in the balances and found wanting goes most heavily against religion. In this crisis, it is being written on a global wall for all to see that Judaism, Christianity, and Islam have reached a point of virtual moral bankruptcy.

It was scandalous to hear the pious mouthings of both Saddam Hussein and of George Bush as the final deadline of January 15, 1991, grew near. Each was obviously relying upon his god to give the victory. Each was said to be utterly serene and contented over the decisions he had reached. Each was convinced his side held the only truly moral ground.

But Judaism, Christianity, and Islam all teach that peace is God's will, and that it means not simply the absence of war but *the presence of justice*.

We pay verbal homage to this principle. But once again it has seemed easier to wage war than to face the pain and cost that the quest for authentic world justice would entail.

— The Gulf War, III —

If this war holds, as George Bush believes, "the promise of a new world order," God help us all.

Morality and war are obviously and mutually contradictory. It has been one of the Church's greatest betrayals of Jesus to have dropped his teachings on violence in favour of the theory of the so-called just war.

Justice, like truth, is among the first casualties of any war. Certainly this insane Gulf war is not just by any standards. Not even Billy Graham, pouring holy water over it by staying with George Bush on that fateful night of January 16, or by praying with him for victory at a church service the next day, could make it just. Graham would have been truer to his calling and his Master if he had joined the protesters in Lafayette Park and called for peace, instead of being entertained at the White House. (Only if you can imagine Jesus Christ at ease as court chaplain in the palace of Herod or Pontius Pilate does the Graham scenario make any sense.)

Yet, complex as it is, we desperately need to try to pierce through the miasma of lies and propaganda that surrounds this present crisis to find some basic truths.

That's what one teacher at an American college has tried to do. Last fall, Michael Rivage-Seul, an associate professor at Berea College, Berea, Kentucky, set his students a semester-long project to research the Gulf conflict and the reasons behind it. The results, summarized by him as the main feature in the January 11, 1991, issue of the *National Catholic Reporter*, are worth repeating here.

What the crisis is not about:

The students found that it is not about stopping "another Hitler." Saddam Hussein is not a world-class threat. He's a regional dictator of a medium-sized, Third World country. He is no more or less evil today than when he was the recipient of massive U.S. support against Iran in that eight-year war. His much hyped "military machine" was unable to overwhelm Iran.

It's not about defending democracy. Neither Kuwait nor Saudi Arabia is a democracy; they are feudal oligarchies that have monopolized their countries' enormous wealth for their own luxuries. They want to keep it that way.

Clearly, it's not about upholding the rule that larger countries must never invade smaller ones. The U.S. has never subscribed to that ethic: "History shows the U.S. has virtually written the book on shaping the destinies of weaker neighbours." The students cited the 1983 invasion of Grenada, the ravaging of Panama in

December, 1989 (condemned as illegal by the U.N.), the ten-year war against Nicaragua.

Nor is the war about maintaining "the international rule of law," they found. Indeed, the U.S. has a very uneven track record in this area: "It supports U.N. and World Court decisions only when these coincide with U.S. self-interest."

The most glaring example of this is the way the U.S., along with Israel, has simply ignored the various U.N. resolutions demanding the withdrawal of Israeli troops from their twenty-three-year occupation of the West Bank and Gaza. Similarly, in 1986, the U.S. flatly refused to abide by the World Court's decision to stop its Contra war and to pay reparations to the Sandinista government in Nicaragua.

The conflict is not even about protecting innocent people from atrocities carried out by brutal military dictators or others. The students quickly realized that the U.S. has never backed away from supporting leaders with the most abysmal of human-rights records – Marcos in the Philippines, Samoza in Nicaragua, and Pinochet in Chile. The list is almost endless. Coalition member Hafez Assad, of Syria, is the latest embarrassment.

The students "discovered" as well that U.S. Gulf policy has little to do with a consistent opposition to chemical weapons or nuclear proliferation. Over the years, the U.S. has "staunchly opposed treaties controlling the production of chemical weapons."

And the U.S. has shown little if any concern about nations it approves of, such as Israel, having nuclear weapons. What's more, the U.S. has consistently and steadfastly refused to sign any treaty aimed at ending the testing of even more nuclear weapons in the future. Its latest refusal came virtually on the eve of unleashing the present high-tech blitzkrieg against Iraq.

The students' research is correct. It highlights the abysmal hypocrisy of the loud claims to righteousness of the U.S., Canada, and the rest.

In an interview in the January 7, 1991, issue of *Time* magazine – the one with the remarkable double-exposure shot of the two faces of George Bush on the cover under the title, "Men of the Year" – Bush, who was speaking of his domestic policies, said: "We have the kinder, gentler approach. It is catching on. They used to laugh about the thousand points of light...."

There are ten thousand "points of light" raining down over the civilian population of Iraq every twenty-four hours from U.S. and other Coalition planes. They are bringing death and destruction to innocent people.

We speak, rightly, of Saddam's "terrorism." But nothing equals the terrorism now being used against the Iraqis in the cause of "peace." It's an outrage against our common humanity and must stop, in God's name.

— The Gulf War, IV —

Previously I wrote about the professor at Berea College who set his students a semester-long project to research the Gulf conflict and the reasons behind it. Here are their views on what the war *is* about:

• From the Iraqi side, the crisis is about Saddam Hussein's "arguably legitimate claim" concerning his country's relationship with Kuwait. The students noted that Saddam is the leader of Iraq's Ba'ath party. This is a Pan-Arab organization of Arabs who affirm the unity of their race and who refuse to be bound by the boundaries arbitrarily established by the British occupying forces earlier this century. Pan-Arabs claim the whole Gulf territory as Arab property belonging to the tribes who lived there before colonial powers carved up everything to ensure foreign control of the oil first discovered in 1908.

Apart from puppet kings and emirs set up by the occupying forces, the majority of Arabs in the region have never accepted the artificial division of their land. In particular, Saddam holds that Iraq never recognized the creation of Kuwait – invariably considered part of the Ottoman Empire's Basra province, which became part of Iraq.

What's more, the creation of Kuwait immediately deprived Iraq of access to the Persian Gulf, a route held essential to Iraqi trade ambitions. (Significantly, in the January 28, 1991, issue of *The New Yorker*, William Pfaff points out that Saudi Arabia, Kuwait, the Emirates, Syria, and Jordan are "inventions of this century, lacking historical roots and national integrity." Saudi Arabia had no international political identity until 1932. Kuwait was the result of an agreement between the British and an Arab leader. By contrast, Iraq has a ten-thousand-year legacy behind its modern state.)

Thus, for Pan-Arabs, the invasion of Kuwait is "an act of liberation" rather than of aggression, the students wrote. For Arab masses, as opposed to their leaders, Saddam is a leader who is finally ready to do something about Arab reunification rather than engage in more talk.

• The crisis is about Kuwait's alleged recent looting of Iraq's southern oil fields. Saddam says that, while Iraq was busy fighting Iran, Kuwait pumped oil from its neighbour's vast Rumaila field, which extends into the disputed area between Kuwait and Iraq. That, in Saddam's eyes, was a case of brazen theft.

• To this was added a further aggression, he argues. In 1986, OPEC members agreed to put the price of oil at $18 a barrel and to keep production in line with that price level. But, ignoring Iraqi protests, Kuwait and the United Arab Emirates exceeded production quotas, depressing oil to $13 a barrel and costing Iraq billions in revenues. (Iraq's oil counted for 95 per cent of its exports.) Hence Saddam's charge of "economic war" by Kuwait.

• For the U.S., the conflict is partially about establishing an international order "that is both new and old." It's new in that U.S. intervention in the Third World can no longer be justified in Cold War terms as resistance to Soviet aggression. In the new era, "leaders like Saddam, Libya's Gadhafi, Nicaragua's Ortega, and Panama's Noriega must be portrayed as madmen on their own."

The order is, however, also old. The students said its rationale was frankly described by George Kennan in 1948 when he was head of the State Department Policy Planning Staff. He wrote then: "We have about 50 per cent of the world's wealth, but only 6.3 per cent of its population.... In this situation, we cannot fail to be the object of envy and resentment. Our real task ... is to devise a pattern of relationships which permit us to maintain this disparity without positive detriment to our national security.

"To do so we will have to dispense with all sentimentality.... We need not deceive ourselves we can afford the luxury of altruism and world benefaction.... We should cease to talk about vague and – for the Far East – unreal objectives such as human rights, raising standards of living and democratization. The day is not far off when we are going to have to deal in straight power concepts. The less we are hampered by idealistic slogans, the better."

• Specifically, the conflict is over control of the Gulf oil fields and other Third World resources by the big multinationals and those they can manipulate, according to the students. That was the point of the Mid-East boundary setting in the first place. The various kings and emirs extended "sweetheart" oils deals to the foreigners, insuring a flow of cheap oil to the West. The puppets' families grew fabulously rich; the Arab masses continued in poverty. Saddam, and others like him, now threaten our proxy control. They face us with the terrifying prospect of an era in which Third World peoples will actually control their own resources.

• The crisis involves the US military-industrial complex. This powerful nexus was in turmoil for months as everyone talked about a hoped-for "peace dividend" from the demise of the Cold War. Such talk has now ended. For the defence industry and the Pentagon, this war is heaven-sent.

Well, there you have some American students' findings. As for George Bush, he claims the war in the Gulf is about "good versus evil, right versus wrong." Smiling, he says: "It has everything to do with what religion embodies."

— The Gulf War, V —

Every culture likes to think of itself as morally superior to all others. This is certainly true today and applies particularly to the so-called First World countries or western nations. Among these, the United States, in its current mood of jingoistic euphoria (closely echoed, as always, by Canada), claims absolute supremacy.

The truth, however, is that the whole of the West is presently in a state of gross spiritual and moral decline. Decline is actually too light and facile a word to describe the rot at the core. It's more accurate to say that the traditional moral values of our Judeo-Christian heritage have been subverted and turned upside-down.

Consider this. If it were to be discovered tomorrow that George Bush had several mistresses, or that he had had a recent fling with a model, his standing in the polls and his chances of re-election would plummet. But when he wages a horrendous war, preferring force to sanctions, when he destroys Baghdad and turns the desert into a killing field, even using napalm to obliterate Iraqi troops, he is hailed as the embodiment of righteousness.

Adultery is considered immoral. The murder of innocent Iraqi civilians, or the maiming and killing of thousands of young soldiers on all sides of the conflict – for the sake of oil and American hegemony over the Third World – is esteemed as a virtue.

I am reminded of a conversation I once had with John Lennon in 1969 when the war in Vietnam was at its height. I was then host of an open-line radio show on CFGM in Richmond Hill, Ontario. Lennon, together with Yoko Ono, Tommy Smothers, my friend the late Rabbi Abe Feinberg, and a host of others had just made their recording of "Give Peace a Chance" in a Montreal hotel. It was during the famous "bed-in for peace."

CFGM linked me by phone to room 1742 of the Queen Elizabeth Hotel, and Lennon, occasionally interrupting our talk to try to dull down the roar going on all around him, spoke earnestly about his controversial remark that the Beatles were more influential among youth than Jesus Christ.

Lennon made it clear that he wasn't (contrary to what shocked Church people everywhere had assumed) trying to put down Christianity. His thesis, argued most articulately, was that Christians had betrayed Christ's teachings, and that young people, seeing through the hypocrisy, were more tuned in to what the Beatles were singing than to the Church and its message.

That's my point. It can best be illustrated by looking at what we have done with the heart of Christian ethical teaching, the Sermon on the Mount. The Beatitudes say: "Blessed are the poor in spirit; Blessed are they that mourn; Blessed are the meek; Blessed are those who hunger and thirst after justice; Blessed are the merciful; Blessed are the pure in heart; Blessed are the peacemakers."

This is truly radical stuff, but we have turned it all inside-out. North American society believes none of it, though it still pays it lip service. Interestingly, American presidents like most to talk about God and to be seen attending church precisely at those times when this lip service is in danger of being exposed for what it is.

Here is the version of the Beatitudes we prefer to the original: Blessed are the arrogant – and too bad about the poor in spirit, for they are destined to be trodden down even further; Tough luck about those that mourn, they should have known better than to get in our way or dare to question our right to the lion's share of the world's resources; Blessed are those with the most sophisticated means of mass destruction, for what is left of the Earth when they're through is theirs; Blessed are those who hunger and thirst for affluence and power, for they shall be glutted; Scorn the merciful, they're nothing but bleeding-heart appeasers anyway; above all, Blessed are those who always use more violence to "end" violence, for they are the true children of peace – and besides, they know what's good for business, don't they?

Speaking of business, according to the latest figures, the war in the Gulf will have cost from $58 to $77 billion (U.S). Of this, the United States expects to pay about $15 billion. According to Finance Minister Michael Wilson in his budget speech, the cost of Canada's role could reach nearly $1 billion.

There is no money to end the scandal of millions of the world's children dying of hunger, disease, and exposure right at this moment, but there is money for war. The Canadian government has to cut back on foreign aid and on a range of social services here at home, but there is money for war. Hundreds of battered women have to go back to the hell of living with violent men tonight because this country hasn't got nearly enough shelters to protect them, but there is money for war. *There is always money for war.*

Our young people today are brighter, better informed than a generation ago. Like Lennon, they see through all the hypocrisy and double-talk. Is it any wonder they're dismayed, confused, and sometimes in despair?

One has to weep for them. They too are casualties – in some ways the most grievous – of the U.S. "victory" in the Middle East.

— The Gulf War, VI —

No matter how we feel about the recent conflict in the Middle East – jubilant or despondent, critical or complacent – every responsible person has some hard thinking to do just now. Otherwise, we will have learned nothing whatever from all the devastation, killing, and maiming that has been inflicted.

There is a huge temptation to turn away from the entire mess and simply get back to the seductive normalcy of making a living, enjoying ourselves, or being absorbed by our own problems. But that would be to make an even greater tragedy of what has transpired.

The thing that really concerns me in the wake of the cease-fire in the Gulf is our all-too-human propensity for self-deception, our eagerness to swallow lies that most fit our own interests or our longing for placebos. As a religious philosopher recently pointed out to an international gathering of scientists in Washington, animals might deceive predators to stay alive, but only humans deceive themselves – constantly.

The greatest delusion being greedily consumed just now is that the consummation of the twenty-eight-nation coalition's aims in

the Persian Gulf region – the pulverizing of Iraq and the uncondi-
tional withdrawal from Kuwait – constitute a great victory for freedom, democracy, and the rule of law.

Anyone blind enough to believe this wouldn't recognize the
truth if it turned up for dinner. This was no victory for anybody.
What this unhappy cataclysm represents is yet another massive
failure in our longing and endeavours to banish war and to solve
global tensions through diplomacy. It only proves once again
Mao's dictum that, ultimately, might and right come from the
barrel of a gun.

Those whose self-interest makes them want us to believe that
the horrible violence of these past few weeks is really a fulfilment
of the United Nations' true mandate and the harbinger of a "new
world order" must be exposed for the hypocrites they are. Even the
lame-duck secretary general of the U.N., Pérez de Cuéllar, has
candidly told reporters that the war in the Gulf was a U.S. war and
not a war waged by the U.N. itself. He hardly needed to say that
when the facts have jumped out at everyone who could read a
newspaper or watch the television coverage on their own.

In fact, as a few of the bolder commentators have noted, the
U.N. itself might be one of the most serious casualties of the whole
affair. Clearly the U.S., whose support, both financial and otherwise, for the international body was far less than enthusiastic prior
to the invasion of Kuwait, has cynically exploited the U.N. as a
pious cover for its own purposes.

But reflection on the ease with which the war option was so
quickly sold to and accepted by the majority of people in the coalition countries – remember how eagerly people believed the lie
that the captured airmen shown on Iraqi TV had been beaten up? –
lays bare an even more insidious form of self-deception at work.
While perhaps outwardly indicating to others a sense of
abhorrence that it had to come to violence in the end, a scary element in human nature, just below the surface, caused not thousands but millions to feel a kind of vicarious thrill and excitement
– even exhilaration – as the war unfolded.

Human beings, all of us, have deep wells of aggression and

hostility within. You can see it every day on the nearest rush-hour route, as normally composed adults of both sexes become almost raving lunatics when some other driver offends them, either deliberately or unconsciously.

I myself know several otherwise peaceful businessmen who couldn't wait to get home from the office every night from January 16 on to prop themselves before the TV and watch yet another retired general gleefully expound on the glories of "smart" bombs or "Patriot" missiles. War fascinates even as it repels – provided it's somewhere else and risks somebody else's life and homeland.

Everyone knows intellectually that war is hell and that it is obsolete as a tool of international justice and peace. But it will never be discarded as an archaic barbarism until humanity faces the unpalatable truth – stated long ago in the Bible and elsewhere – that in the end it flows out of the heart and mind of every individual on the face of the Earth. We can't stand apart from the Gulf war and say "Saddam Hussein did it" or "George Bush and U.S. militarism did it." We all did it. We all allowed it to happen. And unless there are some profound changes made, make no mistake, we will do it again. There will always be an enemy.

One of the wisest and most profound books I have read touching on this problem is by the great psychoanalyst Dr. Carl G. Jung. It is called *The Undiscovered Self*, and its thesis is that, unless each of us is willing to face the "shadow side" within, there can never be peace.

The Gulf war will not have been wholly in vain if we are able to cut through the deceptions and to realize, in the oft-quoted words of the comic character Pogo: "We have met the enemy and he is us."

PART FOUR

THE ENVIRONMENT

Chief Seattle's Speech

There has never been a more eloquent or more deeply moving expression of the ethical and spiritual values at stake in our relationship to Earth than the famous speech of Chief Seattle. Although there is some debate now about additions having been made to the original speech, it remains a powerful testimony.

Snippets from this address, made in 1854 when some of his people's ancestral lands were coveted by the U.S. government, are widely quoted by environmentalists. The full text, however, is seldom seen. It was sent to me recently by a reader, and I reproduce most of here since it deserves to be known by everyone, especially our young people.

Seattle, chief of the Squamish tribe in the territory that is now the State of Washington, had this to say:

"The Great Chief in Washington sends word that he wishes to buy our land. He also sends us words of friendship and good will. This is kind of him, since we know he has little need of our friendship in return. But we will consider your offer. We know that if we do not sell, the white man may come with guns and take our land.

"How can you buy or sell the sky, the warmth of the land? The idea is strange to us. If we do not own the freshness of the air and the sparkle of the water, how can you buy them?

"Every part of this Earth is sacred to my people. Every shining pine needle, every sandy shore, every mist in the dark woods, every clearing and humming insect is holy in the experience of my people. The sap which courses through the trees carries the memories of the red people.

"The white people's dead forget the country of their birth when they go to walk among the stars. Our dead never forget this beautiful Earth, for it is the mother of the red people. We are part of the Earth and it is part of us. The perfumed flowers are our sisters; the deer, the horse, the great eagle, these are our brothers; the rocky crests, the juices in the meadows, the body heat of the pony and humans – all belong to the same family. . . .

"The shining water that moves in the streams and rivers is not just water but the blood of our ancestors. If we sell you the land, you must remember it is sacred and you must teach your children it is sacred, and that each ghostly reflection in the clear water of the lakes tells of events and memories in the life of my people. The water's murmur is the voice of my father's father.

"The rivers are our brothers, they quench our thirst. They carry our canoes and feed our children. If we sell . . . remember, and teach your children, the rivers are our brothers, and yours, and you must henceforth give the rivers the kindness you would give any brother. . . .

"The air is precious to us, for all share the same breath – the beast, the tree, the people. The whites do not seem to notice the air they breathe. Like a man dying for many days, they are numb to the stench. But if we sell you our land, you must remember the air is precious to us and shares its spirit with all the life it supports.

"If we decide to accept, I make one condition: the white people must treat the beasts of this land as their brothers. I am a savage and do not understand any other way. I have seen a thousand rotting buffaloes on the prairie, left by the white man who shot them from a passing train. . . . I do not understand how the smoking iron horse can be more important than the buffalo that we kill only to stay alive.

"What is man without the beasts? If all the beasts were gone, the people would die of great loneliness of spirit. For whatever happens to the beasts happens to the people. All things are connected…. This we know. The earth does not belong to the people; the people belong to the Earth. This we know. All things are connected like the blood which unites one family.

"Whatever befalls the Earth befalls the children of the Earth. The people did not weave the web of life but are merely a strand in it. Whatever we do to the web we do to ourselves.

"…. It matters little where we spend the rest of our days. Our children have seen their fathers humbled in defeat. Our warriors have felt shame, and after defeat they turn their days in idleness and contaminate their bodies with sweet foods and strong drink…. A few more hours, a few more winters, and none of the children of the great tribes that once lived on this Earth or that roam now in small bands in the woods will be left to mourn….

"One thing we know, which the whites may one day discover – our God is the same God. You may think now that you own God as you wish to own our land, but you cannot. God is the God of people and God's compassion is equal for the red and white people. This Earth is precious to God, and to harm the Earth is to heap contempt on its Creator. The whites too shall pass; perhaps sooner than all other tribes. Continue to contaminate your bed, you will one night suffocate in your own waste."

— Nature Defiled —

Reginald Heber, who lived from 1783 to 1826, is responsible for some of the best-known hymns in any hymnary. Heber wrote the famous missionary hymn "From Greenland's icy mountains." Just thinking of it brings a rush of memories from my boyhood days as a chorister at an east-end Toronto church.

There was one line of this hymn, however, that grated on me then and throughout the years. Describing the glories of nature, it says:

Where every prospect pleases
And only man is vile.

Significantly, the stanza in which this occurs was dropped from Anglican and many other hymnbooks in the 1940s. It was thought to hold an unduly pessimistic view of *Homo sapiens*.

Frankly, however, there are days now when I'm not as sure about this as I once was. I'm not just thinking about the stories of crime and human shame that seem to flood the media at present. I'm thinking in particular about the way we are much worse than pigs when it comes to our treatment of the Earth around us.

If I sound angry, I am. One day recently (during Earth Week no less) I went for a morning hike over one of the most gorgeous, as-yet-undeveloped pieces of the Oak Ridges Moraine, a couple of kilometres from home. I hadn't walked there for several weeks.

It's a rolling terrain, roughly two kilometres square. There's a series of ponds where some rare species of waterfowl nest, and a prime hardwood forest where one of the best displays of trilliums in the Metro Toronto region bursts forth each spring. Even though it begins just a few feet away from Yonge Street (Highway 11), it is home to deer, brush wolves, foxes, and many other small mammals. If I could afford it, I'd buy it and preserve it as a park forever.

Imagine my feelings, then, on the day in question. I climbed to a favourite lookout spot only to find a hundred or more used tires strewn all over the hillside. Further down the slope I could make out another chaotic heap of them flung in all directions.

That was just the beginning. As I continued my walk, there were piles of building blocks, heaps of old, asphalt shingles, worn-out appliances, chunks of concrete – you name it. A wrecked, rusting VW Beetle blocked the main footpath through the woods.

Nearby, I discovered that another large parcel of land – formerly a sand-and-gravel site now healed over by nature and possessing a pond where there are northern pike – has become almost overnight an even more obscene dump. Along the shore of the pond, where in the past I have seen both green and great blue herons fishing, filthy garbage has been scattered far and wide.

There were heaps of rubbish from construction sites, the twisted, burned-out bodies of at least eight or nine cars, old sofas and mattresses – all the detritus and scourings of a sick, consumer society as far as the horizon. In a patch of woods where a few months ago I saw two does and a fawn, I found yet another mountain of discarded tires. There were more thrown into a small stream that ultimately feeds our lake.

I don't pretend to understand the kind of mentality that can desecrate natural solitudes like that any more than I can comprehend the joy of the idiots who defile the silence and tear up the Earth on their pestilential dirt-bikes. But it's an increasing trend. In recent months I have noticed that at almost every ditch or gate along some of the loveliest country roads around Greater Toronto, people are dumping their heavier junk under cover of darkness.

What I think we're seeing, in part at any rate, is the paradoxical, reverse side of mounting concern about the environment. As controls over what can be put out as garbage by ordinary citizens are sharply tightened, and as waste-disposal sites charge ever higher amounts for home renovators or construction firms to dump their refuse, some people are opting for the cheapest solution of all.

This problem is one that cries out to be thought through and dealt with quickly, before we completely bury whatever green spaces we still have left around our urban areas. The stupidity (and myopia) of what is going on is difficult to surpass. Cleaning up the two areas I first described – if it ever happens, and I honestly fear it won't – will cost infinitely more than if there had been a proper disposal of the waste involved in the first place. Of course, the money will now have to come out of everybody's pockets instead of those of the dumpers.

If nothing is done, since garbage attracts garbage, something priceless will have been lost forever. There seems little point in the rest of us recycling, composting, and cutting back if the yahoos are to be allowed to run rampant. Since reason can't reach them, we should lobby hard for massive fines, the impounding of trucks, and the cancelling of all building permits for anyone convicted of illegal dumping.

I can see no alternative.

— The Holy Land —

Autumn, my favourite time of the year, always brings with it so many warm memories – trips to the cottage as a child, the many harvest home services at various churches over the years, my first ramble around Addison's Walk in Oxford as a gangling undergraduate fresh from the "colonies," or walking under the falling leaves by the banks of the Tiber on my way to the Vatican for an October synod.

But, above all, it seems that fall, more than any other season, reminds us of our deep connection with the Earth, with the cycles of nature, and with the wider, swirling energies of the cosmos itself.

It's a good time at which to ponder again that most pressing and fundamental concern of whether future generations, too, will be able to celebrate this or any other season. What is going to halt the unbelievable process of degradation and pollution that we know now threatens to shut down the biosystems of our planet?

My own interest lies not so much in the issues of managing waste, recycling projects, or on the promotion of "green" consumer items – many of which unfortunately fall into the category of mere fads. I'm more intrigued by the underlying questions that have to do with the necessity for a new kind of humanity. We need a new way of relating to the natural world, and thus a new way of being human.

Without basic, unprecedented changes at this level, nothing will happen, except that we might slow down the process of ultimate ecological extinction by a few decades or so.

Like many, I have come to believe that religious ideas have had a crucial and often deleterious part to play in our relationship to Earth and its other creatures. In particular, I'm thinking now of one concept, common to Judaism and Christianity, and to some extent shared also by Islam – that parts of the Middle East constitute what is known as the Holy Land, the Promised Land.

This idea centres on the belief that this one specific region of the Earth, which witnessed God or Allah's revelations – first to

Jews, then to early Christians, then to the Prophet Muhammad – and which contains the "holy places," is somehow more sacred than anywhere else. But if this particular region is holy, then it follows (or so the logic has led) that all other places are less holy, less open to God's Spirit, less likely to be sites of revelation or of special promise.

This has led to an enormous failure to grasp the sacredness or holiness of the ground upon which all others live, and of those areas of the globe we call "wilderness."

Sacredness of land is understood by Native peoples the world over. They are deeply aware that the land that gave them birth and sustains them is holy, worthy of the deepest respect, and the source of *spiritual* as well as physical well-being. But for western culture, the Promised Land, the Holy Land, has always been somewhere else. We see the beauty but we do not perceive the sacral character of rocks, forests, rivers, lakes, and mountains in our native Canada.

What follows inexorably from this is that we do not then look for the special revelation of the Creator Spirit that can come from a close communion with this great land and its inner secrets. Our spiritual gaze is always fixed far away.

This largely explains why so much theologizing and so much religious talking by Canadian spiritual leaders is merely a rehashing of old mash from a distant past. We can't hope for any originality or authenticity in our spiritual thinking when we continually neglect the unique vehicle God has given to us – our own continent, landscape, and skies.

This has a deeply personal reference. Joseph Campbell, for example, the expert on myth, was right when he said that if anyone wants to know where the Promised Land for him or her is – the place of revelation and self-fulfilment – it's right where they stand. It's their own chosen space or turf.

What's more, from the point of view of the environment, if you see springs, lakes, fields, mountains, and all of nature here where we live as holy, as our Promised Land, the place where Gods speaks to us, it becomes not just imprudent or uneconomic to foul them. It becomes (what it really is) a form of sacrilege.

You begin to realize the implications of this approach when you ask how much defilement of churches, synagogues, or temples would corporations or individuals be allowed to get away with on the basis that these are "acceptable levels"? If the St. Lawrence or the Great Lakes were viewed as sacred, how long would the raw sewage that daily flows into them continue?

The Bible says the whole Earth "is the Lord's and the fulness thereof." If we really believed that we'd never treat it as we do.

— The Mantle of God —

"Christianity is the most materialistic of all the religions." This saying of Most Rev. William Temple (1881-1944), probably the finest Archbishop of Canterbury Anglicanism ever produced, has a particular relevance today.

We need to be reminded of it because matter and spirit have so often been misunderstood as deeply opposed to one another. The resulting dichotomy has been disastrous for us all.

Derived in western thought from Platonic roots via St. Augustine, the spirit-matter split has led, among other things, to the Church's colossal distrust of the body (hence the absence of a proper theology of the body and of sexuality) and to our radical abuse of the natural world. The mind-set that treats all of the Earth and its resources as an "it" to be exploited, manipulated, and ultimately degraded beyond all recognition stems from a loss of the sense of the sanctity of matter itself. The so-called pagans knew better!

The feeling that the body is evil, the negative attitude to sex, and the centuries of viewing women as the cause of temptation and even of the primal "Fall" all spring from the same source.

By saying that Christianity is "materialistic," Temple was referring to the way in which, like its Judaic parent, it is committed to the belief that matter, or the basic stuff of the universe, comes from God. It is His creation. I believe Temple would have been most enthusiastic about what is being called today "Creation

Spirituality" (*à la* Fr. Thomas Berry, Matthew Fox, et al.) because it reaffirms a creation- or matter-centred approach.

But it's not just the doctrine of creation that lies behind the need for Christians to see matter as holy. However you understand the Incarnation, the belief that God was revealed in the humanity of Jesus Christ, it predicates taking matter with the utmost seriousness. If our human flesh can become the vehicle of the divine self-revelation, matter matters incredibly. Whether we look at the majesty of the planet and the vast galaxies beyond or at the Gospel story, it is clear that matter is the robe and mantle of the Almighty.

But even here we must be careful. Matter, as the most recent work of the physicists reveals, is not some kind of irreducible, fine atomic mist (from the Greek *atoma*, that which can't be cut any smaller) but rather a "dance of energy." Moreover, in saying that matter is the mantle of God, I do not mean that God is to be understood as a Being above or beyond or outside of the cosmos. That is, in effect, a kind of dualism. Rather, matter is "in God" and God is in matter.

This is what the great medieval mystic Meister Eckhart is talking about when he writes: "Apprehend God in all things, for God is in all things. Every single creature is full of God and is a book about God. Every creature is a word of God. If I spent enough time with the tiniest creature, even a caterpillar – I would never have to prepare a sermon. So full of God is every creature."

Eckhart goes on to say, "All hiding places reveal God. If you want to escape God S/He runs into your lap. For, God is at home. It is we who have gone out for a walk."

Or, as St. Paul said centuries earlier, quoting a pagan poet: "In Him we live and move and have our being."

In our present age we need to recover this awareness of the underlying unity of all things great and small, and of the divinity that dances in the rocks and trees as well as in the distant stars. This will mean avoiding at least two things: any attempt to put asunder "that which God hath joined together" (that is, spirit and matter) and a phoney materialism that in effect really turns its back upon both.

Let me explain the latter. It's falsely assumed by some that because we live in a consumer culture we are therefore the ultimate materialists. But the opposite is true. Consumerism, while appearing to worship material things and therefore to honour matter, actually trivializes matter entirely. It's nothing but an abasement and abuse of matter to treat it as existing simply for one's own private amusement or sensual satisfaction.

A throw-away, conspicuously consuming lifestyle knows, as has been said, the price of everything and the value of nothing. Nothing is sacred. At no point in the daily round comes there a moment when an inner voice bids one: "Take off your shoes, for the ground you tread upon is holy ground."

What a loss! What a terrible plight, not just to have nobody to thank for all the gifts of the material universe but never even to feel the rising up of gratitude within.

That's what's so hollow about the beer commercials, the car commercials, and all the other consumer hype. They're not materialistic in Temple's sense. They celebrate nothing but money, greed, and self.

— The Diaper Disaster —

This essay, first published August 7, 1988, prompted an incredible response across the country. Numerous new cloth diaper services were launched as a result.

For centuries before the coming of the Europeans, and right up until quite recently, Canadian Indians had a unique method of diapering babies. They would dry sphagnum or other mosses and then pack this light and fluffy material around the baby inside the *tikinagun*, or back-pack-type carrier. This cost nothing except the labour to gather it; it was easily disposed of; it was highly absorbent as well as hygienic; and, above all, it was completely biodegradable.

One of my first memories of entering an Indian summer encampment near Hudson Bay, as a student teacher, was the moss hanging out to dry on sharp sticks around nearly every tepee and cabin. Today, however, all that has changed. The so-called disposable diaper has hit the North with a vengeance – and in many ways has become a curse.

"The disposable diaper is one of the worst disasters ever to happen to the Canadian North," a bush-pilot told me in a radiophone interview from a northern post recently. He confirmed my own observations that piles of these nearly indestructible products of our technology now disfigure almost every Native settlement in the bush. Soaked with faeces and urine and laden with plastic, these diapers resist fire or any other natural method of disposal. They yield to neither rot nor rust.

What's more, the pilot said that as he flies over the bush these days he can see that "there is garbage nearly everywhere, and a lot of it is undoubtedly made up of disposable diapers." When I remember how pristine and lovely this same wilderness area of which he spoke used to be when I first canoed and portaged through it, I could almost shout with anger.

But it is we in the South who have shown our Native people the way in this desecration and waste. According to Pollution Probe, these same diapers generate 20,000 tonnes of garbage annually for Metropolitan Toronto alone. The estimated figure for the entire country is approximately 200,000 tonnes!

This is a staggering figure when you reflect that we are, as a throw-away society, already drowning and suffocating in our own waste. As Fr. Thomas Berry says, our society needs to be "toilet-trained."

If the diapers are incinerated, the toxic gases from the plastic add to the deadly smog already contaminating the very air we breathe. When they go to landfill sites, the human waste, mixed with other harmful substances, can form a highly dangerous mess.

Nobody likes to think that the amount of waste caused by his or her particular lifestyle makes much difference to the overall problem. But when you consider that the average child goes through some 7,000 diapers from birth until about two years of age, this is an area where the cumulative effect of *one* family's habits in just *one* aspect of living can have an enormous impact.

That's why environmentalists are lauding the decision of a Markham, Ontario, woman to start up a cloth diaper service.

Deborah Summerfield, who is on maternity leave from IBM Canada Ltd., says news that Toronto's only cloth diaper service, Stork Diaper Ltd., was ending prompted her to act.

Her service, run from her suburban home, (which she mortgaged to get the more than $100,000 capital), will cost $14 to $15 a week and supply seventy diapers. The same number of disposable diapers can cost up to $23.60, she says. Yet even though the cloth ones are cheaper, are delivered to the door, and are ecologically so much better, Stork only had 1,800 customers in a population of about 2.5 million.

I want to wish Summerfield every success and state my hope that she is the harbinger of a new trend that will not just make her rich but will signify our society's renewed determination to act in all things, big or small, to protect our Earth home.

For the makers of Pampers, Luvs, Huggies, Snuggies, and all the rest, I have a suggestion. In fact, it's offered freely to anyone. I suggest they send a researcher into the bush to take a fresh look at the moss nature has provided with such abandon – billions of tonnes of an ever-renewable resource.

Properly dried, cleaned, and combed, it could be made into a soft, absorbent lining for an entirely new kind of throw-away diaper. By using a moisture-proof outer layer of towelling, also made from moss (processed), all need for plastic would disappear.

They'd be doing not just our Native people but all of us a big favour.

The diapers could be called "Mossies." I can see one marketing slogan now: "Begin at the bottom with Mossies for a cleaner environment."

At present, we're creating a mess in the future for the babies we're diapering today.

— The Third Stage —

While it is important to be informed about the alarming scale of the ecological crisis, this in itself is far from enough.

In fact, if the environmental prophets only tell us how bad things are and how they are inevitably getting worse, their broadsides could have a paradoxical effect. They could lead to a paralysis of despair. That, in turn, could abort the possibility of any remedy whatever.

We need more than stories of rain forests being destroyed or of rapidly vanishing species. Much more thought and space must be given to positive suggestions on ways out of this catastrophe. In addition to the best thinking of the brightest scientific minds applied to specific problems such as clean air, clean water, or population control, we need philosophers, psychologists, sociologists, theologians, and others thinking about the wider picture.

Make no mistake, the situation before us is so dangerous and so unprecedented that technological tinkering or more waste-management programs will never suffice. We need nothing less than an inner revolution, a mental and spiritual "conversion" to a radically new way of being human. Without this, our patterns of consumption will stay the same; our relationships with other species and with the whole of nature will rest unreformed; and the process of destruction, while perhaps slowed down, will not abate.

In a feature called "The Search for Modern Humans" published in the *National Geographic* magazine (October 1988), a physical anthropologist from the University of Witwatersrand, Johannesburg, Phillip Tobias, had this to say:

"From my lifetime of studying hominid fossils, I know we've hardly shown any anatomical changes in our bodies for 100,000 years. And I don't think we're suddenly going to start again showing anatomical change. I believe that our physical and anatomical evolution has become less and less significant, whilst our cultural, behavioral, linguistic and *spiritual* evolution has become more and more important" (italics added).

It seems to me that Tobias is right, and that the global challenges now before us – of the environment on the one hand and of peace and justice on the other – might be the levers to shift us towards this spiritual, evolutionary leap.

There are many signs of hope that a basic change in human consciousness is already in the works. These include the growing Green Movement around the world; however gradually, there is a heightening of awareness that this planet is the only home we have.

Included too is the slow but certain emergence of the feminine principle into the forefront of human thinking and imagination. We're talking here of something much greater than the feminist movement, though it has some common elements. The feminine principle or archetype constellates around the qualities of receptivity, mutuality, resonance, co-operation, and intuition. It belongs to men as much as to women and is the only thing that can save males from the prison of competition, workaholism, solely linear thinking, and fear of intimacy. It is the total opposite of the purely male principle, which, unchecked, has brought us the legacy of nuclear terror and a plundered planet.

A further hopeful indicator lies in the gradual lessening of East-West tensions and the beginnings, however tentative, of the reduction of nuclear weapons. Leaders on all sides appear to be getting the message that the mass of ordinary people will no longer tolerate even the contemplation of a future nuclear war.

I would add one more sign – a growing sense of mysticism. Let me explain.

As a baby, during the first months of our lives, we only experience ourselves or beingness in union with our mothers. We can't distinguish between self and not-self. The sense of being an entity on our own, and that we constitute an "I" quite separate from the world around us, comes gradually as we go from toddler to young child.

The third stage towards maturity is the awareness of others and their needs, the limits to our egocentricity, and, eventually, our interdependence and unity with the whole world, both human and non-human.

This individual pattern is a microcosm of the human story. Early humans made little distinction between themselves and nature. In the sixth century B.C., however, we entered the second stage – awareness of ourselves as subjects with the natural world as object – through the explorations of such pre-Socratic philosophers as Thales, Anaximines, and Heraclitus.

They began the impulse that led ultimately to the birth of western science and technology. This brought incredible blessings, but it also set the scene for the rape and exploitation of the Earth.

We need and are ready now as a species to enter the third stage – the mystical awareness of the unity of all things, the interdependence and oneness of all humanity and of the cosmos.

Thankfully, this conceptual change has already begun.

— Deadly Enemy —

I was in a local coffee bar recently when a man of about thirty-five, with a belly like Friar Tuck, began to boast loudly about his hunting exploits.

"There I was, driving my pickup along the sideroad, when out steps a big bull. Easiest moose I ever shot. I just stopped, loaded up, and bang! He couldn't have been more than thirty feet away. Had a great rack [antlers] on him, too."

I had to use a lot of self-restraint to keep from telling him I'd think a lot more of his sporting tales if moose carried guns as well.

The idea of a man with a high-powered rifle killing a magnificent, enormous creature such as a moose at point-blank range, not out of necessity but for "fun," sickens me. I used to hunt rabbits and partridge, but I long ago lost any delight I had in killing. I see a lot of things differently today.

I'm not knocking those who *must* hunt to live. I can't go along with those who fanatically oppose the trapping of fur-bearing animals by Indians and Inuit. Certainly we should lobby for the most human possible kind of live-trap rather than the cruel leg-hold. But, however regrettable, the fact is that if all trapping is outlawed, then unemployment among Native peoples will be 95 per cent instead of an already scandalous 40 to 50 per cent.

We have oppressed and deceived the Native peoples enough without stripping them of their way of life today. It would be ironic and inhumane to have made them rely wholly on trapping for their economy over the centuries and then turn around and tell them we've now decided it's a sin.

Nevertheless, with our new understanding of the cosmos, we are aware that all things, living and inanimate, had a common origin in the primeval fireball 15 billion years ago. It is increasingly obvious that birds and animals are truly our "sisters" and "brothers."

When St. Francis spoke in these terms over seven hundred years ago, he was using the language of mysticism. But modern physics has now shown that this mysticism was actually based upon hard, scientific fact. We are fundamentally one with the elements, the winds, the plants, the oceans, and the spiralling galaxies.

Native peoples everywhere have always known this basic kinship with all creatures great and small. But we who pride ourselves on our sophistication and modernity have suffered for ages from what is called "anthropocentrism," the false creed that we are not only apart and different from other species but that everything exists purely for our sake.

Bible verses indicating that mankind was meant to exercise responsible stewardship of the planet have long been misinterpreted to justify our lording it over the rest of creation.

Whereas the despised so-called pagan religions believed God (or the gods) was working in and through the natural world, the Judeo-Christian tradition has been distorted to put God "Out There" somewhere. The created order has been regarded as an artefact, an object made by God strictly for man's pleasure and exploitation. As a result, we have treated our environment with contempt, losing both it and our sense of the immediacy of God's presence in the process.

Thank God, in the face of impending ecological and spiritual ruin, we are beginning to wake up. Theologians are beginning to listen to the physicists and vice versa. We no longer view the cosmos as an object God made as one would make an alarm clock.

Instead of the force that wound up the universe and then let it run down on its own, God is more and more seen as the dynamic energy or force within as well as outside the cosmic event. The universe is not just "there" as an accomplished fact; it is an emergent, evolving, as-yet-unfinished process. We do not yet see what is coming into being.

At the moment, it is, as Fr. Thomas Berry and others have pointed out, the unique role of humans to be the "point at which the universe comes to full consciousness of itself." We have this distinction that, as far as we know right now, we are the only creatures able to be self-reflective enough to celebrate creation's glories.

When the osprey plunges and takes a fish just a few feet from our dock – a pair of them have been visiting our lake over the past few weeks – it's a thrilling moment. To see a fish eagle rise from the water with its prey, shake itself like a dog to get the excess moisture out of its feathers, and then soar off is to glimpse a primal beauty.

As far as the osprey itself is concerned, though, it's simply obeying its instincts. Reflecting on what it is doing or celebrating its beauty is the farthest thing from its brain.

Our Earth has produced humans to be its highest self-consciousness and vehicle of celebration. Why must we so often act like nature's deadliest enemy instead?

— Muzzle Not the Ox —

My wife says I'm the only person she knows who would go from playing with the cat to speculating whether Christianity would have been different if St. Paul had had a pet. She said this as I was rambling on over dinner one night.

We both have always been "dog people." After our dog, Morgan, had to be put to sleep, we went for a couple of years without pets. Eventually, however, we went to the Humane Society and brought home a four-year-old male cat who was sitting forlornly in a cage with a note that read: "Likes to cuddle; take him home."

We took Percy home, and for the first six weeks all he would do was hide – in the furnace room, under beds, anywhere that was safe and out of sight. Cuddling was the last thing on his mind. We almost gave up on him.

But miraculously all that changed. He is now sitting outside my study peering through the French doors at me, desperately wanting to come in. He'd be welcome except that he wants to sit on my shoulder and rub his chin on my beard as I work.

But what has any of this to do with Paul or the development of Christianity? Thereby, as they say, hangs a tale.

It's only very recently that Christian thinkers have begun paying attention to the fact that proper respect for animals and their innate rights has been neglected. The Church – apart from St. Francis and one or two others – has exalted humans far above all the rest of creation. Animals have been treated as though they existed merely for the sake of our unbridled pursuit of greed and/or pleasure.

Why? I believe part of the answer lies in some significant differences between Paul and Jesus. Their attitudes to nature and the world of living things are strikingly opposite.

Jesus was, above all, a rural person. This is evident not just from the fact that he spent most of his life in tiny villages or in the open country, but also from his use of language. The imagery of the parables and one-liners of Jesus is that of a person perfectly at home with fields, birds, animals, and growing things. He likens himself to a mother hen with her chicks, or to a shepherd with his flock. He rebukes Herod as "that fox." His great metaphor for the dying-renewal process is the death and rebirth of a grain of corn. His express teaching is that God cares not only for each of us but also for the humble sparrow and for the lilies of the field.

Contrast this with Paul. This brilliant, highly educated man was most at home in the urban culture of the sophisticated Hellenistic world. Certainly he could rough it with the best of them when necessity called, but his thought, his style, his point of view are all permeated with the spirit of cities such as Tarsus, where he was born. Paul's language sparkles not with images of field and stream but of human endeavour. His metaphor of the Church as a building is but one example.

What put me on to his near-contempt for animals, however, was a singular passage in one of his letters. He is arguing that, as a minister, he has a right to be supported, and he cites a verse from Deuteronomy that says: "Thou shall not muzzle the ox that treadeth out the corn."

This text is clearly part of rules laid down for the humane treatment of working animals. The ox is hard at work, surrounded by food. It would be inhumane to muzzle him so that he cannot eat a little.

Paul, however, twists the verse. Having quoted it, he says: "Does God care a fig about oxen?" (The answer he expects is clearly a "no.") Then he continues: "Isn't God saying this really for our sake?" That is, isn't the reference here to humans and not to animals at all? Paul concludes that the latter is indeed the case!

This, to my mind, is a quite extraordinary revelation of an anti-animal bias, as well as a clear example of the way in which he did not hesitate to use texts to his own advantage when it suited.

I know that in the presence of Paul we are in the presence of one of the great minds of all time. But he never claimed to be infallible. And obviously he wasn't – about women, about slaves, about animals.

If Christianity had paid more attention to Jesus in regard to all three than to Paul, a lot of grief down the ages, both human and animal, might well have been avoided.

— Out of Control —

One of the greatest misuses of language is to say that when a person acts in some grossly outrageous fashion he is behaving "just like an animal."

With rare exceptions, animals do not torture and kill their own kind. They do not attack unprotected females or rape their own young. They do not destroy the very earth, air, and water that give them life.

Above all, the higher the animal's intelligence the less likely it is that it will reproduce indiscriminately or harm other species with its waste. Even the common cat will bury its own excrement rather than foul the elements. Wolves and many other higher vertebrates carefully control their birthrate so as to avoid famine for themselves and others.

Yet we humans, who contribute nothing to the Earth's well-being or to the sum of its ecological "gross national product" – who indeed do the very reverse – have the audacity to describe those who succumb to greed, lust, or violence as "animals." We need to look at the deep, philosophical implications of this paradox, or, in spite of all our recycling, emission controls, and "Green" campaigns, the devastation will accelerate.

Looked at objectively, *Homo sapiens* is a species that is multiplying out of control. We are collectively the most virulent plague ever to afflict this fragile ecosystem. According to the latest figures released by the United Nations Population Fund, Earth's population is increasing by three people every second, or about 250,000 daily. In 1990 alone, 90 to 100 million – about the combined population of the Philippines and South Korea – will be born. In all, about one billion people will be added to the present 5.2 billion before this decade is over. Most of these new arrivals will be in the poorest countries in the world, the ones least equipped to handle more.

Quite bluntly, this is like a monstrous cancer on the Earth and is destined to strangle both the planet itself and everything on it. There is little use in finding ways to cut waste and consumption if the number of people producing the waste and doing the consumption is allowed to expand exponentially.

I don't buy into the theology of an inevitable doomsday. Since human intelligence got us into this mess, it can also get us out of it. But there is a huge proviso. We must *use* this God-given asset of intelligence properly. At the moment we are not doing so. Since we have overcome all or nearly all of the checks and balances set down by Earth itself for its own survival as a living system, our population will only be controlled if we ourselves control it.

This seems obvious, but obviously it isn't. As proof, I need only cite the current, disastrous policies of the blinkered men of the Curia of the Roman Catholic Church. Recent pronouncements from the Vatican show that these men have finally discovered the moral issue of the environment and want us to be concerned about it. Yet all of that is merely platitudinous or worse if they not only continue to condemn the best means of birth control human intelligence and research have so far been able to devise but even encourage those less able to do so to bear and raise more children!

I have no animus against the present Pope, but I cannot with integrity join the ranks of those who praise him as a great moral leader in our time. When you have been present on his tours, as I have, and heard him telling poor peasants, already burdened with poverty and more children than they can raise, to have larger families, you know in your mind and heart that he is more than wrong; he is wittingly or unwittingly a source of great harm.

In 1968, Pope Paul VI, with his document *Humanae Vitae*, went against the judgement of his own special committee of advisers and banned artificial contraception. Many will say that it is therefore unfair to lay the blame on John Paul II. They forget, however, that Paul was *laissez-faire* on this matter in comparison with the present Pope. Paul didn't spend half his time or more visiting the impoverished nations of the world and constantly restating the ban. Paul, to my knowledge, never went about telling the faithful that to disregard the ban was to be in mortal sin.

Critics will say it is anti-Catholic to criticize the Pope for this. If so, the vast majority of North American Catholics, including priests, bishops and academics, must also be anti-Catholic. They certainly don't believe he's right.

This is not an anti-Catholic position. It is deeply pro-truth and pro the life of generations to come.

— The Glory of Nature —

Back when I was a professional cleric, I shared the scorn of the ecclesiastical establishment for the "excuses" offered by those who seldom or never came to church.

We even had names for them: the "Sunday School dumpers" – parents who, often still in pyjamas, dropped their children off at the church door each Sunday and hightailed it back home to bed; the "would-be agnostics," who didn't have a clue what the word meant but used it as a chic-sounding cachet to hide their general indolence; and the "blue-domers," who claimed to worship God on the ninth tee under the great blue vault of heaven, but who probably didn't give a thought to anything out on the course except their next swing. The phrase "nearer to God in a garden than any place else on Earth" was likewise greeted with priestly derision.

But without making judgements about their sincerity, the "blue-domers" and the gardeners had a point. There is an inescapable connection between the natural world and the inner, spiritual life of the human species. This explains the fact that there is currently an intense spiritual hunger and searching on the part of all humanity. It correlates exactly with the time of the greatest impoverishment and degradation of our planet home.

Any comprehensive knowledge of the world's religions shows just how profound this relationship between Earth and our understanding of spiritual reality actually is. The great prophets and founders of the various faiths have all come out of the "wilderness" with their vision of the Ultimate. Even St. Paul, a city man, spent three years alone in the wilds of Arabia after his conversion experience and before launching his ministry.

The springs of Hinduism flow from the great *rishis* who meditated in the Himalayas before our history began. The mountains, the sources of the great, sacred rivers, the fertile plains, and the lushness of the jungle all played their part in shaping the Hindu soul. The plethora of gods in Hinduism (all expressions of the one, eternal Atman) reflect the energies and forces of nature.

The Buddha found his Enlightenment not in the palace or the city but under the Bo tree. Moses saw his vision of God out in the wilderness at the burning bush and received the Law on a lonely mountaintop in the Sinai. Muhammad received his revelations while meditating in a cave on a mountainside, out in the desert.

Jesus was raised in the hill town of Nazareth, with its vast, panoramic view of the surrounding countryside; he came out of the Judean wilderness to begin his ministry, and he spent almost the entire period of his teaching hiking around what is now Israel with his disciples.

Many people today criticize the Bible for the negative influence it is alleged to have had on the environment and related issues, citing such texts as "Be fruitful, and multiply, and replenish the earth and subdue it: and have dominion over ... every living thing." But you can't understand the Bible unless you look more deeply and realize that it is the natural world that is the primary locus or agent of revelation of the Ultimate.

I suggest to all of you a new way to read the Bible – one that will make it come alive and achieve a unity in your mind that will be fresh and different. You can skip over genealogies, detailed ritual regulations, or other more or less tedious passages and concentrate upon the extraordinary extent to which nature or the creation underlies and infuses the whole.

Fr. Thomas Berry – the author of *The Dream Of The Earth* and, in my view, today's outstanding "geologian," as he calls himself – is right when he says that if we lived on an empty, dusty planet – something similar to our moon – we would have a God or gods reflecting that reality.

If we reduce our Earth to a reeking, wasted, garbage-glutted parking lot, our God will have shrunk to a hateful, fiery, all-consuming monster.

The God worshipped by Jews, Christians, Muslims, and others is described by Isaiah thus: "He shall feed his flock like a shepherd: he shall gather the lambs with his arm, and carry them in his bosom, and shall gently lead those that are with young."

Going on, the prophet asks: "Who hath measured the waters in the hollow of his hand, and meted out heaven with the span [the rainbow], and comprehended the dust of the earth in a measure, and weighed the mountains in scales, and the hills in a balance?"

It is because of this vision of God in nature that he can conclude with such ringing confidence: "They that wait upon the Lord shall renew their strength; they shall mount up with wings like eagles; they shall run, and not be weary; and they shall walk, and not faint."

Nature came first. The Bible reflects its glory.

— Armageddon? —

One of the few predictions that can be made with accuracy about the 1990s is that it will be a time of rising emphasis upon the End of the World. In fact, I predict the emergence of a rash of fresh cults and sects based upon this apocalyptic vision, in addition to the numerous more or less respectable denominations already obsessed by it.

This kind of end-of-the-age ferment occurred immediately prior to the year 1000. Today, with so many global threats on the horizon, the justification for targeting the year 2000 or thereabouts for Armageddon is virtually overwhelming – in some fanatical circles.

Already, if you watch religious advertising or follow the utterances of what once were considered fringe groups, the message is clear. Earthquakes, plagues such as AIDS, famines, declining church attendance, and the rise of humanistic secularism – not to mention the sad litanies of the ecological doomsayers – are all being taken as divine signs that "God is about to wind things up."

While professing to believe in a loving God, the Ground of all hope and Lord of the cosmos, people with this mind-set are actually committed to a God of pessimism and despair. Confused and anxious as they look out at a troubled and (to them) God-hating world, they take refuge in the belief that only divine intervention can save them and theirs.

Conveniently, they overlook the plain truth – that their

approach plays into the hands of the military-industrial complex behind the scandalous international arms trade and the arms race itself. They argue that since Armageddon is coming, the side with the most sophisticated nuclear or other weapons gets in the last licks.

They ignore as well the irrefutable point that eager expectation of the alleged end gives them the perfect out from all responsibility to work to prevent war, famine, poverty, or environmental collapse. Taking a few verses that Jesus probably never spoke and whose meaning is ambiguous to say the least, they turn their backs upon the main body of his teaching. They scorn as well the thundering, ethical imperatives of the great Hebrew prophets in what Christians call the Old Testament.

Since we are a culture in dire spiritual need, we must studiously resist the seductiveness of this gathering trend.

Increasingly, I find that the conclusions I have been coming to in my own thinking about the future are shared by a growing range of thinkers in allied or completely different fields, from physics to anthropology. While expressed in widely varying ways, the message is essentially the same: Only a spiritual revolution or quantum leap ahead will enable us to meet the manifold dangers we face. If this does not occur, we won't need an act of God to end history. We will manage it quite well by ourselves.

There are some voices suggesting that this quantum leap to a more spiritual humanity will happen of itself – a sort of predetermined evolutionary mutation. I do not share this Pollyanna-type optimism. It will only happen if, by God's help and grace, we make it happen.

Fr. Thomas Berry agrees. He is convinced that we must "reinvent the human" or perish in a devastated planet, and with this he has put his finger on a crucial matter. All other living species are what they are because of their biological coding. An acorn becomes an oak, a kitten becomes a cat, and so forth. With humans, however, it is different. There are instincts to be sure, but what we are is not all carried or predetermined in our DNA. In addition to genetic coding, we have cultural coding to shape our identity, our humanity. The laws, literature, music, art, mores, religions, architecture, and lifestyles of any given culture tell us what it means to be human at that period in time.

Humans belong to the only species that creates its own meaning, identity – and future. We not only must, we can reinvent what being human is all about.

When we refuse to accept the definition of ourselves as "consumers" merely or chiefly; when we see ourselves as servants of Earth rather than as its masters; when we base our economies on global justice instead of private or national greed; when we realize that war is suicidal insanity, no matter what fancy causes are trumped up to justify it; when we acknowledge that racism and religious prejudice are the worst kind of blasphemy – then we will have begun to reinvent ourselves.

The year 2000 is not a point of menace but a gateway of hope.

— The Real Cost of Meat —

The old slogan "it's mainly because of the meat" can be taken in more than one way. Today, health experts and environmentalists alike are telling us that our overconsumption of meat products is a trend that must be reversed. It's mainly because of the ecological costs of expanding, global meat production on the one hand and the dire risks to human health (from too much meat and dairy products) on the other that there is an urgent need radically to rethink our western diet.

My concern is with the environmental impact of our love affair with meat and the consequent excessive proliferation of livestock. According to one of the most respected private policy-research think-tanks in North America, the Washington-based World-watch Institute, we in First World countries will have to begin to eat less meat (as nutritionists also advise) while Third World nations keep their meat consumption low.

In a special report, Worldwatch Paper 103, "Taking Stock: Animal Farming and the Environment," the authors document the following thesis: "Too much meat consumption leads to illness. Too much meat production leads [many poorer nations and dozens of middle-income countries] to dependence on grain imports, a food system skewed against the poor, and a worsening environmental predicament."

Vast areas of the world's croplands now produce grains to feed livestock, which provide meat for the rich rather than the basic foods of the majority. Earth's forests, which are so vital to planetary health, are being cut down at an alarming rate, not just in the Amazon basin and in Central America but anywhere in the world where ranchers, often a front for land speculators, can persuade or dupe governments into believing this will create "productive" land. Nearly 70 per cent of deforested land in Panama and Costa Rica is now pasture. In Mexico, about 18 million hectares of pasture was once forest, and 5.5 million of that was tropical forest.

The social justice issues raised around this issue are enormous. In Latin America no other major agricultural enterprise creates fewer jobs per hectare than ranching – for example, one worker per 1,500 hectares in the Brazilian Amazon.

Removing rain forest for pasture sets up an inexorable chain of tragedy: "Shallow, acidic and nutrient-poor tropical soils lose … nutrients.… Most pasture is abandoned within a decade for land newly carved from the forest." The amazing diversity of life in these forests vanishes with the trees. As we know, the rain forests, covering just 7 per cent of the Earth's land surface, contain about half the Earth's species.

Deforestation for ranching also makes for climate change. As living plants are burned or decompose they release carbon into the atmosphere as the "greenhouse gas," carbon dioxide. This traps the sun's heat and warms the Earth. Since 1970, expansion of pasture at the expense of trees in Latin America has released 1.4 billion tons of carbon to the atmosphere, more than the U.S.A. (the world's leading carbon emitter from all sources) released in 1990.

What's more, livestock are a significant source of the second most important "greenhouse gas," methane. The report says "perhaps 80 million tons of the gas are released each year in belches and flatulence, while animal wastes at feedlots and factory-style farms emit another 35 million tons."

The report notes that the countless tons of animal waste that now accumulate around modern livestock production facilities can pollute rivers and groundwater. "If they get into rivers or lakes, nitrogen and phosphorus ... over-fertilize algae, which grow rapidly, deplete oxygen supplies, and suffocate aquatic ecosystems. From the hundreds of algae-choked Italian lakes to the murky Chesapeake Bay, and from the oxygen-starved Baltic Sea to the polluted Adriatic Sea, animal wastes add to the nutrient load from fertilizer runoff, human sewage, and urban and industrial pollution."

Worldwatch researchers are not urging vegetarianism or an absolute abstention from eating meat – although they note that most North Americans consume twice as much protein as they need. (They quote with approval Cornell University professor Colin Campbell's view that "we are basically a vegetarian species and should be ... minimizing our intake of animal foods.") Their real point is that "a meat-fed world now appears a chimera.... Supporting the world's current population of 5.4 billion on an American diet would require two-and-a-half times as much grain [for livestock] as the world's farmers produce for all purposes. A future world of 8 billion to 14 billion eating the U.S. ration of 220 grams of grain-fed meat a day can be nothing but a flight of fancy."

From reading the Worldwatch study paper, and from many other observations (average red meat consumption in the U.S. has fallen 14 per cent since 1976 while in the U.K. an estimated 6 million people voluntarily dine meatless most of the time), I believe a quiet revolution might be underway around the matter of meat, especially among the young. It *can* make a difference.

— The Killing Floors —

"If people want to eat meat, it has to be killed, and that's never going to be pretty." (The foreman of a slaughterhouse, who asked to remain anonymous.)

In one of the ancient Greek mystery religions, the initiate stood under a grating while a bull had its throat cut above. He was thus bathed in the cascading blood. This and all other primitive forms of animal sacrifice seem quite barbarous to us today. Yet our civilization runs by the shedding of literal rivers of blood from millions of animals sacrificed to satisfy our demand for meat.

I don't want to be dramatic, nor do I wish to offend. However, what follows might well disgust some and anger others. It's an objective report of how the meat we see so neatly wrapped or hanging in our food stores is slaughtered.

As a journalist concerned with religion and ethics, I was keen to visit an abattoir and see for myself how steers, calves, and pigs are killed. As a person who once hunted but gave it up years ago after hearing a wounded rabbit scream, and who now has a normal sensitivity to bloodshed, I was reluctant to go anywhere near a slaughterhouse. Eventually, however, I visited three. I don't recommend it, even supposing you were able (and it's far from easy) to get the necessary permissions.

First, the good news. I came away from all three meat-packing plants, with their killing floors, impressed by the following observations:

• The meat industry is highly regulated. The largest facility had thirteen federal inspectors and four or five veterinarians always on hand watching over every stage of the process. The other two had the same system scaled to match their size.

• Great attention is paid to the health of the animals before killing, and to the quality and hygiene of the final product.

• The people working in such places – cutters, packers, and so on – work very hard. They stand or sit shoulder to shoulder, their hands flying to keep up with the endless hooks or trays on conveyor belts bearing carcasses or parts. Observing the sawing, cutting, snipping, and hacking, I was struck by the aptness of the remark made by one official: "It's just like an assembly plant only it's in reverse. Here, we take things apart."

• Those who direct or do the actual killing are decent, humane people who try to see that the animals don't suffer unnecessarily. They are doing a dirty, smelly, unpleasant job for the rest of us in a society that would prefer not to think about this aspect of diet at all. You won't see what I saw on your TV set.

• There was little waste. Everything – noses, lips, tongues, feet, hides, fat, bones, and even blood in some plants – goes for food or some industrial purpose.

My first visit was to one of the largest beef-packing plants in the country. (The stench outside was horrible.) Here, daily, hundreds of steers arrive, are kept in large pens, and are then herded and prodded into a tightly confined conveyor where, struggling and in obvious panic, they are stunned by a bolt fired into their skulls. As I watched, one steer took three shots from the gun before falling and being dumped on the floor. Many are still kicking – just nerves? – as they are strung up by a chain around one leg and hoisted to be moved along to where their throats are cut. Gouts of blood splatter on the grating below.

These animals did not suffer long, but they plainly sensed what was coming before it happened. I will never forget the eyes of about five steers who stood like deer at bay before being driven into the fatal chute. It was the look of fear in beings that realize they have been lethally betrayed.

Next I visited one of the largest pork-producing plants in Ontario. Some 20,000 pigs a week enter its doors to be turned into bacon, ham, or chops. Here, I thought the killing was slightly more humane than with the cattle. The pigs, two at a time, locked in a small cage, were dropped about nine metres below the killing floor and given a shot of carbon dioxide. They were brought up unconscious, rolled out on the floor, strung up by one foot, and had their throats cut so they would bleed to death before regaining consciousness.

However, I can't soon forget the screams and struggles of these pigs as they had to be driven with electric cattle prods up the final ramp to the gas chamber. Pigs are very intelligent animals with highly sensitive noses. It was clear they could smell the blood and could tell they were about to die. They, too, were filled with terror at the end.

The worst experience was at the third site, a packing plant for veal. The people were nice; the plant was clean; there was a veterinarian and a federal inspector. But these 180 to 200 kilogram calves were being slaughtered kosher. This means their throats were sliced open while they were fully conscious.

I know this method is permitted to Jews and Muslims for religious reasons, and that it is argued it is just as humane as the other methods described. I know also that many Italian, Greek, and other Christians kill lambs and goats in the same way at Easter. Personally, I found it deeply repugnant.

— Ritual Slaughter, I —

Schoolchildren are taught a number of lies. There's no conscious conspiracy, though. Often, parents and teachers are so brainwashed by the prevailing culture that they're unaware of propagating illusions and falsehoods. One could cite a list of such lies – such as the ineluctability of human progress or the capacity of our technology to solve all problems. However, my concern here is with the lie that meat is an *essential* part of our diet. Selling this lie involves, as with most lies, other lies to lend support.

The chief ancillary lie in this regard is that livestock are the trusted, loved friends of humankind. Pictures in children's books, as well as those adorning the propaganda of the meat industry, show smiling, contented animals frolicking in their delight at being part of the human food chain. Nowhere is the ugly truth shared that we humans are the only higher species that cultivates its intended victims as friends right up to the point of killing and then devouring them. Nowhere in all the pretty books do children see the killing floor, the terminal panic of our "friends," or the welter of their blood. Not surprisingly, few adults – never mind children – give this matter a thought.

In order to describe the no-stun method of killing, I visited another slaughterhouse. Please bear in mind that while it was an Orthodox Jewish ritual I witnessed, virtually the very same methods are used by devout Muslims as well as by those ethnic Christians who eat lambs or young goats at Eastertide.

Wearing a gown and rubber boots because of the water and gore, I watched as a series of veal-calves had their throats cut. There were about 115 of them, mostly young bulls from dairy herds, in a holding pen to our right. Each was led into the chute and finally into a metal box about three feet in front of us. The calf naturally thrust its head out the only "window" in the box, and this opening was then constricted so that it could not withdraw.

The ritual slaughterer (*shohet*) then pushed a button causing a lever to force the calf's head up so as to leave its throat thoroughly exposed. Then, using a razor-sharp knife, about 46 centimetres long by 3.5 centimetres wide, he made a swift cut from side to side to sever both jugular veins, the two carotid arteries, and the esophagus, in a single stroke. The head was then forced higher as the blood spurted forth. In about five or six seconds – it seemed much longer – the eyes glazed, the side of the box opened to disgorge the twitching corpse, and it was strung up by one leg to "bleed out."

In Canada, livestock must be stunned by electric shock, gas, a blow on the head with a sledgehammer, or a shot between the eyes from a spring-loaded bolt before being hung upside-down and slaughtered by having their throats slit. But there are exceptions. In kosher and halal slaughter, the animal's throat is cut first, while it's conscious and unbruised, according to special rules aimed at ensuring a quick demise.

There's no doubt that, where the cut is done expertly, death follows almost instantaneously. The cutting of the arteries means that all blood flow to the brain stops. The twitching and kicking I saw in some calves, even after they were hanging, was explained by the *shohet* as "reflex muscular action." However, a federal inspector (with over twenty years' experience) who stood nearby told me he thinks the process is: "one of the most inhumane things I have seen in this business."

Another veteran slaughterer there volunteered the same opinion and added that sometimes a calf with its throat cut will get up and dash back into the holding area. It then has to be retrieved and shot with a stun gun. When I expressed scepticism about this, he invited me to stay for the day and watch. I had already had enough.

Some three thousand years ago, when kosher killing began, it was more humane than the methods used by other tribes and cultures. Today, I believe it's an outmoded archaism that should be banned, as it has been in Iceland and in several countries in Europe. I agree with a liberal Toronto rabbi who says that it should go because, today, it's less humane than the secular method of stunning the animal first. Using gas or electric shock instead of a gun would still leave the animal unblemished, as the rituals require.

Incidentally, since, to be ritually fit to eat, an animal must not just be killed in this way but must also then pass a number of strict hygiene tests (as well as the meat being soaked in salt to get rid of all blood), I was told only about 15 per cent of the calves killed thus that day would end up as kosher. The rest would be sold to regular supermarkets. This also happens in the case of beef. This means one has no guarantee that the meat one buys (except for pork) has not been killed by the no-stun, throat-slitting method. I never knew this before and find it unacceptable. Packaging should be marked to declare how the animal was killed.

My conclusion, after studying the topic of meat, diet, and the environment, is that one useful thing I can do for the planet, as well as myself, is to stop eating red meat. It's a decision my wife and I have now taken together and feel good about. No matter how livestock are killed, they're in terror when they die. In eating them, are we also consuming their fear? Certainly we're sustaining our lives by bloody violence.

Who knows? Perhaps in fifty years humanity will come to view its eating of animals with the same wonder and distaste we now reserve for cannibalism. I hope so.

— Ritual Slaughter, II —

My writings on our excessive dependence upon meat and its effects on the environment and human health have met with emotionally charged criticism from some in the Jewish community, focusing particularly on my comments concerning the no-stun method of slaughter.

To the best of my knowledge, this was the first time a journalist here took a close, firsthand look at the actual process of bleeding calves and other livestock to death without stunning them into unconsciousness first.

Because there are some important issues at stake in this controversy, it's important to give the proper context to what was actually written. What was actually said was that the practice of slitting open the throats of sheep, goats, calves, or other animals while they are fully conscious is part of the religious rituals of devout Muslims and Jews. I added that many Christians from specific ethnic origins use this same method for goats or lambs at Easter.

There was no "attack" upon Jews or the Jewish religion, as some rabbis and others have charged. In calling for a ban on the no-stun, near-decapitation of living animals while there are other (to my mind) more humane methods available, I had no intention of limiting the religious freedoms of any group. The truth is that neither the Torah nor the Quran explicitly says that an animal must watch its slayer wield the knife and be conscious as its life's blood spills forth.

In the case of Jewish slaughter, the explicit prohibitions in the Bible are against bruising or damaging the animal before it is bled. There is obviously nothing to prohibit such practices as electrical stunning or harmless gas, which are now readily available and leave no mark or blemish of any kind.

It is true that the practice of cutting through the two jugular veins, the two carotids, and the oesophagus, as is done in the no-stun method, was originally established in order to be as humane as possible. But if avoiding cruelty is part of what kosher or Muslim ritual killing is supposed to be all about, there should be no objection to a public debate over whether this is indeed the most humane way to carry on today.

My critics say it has been proven beyond the shadow of a doubt that the no-stun way *is* the most humane. I have read some of the relevant literature, and the issue is very far from clear. Some authorities in favour of the method go on to note that it doesn't always work well. Not infrequently, the very sharp knife used actually "seals off" the arteries and/or veins, and the animal remains conscious for much longer than the average five to fifteen seconds cited as the norm.

A number of veterans in the slaughter business — including several federal meat inspectors – have contacted me to say that the "margin of error," even in the case of a skilled ritual slaughterer, is very wide. I have heard a number of accounts at first hand from inspectors who have had to intervene from time to time to stop both Muslim and Jewish slaughterers because of incompetence.

In the prestigious journal *Judaism: A Quarterly Journal of Jewish Life and Thought* (Fall 1990), Professor Temple Grandin, assistant professor of Animal Science at Colorado State University, approves of the kosher method but has some criticisms of certain aspects of kosher slaughter. In particular, Grandin is strongly opposed to the shackling and hoisting method now outlawed in Canada but still practised in some American states. In the same article, she notes that "the cutting technique of the *shohet* [ritual slaughterer] may explain the *great variation* in the results of scientific studies concerning the onset of unconsciousness in calves and cattle" (italics added).

Grandin, who believes kosher slaughter can be made more humane, said she herself has observed that when "a less-skilled *shohet*" was doing the cutting, up to 30 per cent of the calves righted themselves on the table "and some animals even walked on the moving table like on a treadmill." When the *shohet* was highly skilled, he caused 95 per cent of the calves to collapse immediately. Grandin, in a note to me, said she has since learned that "the problem can be prevented by changing the cut location."

The charge from some in the Jewish community that I am consciously or unconsciously anti-Semitic for raising this whole issue is so absurd that I would not mention it except for the fact that I'm shocked at how glibly it runs off some tongues at the slightest criticism. Those who have used it should ponder the fact that the no-stun mode of killing livestock – by anyone – has been banned in Sweden, Holland, Norway, Switzerland, and Iceland. These are hardly countries one would call anti-Semitic by any stretch of the imagination.

What is most interesting in this whole debate is that none of the critics of my stand on no-stun slaughter have addressed this very real public issue: a large quantity of meat from animals killed by the no-stun, slitting of the throat method, goes to our meat-markets for general consumption. Nobody I have talked to seemed aware of this fact before I brought it to light.

I believe it is important to respect the rights of all minorities. But what about the rights of those who would not buy meat at all if they knew it was killed in a way they consider less humane than the normal, secular method? At the very least, there should be a labelling system so that people can be clear about what is going on.

PART FIVE

RELIGION TODAY

— Stolen Dreams —

The fact that justice for our Native peoples is one of our most urgent ethical problems has now been forced to the surface of our Canadian consciousness. But there is a long road to travel before we will even have begun to make amends for the injustices of the past.

Too many Canadians are still reluctant to face the reality of the terrible devastation wrought, especially among the Indians, by centuries of exploitative contact with whites. We might come to know it with our heads and still not feel it in our hearts.

It's not just that we took their land and rode roughshod over their culture. We robbed them of their inner life, their dreams, and their sense of who they were. We left them like passive, dependent children, unable to go back to the life they once knew and yet unprepared to "fit in" to a society totally foreign to their own spirituality.

I got a renewed glimpse into the dimensions of this tragedy this week when I came across a passage in Carl Jung's book *Memories, Dreams, Reflections* in which he describes his visit to Africa in 1925. Jung tells of meeting with a very elderly *laibon*, or medicine man.

When he asked the *laibon* about his dreams, the old man answered, with tears in his eyes: "In the old days the *laibons* had dreams, and knew whether there is war or sickness or whether rain comes and where the herds should be driven." His grandfather, too, had still dreamed, he said. But, since the whites were in Africa, no one had dreams any more. "Dreams were no longer needed because now the English knew everything," he said.

Jung comments that this reply showed him that the medicine man had completely lost his *raison d'être*. The divine voice that counselled the tribe was no longer needed because "the English knew better." In former times, the medicine man had negotiated with the gods, or destiny, and had advised his people. He had exerted great influence, and the tribes had flourished. Now his authority had been replaced by the District Commissioner, a total outsider.

Aware of their great spiritual losses, Jung comments: "The value of their life now lay wholly in this world. It seemed to me it would be only a question of time and of the vitality of the black race before the Negroes would become conscious of the importance of physical power."

The Swiss doctor was making a sad prophecy whose fulfilment is still being savagely expressed in the tribal strife going on in South Africa today. The confrontations at Oka, Quebec, in 1990 and other threats of violence – for example, over the planned expansion of Quebec Hydro's massive James Bay project over more of the Cree's traditional lands – are symptoms here also of a similar, inexorable process. If you destroy a people's vision of how they fit into the cosmos, if you crush their relationship to the Earth, to each other, and, eventually, to their own spirit or Self, you leave them no alternative but either to be destroyed or to take a stand and, if pushed, opt for the one value their oppressor knows well, "physical power" or force.

When I was nineteen, I had an experience in our North similar to Jung's. On a remote Cree reserve at Big Trout Lake, Ontario, which is still today inaccessible except by air, I found the Native people utterly demoralized and reduced to total dependency upon white authority figures.

As a teacher for the summer – the sole time the Cree were not scattered on their traplines – I was the "school boss." Inexperienced as I was, I nevertheless had absolute sway as far as what or who was taught. Native input was nil.

The missionary, a sincere man, was the "church boss." Indian spirituality was nowhere to be found. Anglicanism, complete with prayers for Her Majesty's good health, had banished the elders and medicine men to oblivion. The Hudson's Bay Company manager was the "big boss" because he held the economic lives of the entire band in his power. If he wouldn't advance enough "debt" in the fall to see a family through the winter, or if he refused to buy the furs in the spring, a trapper and his family could perish.

Once a year, the ultimate boss, the Indian agent, would come in to pay treaty money. If they were lucky, the Indians would also see a doctor, the "healing boss," at the same time. Traditional Indian healing had long ago vanished.

There was, of course, a chief and council, but they had no authority that mattered. White bosses, including the "weather bosses" at the Department of Transport station, ran everything.

I have never in all my travels and experience since then encountered a situation where a once-proud and thoroughly capable people has been more completely dominated, lorded-over, and rendered spiritually and politically impotent than during the summers I spent there. A form of apartheid was going on in our North as surely as it was in South Africa at that same date. The only difference was that, for the Indians, the violence was muted by the remoteness of the victims and the smaller numbers involved.

Some seem surprised, even shocked, when they see expressions of Native anger today. The truly surprising thing is that Indians are still willing to attempt a dialogue with the rest of us at all.

— Travelling Light —

I once spent a week on an island in the middle of Lake Nipigon. I was there with three other men, fishing for speckled trout.

We almost drowned on the way in because our small boat was

overloaded. The man entrusted with buying the supplies had forgotten the first rule of trekking in the bush – travel light. Instead of dried foods, he had turned up with a mound of canned stuff that weighed a ton!

My deep conviction is that if Christianity is to survive it must begin to travel light. This means some radical change. We have passed the stage where just tinkering with the details can help. That's why adding this or that prayer to the worship or using trendy language in sermons is of little avail.

Failure to reach young people makes the point. We are seeing the first generation in Canada to be raised as religious illiterates. The majority of youth see religion answering questions they're not asking, in concepts they can't comprehend. The spiritual path seems equated with what is hoary with age, tied to an outmoded worldview, and synonymous with the dull and the irrelevant.

This is tragic when true spirituality – the inner journey with its lived-out results – is the most relevant, riskiest adventure life affords. It's precisely what youth, with all its aspirations and fears, needs and wants. Yet the communication gap and the estrangement from religion remain.

One way to help bridge this is to recover and reinterpret the most powerful metaphor of spiritual life. It occurs in every religion: that of the heroic journey, trek, or pilgrimage. It runs throughout the Bible and in classics down the ages, from Bunyan's *Pilgrim's Progress* to Tolkien's *Lord of the Rings*.

The wandering of the Israelites in the wilderness can be dusty reading until you realize it's a symbol of the quest of every soul. The story is about *us now*, not just about *those then*.

In the New Testament, one author explains what Jesus was about and what the Christian life is like in terms of that forty-year wilderness trek. He reminds us of what every real hiker knows: that when you're on a wilderness trip, the camp each night is the place of order, of safety, of refreshment and rest. But it is never an end in itself. It is always impermanent, a means to an end.

For the Israelites, it was also the holy place where the Ark of God's presence was. Outside the camp was considered profane.

However, once the tribes reached the Promised Land, the "camp" became permanent in the City of Jerusalem. Everything was built and hedged about with walls of stone. Instead of being the God of the journey, moving ever onwards, God tended to become the God of the static, of the rigidly enclosed.

But the author of Hebrews says: in suffering and dying outside the walls of Jerusalem – out on the profane or secular ground where criminals were executed – Jesus went "outside the camp." He broke through to the place not of safety, of rest, of order, or of the conventionally "holy"; his journey took him out to the place of risk and of high adventure, because of his obedience to God's call. Significantly, our author then makes this startling challenge to the people and Church of his time – and hence to Christians today: "Let us then go to where Jesus is, outside the camp, bearing his reproach."

For the Church, the camp now represents not old Jerusalem but all that is too comfortable, rigid, safe, or static in its understanding of God's will for individuals and for the world. Theology, structures, worship, ways of communicating the faith to others, whatever has served in the past as means to an end but has now become petrified as if it were the end itself must be challenged. Excess baggage must go.

To go outside the camp now is to recognize that our former ideas of God, of what is sacred or secular, of who is or is not "saved," of which religion has or lacks "The Truth" may all have to change. We are all pilgrims, all on trek, and none of us has yet "arrived" at the fullness of our destination. It is this sense of openness and this awareness of the spiritual journey – of movement, however uncertain, ahead – that brings excitement and joy to the way.

While, like explorers, we do not know what lies ahead, we do know that others have heroically gone down this path before. Each faith has its prophets, saints, or gurus who were forerunners and now serve as guides.

For Christians, the "pioneer" of faith is Jesus. His call to God's service is anything but conventional or tame. That's what has to be communicated today.

— Religion and Spirituality —

Recently, I was the guest on CBC Ottawa's call-in show, "Radio Noon." The question put to listeners was: "What does your religion mean to you?" It was a lively program with a wide cross-section of opinions expressed.

Thinking about the experience on my way home from the Toronto studio, however, I realized that I should have done a better job of clarifying several key issues. Because of their wider importance, I'm going to make amends by sharing my thoughts on them with you.

• Whenever you open up the phone lines on the topic of religion, you inevitably hear a lot of griping and negativity. There's no basic problem with that. A lot of people have been or are being hurt by religion in one way or another. What's more, given its history and current difficulties, religion, like politics, presents an enormous target.

As one who cares very much about the future of religion and the various world faiths, I remain extremely critical of certain aspects of institutional religion myself. One's hope is that, by means of informed, constructive criticism, organized religion can be challenged to further renewal and service in the cause of humanity and the rest of creation.

But there's another side to the story, one that often gets scant treatment. I'm referring to the incredible amount of good done by organized religion every day of the week. The radio callers had a lot to say about church "hypocrites" and the very real animosities and tensions caused by religion around the world. There was little appreciation of the unglamorous but vital work done here and abroad by millions of believers of every stripe as they visit the sick, counsel the confused, care for the lonely and the elderly, and give generously of their resources to feed, clothe, and house the needy everywhere.

Believe me, if it were not for the volunteer work done by church and other faith communities members, if it were not for the social service leadership given by clergy and laity of every denomination and belief across this wide dominion, Canadian society itself would be a profoundly more callous, inhuman affair. We pay tribute, rightly, to inspiring giants such as Dr. Robert McClure and Cardinal Paul-Émile Léger. We too easily forget the vast company of those whose names never get in the paper but upon whose diligent caring so much depends.

• The open-line callers talked as though religion and spirituality were synonymous, identical. They are not, and thinking they are can lead to serious errors and misunderstandings. A person's religion has to do with belonging to a particular grouping, accepting certain core beliefs or creeds, and performing specific rituals, meditations, or other prescribed disciplines. It is basically concerned with external matters, with what one professes or performs.

Spirituality, on the other hand, is essentially an internal matter, an affair of the heart. It has to do with a mode of consciousness, a certain way of perceiving oneself, others, and the cosmos. It is the realization, as Jesus said, that the Kingdom of God is within us and around us, that the ordinary contains the extraordinary, that the unseen is more powerful than the seen, and that matter itself is alive with Spirit.

You can be extremely religious, observing every rite, rule, and feast day, and yet be as unspiritual as a lump of clay. There are many today who are deeply spiritual, in tune with the universe and its Maker, and yet are quite outside the bounds of religion altogether. Ideally, all religious people ought to have the inner attitudes and awarenesses suggested by their outward profession of faith. Unfortunately, it frequently doesn't work out that way. As the Bible, for example, puts it, it is possible to spend one's life going to church or temple and saying "Lord, Lord" and still miss the inner reality entirely.

• It's easy to assume from the above (and many critics seem to) that religious rituals, creeds, buildings, and other organizational

structures are totally unnecessary. If the ultimate goal is the transformation of the consciousness of the individual and hence of the
species itself, and if one can be spiritual on one's own, why bother
with all the religious paraphernalia anyway?

This is one of those arguments that appears to carry considerable weight at first glance but collapses on a closer inspection. I am
not personally – and never have been – some kind of religious
anarchist who inveighs against any and all kinds of institutional-
ized religion. As Aristotle once said, "Man [humanity] is a political
animal." He uses "political" in the sense of "intended or meant for
communal life." It's very difficult (impossible?) to maintain one's
spirituality and put it to work for others unless there is the support
and encouragement of those of like mind. You need organization
and institutions to get things done. The forces of irreligion are well
organized!

For me, the big question is not, Do we need organized religion?
but, How can we keep renewing the organization so that it truly
helps people's spirituality instead of getting in its way?

— Sex and Money —

Sex and money. These are two of the most potent forces in any
society. Unfortunately, as a businessman reminded me recently,
they are also the two areas of human life with which Christianity
has always had most difficulty in coming to terms.

Whenever the subjects of sex or money arise, Church leaders
seem overcome by feelings of embarrassment, confusion, and
downright negativity. This is one of the chief reasons why our
religious institutions have such difficulty in getting and holding
the attention of modern men and women, particularly young
people.

The question arises: why, since sex and money are clearly not
only here to stay but are such central themes of living in the real
world, does the Christian faith sound so uncertain a note where
they are concerned? If the Good News is about an abundant life,

how come all the ambivalence and nay-saying at these twin crucial points?

When you believe, as I do, that the parent faith of Judaism is much more positive about both, the mystery deepens further.

• *Sex*: As the early Christians turned more and more to the non-Jewish world for converts, Greek philosophy and religious speculations exerted an ever-greater influence. In particular, instead of a creation-centred spirituality there emerged a strong focus on individual salvation and on escape from this evil world. You had a body-soul dualism in which the body was seen as the prison of the soul, the originator of whatever was crass and evil.

The Christian Church has yet to free itself entirely from this bias. It still lacks a positive understanding or "theology" of creation and of the body. Nor have the roles played in the cultus by the developing dogmas about the Virgin Mary and Jesus himself done much to help this situation.

While believers rightly hold the mother of Jesus in high esteem, there can be no doubt that the concept of womanhood that eventually came to be focused in her has done incredible damage through the centuries. By first stripping her of every possible vestige of full, female sexuality and then exalting her passive submission to God's will as the highest form of feminine self-realization, the Church gave women an impossible, often destructive ideal.

Men, for their part, were left with an ongoing, mind-splitting struggle between the only two options available: seeing woman as virgin or woman as whore. Much male hostility towards women stems, albeit unconsciously, from this schism.

It is by no means accidental that in many cultures where devotion to the Blessed Virgin has been most extreme, the lot of women is often bleakest. It is seen as "normal" (by men!) for a man to have a chaste woman as the mother of his children but a mistress for "the joy of sex."

As I have argued in *For Christ's Sake*, centuries of neglect of the humanity of Jesus have resulted in a Christ who is totally sexless.

Theologians only talk about Jesus' maleness when they want to deny women the priesthood. Any real thought of his having had all the physical experiences that go with being a human male causes nothing but acute embarrassment.

You can listen to clergy expounding what Jesus is said to have said about sex (very little), but where is the model for living out a fully human sexuality as a lover and husband? Certainly not St. Paul. Obviously not a celibate priesthood!

• *Money*: I once had lunch at a select club as the guest of a very wealthy parishioner. At one point he said: "Never worry about money. As the Good Book says, 'It's the root of all evil.'"

As a millionaire, it was advice he could afford to give! But I told him, as gently as possible, that he was one of those "learned enough to misquote." The Bible's actual words are: "The *love* of money is the root of all evil." There's a world of difference!

Scripture nowhere condemns money *per se*. In fact, it recognizes its true nature as a symbol of human energy, work, brains, or creativity, as well as a medium of exchange. True enough, the poor are praised and the way of poverty is commended to those for whom money has become an end in itself and thus an obstacle to inner growth. But there is also recognition that without wealth there would be nothing with which to help the poor. The emphasis is always upon *how* money is made and *how* it is handled – upon proper stewardship of it, and upon using it as an instrument of social justice.

Too often the rich, rather than being challenged to view wealth positively, have been made to feel like sinners simply for *being* rich. Wealth is power. Power itself remains neutral until it is used. With right use, it can be redemptive of society.

You can't *serve* God *and* mammon. But mammon can be used in God's service. For the building of His Kingdom. Now.

⟶ Professional Faith ⟶

On my first day as a freshman in seminary, I met another student who told me his name, asked for mine, and then immediately queried, "Was your father a clergyman?" When I replied in the negative, he demanded, "Then what the hell are you doing in here?"

I was somewhat taken aback. It had never occurred to me that being an Anglican priest might be a hereditary affair. Pursuing the matter, I discovered that the only reason he was there was because his father had been there before him.

It seems that one day, during the Great Depression, his father had been walking the streets of Toronto looking for a job. Happening to pass one of the city's two Anglican theological colleges, he saw a sign in the window: "Wanted, Men For Ministry." He went in and never looked back.

Obviously, as well as thankfully, this does not describe the motivation of the majority who are ministers, priests, or pastors today. But it serves to underscore the undeniable truth that not everyone who dons clerical garb or perorates from pulpits has necessarily received some kind of divine "call" to this exalted state. There are those for whom it is just a job. For some, it's an opportunity to control others, for being centre-stage, for playing churchy games complete with "smells and bells."

But the real question I want to look at here is whether or not we really need professional clerics at all. Is it time – as the iconoclastic social critic Ivan Illich suggested in a monograph some twenty years ago – that we paid our last respects to "the vanishing clergyman"?

• It might come as a surprise, but the idea of a person coming from high school, taking a university degree, and then studying for three or more years at a theological college in order to be ordained as a professional cleric is comparatively recent. There were no professional clergy in the New Testament era, nor indeed for many centuries afterwards. The Church got by almost as long without theological colleges as it did without the invention of Sunday School (1780).

• Several studies have shown that the majority of those who enter training to be clergy are better able to communicate with their fellow human beings before theological college than when they come out! Theology has given them a language and outlook completely foreign to ordinary folk. This accounts in part for the great communication gap between pulpit and pew (never mind pulpit and street).

• The reverse side of this is the way clergy are perceived by the rest of society. They are a kind of breed apart. A third sex. As professionals at holy things, they are either put up on a pedestal or ignored completely.

The Scottish evangelist Tom Allen once said he never wore his clerical collar while travelling on British trains. He liked to talk to people and get to know them, but he had found that "when a man or woman sees you are a clergyman, they stop being the person they really are and try to become the sort of person that they think you think they ought to be!"

• This raises a more serious matter. The various churches for years have debated the role of the laity, the ministry of the laity, "the laity this and the laity that," without changing the situation one jot or tittle. The truth is that as soon as you have a professional clergy, everybody else in the Church (a) feels religiously inferior and (b) subconsciously figures that the professional is really "the Church," and so he or she ought to be left to get on with it.

The result is that, for the most part, for example in the Roman Catholic and Anglican churches, you have a highly clericalized system. The biblical truth that it is the laity (the *laos*, or people of God) who are the true Church is given lip service and little more.

What I am saying is that the existence of a professional caste of clerics has become a major stumbling block to the Church really being the Church in and for the world.

To suggest that this caste should vanish is not a very palatable concept for institutions deeply concerned about their survival. Yet, paradoxically, it might be the only way survival can be ensured – a case of losing one's life to find it.

Of course, there is a need for leadership in the churches, and I'm not arguing against scholarly training in theology. But this is far from the kind of morphological (structural) fundamentalism now at work in denominations that, ironically, abhor Bible fundamentalism like the plague.

The best solution would be worker or secular clergy – people who support themselves by other jobs or professions. Failing that, the next best thing would be for all professional clerics to be given a five-year leave of absence as of now. This would give the faithful a chance to find that they, and not the ministerial hierarchy, really are the Church.

— The Tallest Trees —

As revelation has followed revelation in the ongoing, horrendous story of the violent and sexual abuse of little boys in Roman Catholic-run parishes and orphanages across Canada, there is a crying need for fuller understanding. It is a public insult to be told that this simply shows that priests or religious brothers are "human" like everybody else. It is absolutely outrageous to be told by bishops that "only a tiny percentage of clergy or lay monks are involved," or that "other churches have their problems, too."

How many CF-18s have to crash before we realize that something is dreadfully wrong with either the plane or the training program? How many professional athletes have to be caught using banned drugs before action is taken?

My purpose is not to cast blame, however, but to suggest a path of understanding not yet explored in discussions of what this calamity is really all about.

"Lightning always strikes the tallest trees." This piece of ancient wisdom comes from the same period of classical flowering that gave us the Greek tragedians. There is a deep connection. Like all great dramatists, they were fascinated by the inner events that lead to human greatness or to catastrophic disaster. They identified what is called the "tragic flaw," the weakness in the psyche of the hero that leads to folly and humiliation. With uncanny powers of observation and insight, they were aware that the deadliest and yet most common flaw, in all the sorry catalogue of human vices, is that of hubris.

The Greek word *hubris* has no exact equivalent in English. This is why we keep the word itself. The old-fashioned rendering was somewhat quaint – "over-weaning pride." I translate it as "insolent arrogance." It's not just the pride of "the tallest tree." It's the kind of pride that is so reckless it's openly contemptuous of "lesser breeds" of mere mortals.

You can see it in western society's past attitude to the Earth. Our sadly depleted environment is the end result of ecological hubris on a global scale.

Christianity in general (all denominations) has been guilty of enormous hubris down the ages with regard to one of the most basic human instinctual drives. I'm referring to our sexuality.

Behind all the attempts to control people by manipulating their vulnerability to guilt in this area, behind all the interference in even the most intimate details of married life, there has always been an arrogance or hubris. This has expressed itself in the unfounded belief that church leaders, be they bishops, priests, or evangelists, always know the "mind of God" on sex; that the Bible lays down precise rules about everything from abortion to mastur-bation; and that sexual sin is the basest sin of all.

But in the case of the western wing of the Roman Catholic Church (Eastern Rite churches permit married clergy), the hubris reached its zenith in the lie that sexuality can be completely ignored: "Pray about it and it will go away." Mandatory celibacy became the rule and was exalted to a higher state than marriage.

Ordinary people, conscious of the reality of their own sexual natures and astounded at the lofty spirituality of those who were presumed above such earthy drives, often treated these celibates as little less than gods. The mythology that built up around their much-vaunted chastity lent a power and authority seldom rivalled in any other institution. It also frequently gave to the clergy and religious themselves a totally false perception of their own human-ity. Many were able to function well and lead useful, often heroic lives. But the casualties have been legion.

It is not accidental that the terrible picture steadily coming to light in Canada and elsewhere is one in which perverted sex and incredible anger have combined to bring savage violence to the innocent and shame to the Church. The Greek tragedians would have seen the inevitability of it all. Sexual hubris brings sexual catastrophe.

Little children who are viciously raped, punched in the mouth, or otherwise abused beyond belief by those entrusted with their care all testify to the fury of male psyches themselves violated by unnatural repression and a false denial. A cardinal rule is: "Beware the anger of the righteous." The victims who are now coming forward with their terrible stories of suffering know the truth of this better than any.

There are some important warnings in this whole mess for society at large. The Church is at fault – not least for covering up these scandals for so long. But it is already clear that it never could have done so without the complicity of police and courts, of politicians – and (for many years) of the media, too.

― The Pope's Death ―

"To lose one parent ... may be regarded as a misfortune; to lose both looks like carelessness." (Oscar Wilde, *The Importance of Being Earnest*.)

In the early hours of September 29, 1978, Roman Catholics around the world awoke to find they had lost their second Pope, or "Holy Father," in two months. The sudden death of Papa Luciani, John Paul I, whose election on August 26 to replace Paul VI had surprised everyone, has never been adequately explained.

Some have argued it was carelessness indeed, a failure by Vatican officials to realize that the sixty-five-year-old former Archbishop of Venice was in poor health and under enormous stress. In this view, he died of neglect after a reign of thirty-three days.

Others, most notably the British journalist David Yallop, in his book *In God's Name*, have suggested something much more sinister – murder. The release of the film *Godfather Part III* renewed rumours of possible foul play in the Italian press. In the movie, John Paul I is depicted as the victim of poisoning by the Mafia. I have been often asked by readers for my views on this, particularly since the publication of Yallop's book in 1983.

Those who read my coverage from Rome of the election of Luciani will remember that I was much taken with the new pontiff. His winsome smile alone made him such a refreshing change after the long years of the dour and Hamlet-like persona of his predecessor. What he said about the propriety of speaking of God as mother as well as father, his humour, his track record at Venice of dispossessing the Church of its treasures in order to care for the poor – all this and much more gave promise of positive things to come.

Thus, when the phone rang at 1:30 a.m. that night in 1978, I was as shocked and devastated as the Catholic leaders I then had to call for their reaction. I remember waking Cardinal Maurice Roy, then Archbishop of Quebec and primate of the Canadian Church. As I told him the news, he exclaimed: "It's terrible, incredible.... I just can't believe it!"

Much later that day I was on my way to Rome. When I had dropped off my luggage at the hotel and rushed down the Spanish Steps to get a cab to St. Peter's, I stopped briefly at a kiosk to get a paper. To my astonishment – since the official word was that the Pope had died of a heart attack – a prominently displayed magazine was already on the stand with the accusation that the Pope had been murdered.

There was a cover drawing of Luciani in bed reading Thomas à Kempis's *The Imitation of Christ*. In the foreground, a man in a cassock was looking over his shoulder as he poured a vial of poison into a cup emblazoned with the papal coat of arms. To underline the point, a large caption asked in Italian: "Who killed the Pope?"

Later, at the Vatican press office, it seemed we were given a different version of events every time there was a news conference. They told us first that Luciani had been discovered by his secretary, Father John Magee (now a bishop in Ireland), sitting up in bed with the devotional book still in his hands. Later it turned out he actually had been discovered by a nun, Sister Vincenza. We were told he had been reading a heavy report on troubles in the Archdiocese of Chicago and not the book on Christ. Requests to interview Magee and Vincenza were met by statements that each had left Rome on Church business and could not be reached.

Conflicting stories were given out about the pontiff's state of health. Some sources said that, apart from low blood pressure, he was in first-class shape. The doctor who pronounced him dead was never produced, nor was a death certificate.

Repeated calls for an autopsy by various officials and, in the case of Spain, by the conference of bishops went totally unheeded. One could go on. In truth, either from shocking carelessness or through a misguided cover-up for pious reasons, the tragedy was completely mishandled by the Vatican.

When you realize that at the time the Vatican Bank was embroiled in one of the worst, most complex scandals to hit a Church institution – one that included charges of laundering of Mafia money from the drug trade, bogus offshore companies in the Bahamas, money for Exocet missiles for Argentina in the Falklands crisis, and the deaths of many, including the suicide or murder of "God's banker," Roberto Calvi, head of the Banco Ambrosiano – you can see why speculations about how Luciani died persist.

With me, whether or not he was murdered is still an open question. I don't believe anyone at the Vatican itself would have done it. But there were plenty, including the Mafia, with motives. The opportunity would have been easy enough to arrange.

Godfather III might be right. It certainly wouldn't be the first time in history a Pope was removed by the poisoner's hand.

⏤ John Paul II ⏤

At precisely 6:18 p.m. on October 16, 1978, I was in St. Peter's Square, Rome, awaiting the result of the eighth ballot in an historic papal election. It was a truly memorable scene. The crowd of about ten thousand stood in hushed anticipation. The façade of the vast basilica and most of Bernini's Colonnade flared white in the glare of huge floodlights.

Suddenly, at 6:19, as puffs of white smoke began ascending from the tiny chimney on the roof of the Sistine Chapel, a deafening shout went up. The decision had been made! From every side thousands flooded into the piazza like a mighty torrent. I had to fight against this stream as I rushed to the Vatican Press Office, about a thousand metres away.

I had only a few minutes to get a phone link to *The Toronto Star* to ask them to hold the final edition. By the time I got through to the foreign desk and then paid an attendant to guard the phone at my end, the spotlights were already focusing on the doors above the main entrance to St. Peter's.

As I raced back to the square, the doors opened and a tiny figure in white, flanked by two cardinals, appeared. "*Habemus Papam!* – We have a new Pope!" the loudspeakers boomed. The crowd, already more than ten times its original size, cheered wildly and then waited tensely to hear his name. When the cardinal in charge said, "Cardinal Karol Wojtyla, Archbishop of Krakow," there was a moment of stunned silence.

The mainly Italian throng couldn't believe their ears – the first non-Italian in 450 years! Reporters from around the world were equally shocked. They threw away their elaborate dossiers on the supposed front-runners and began a feverish quest for anyone who knew anything about the man from Poland.

As I turned and ran for the phone, applause for Wojtyla erupted in a crescendo behind me. Breathless, I stammered the story across the miles and managed enough for a front-page bulletin in the final edition. I learned later that, as luck would have it, I had been the first reporter in print in North America with the news.

Within hours of his election, John Paul II, as the handsome, smiling prelate from Krakow had chosen to call himself, was already a familiar face around the globe. He has remained a media celebrity ever since.

However, today, more than ten years into his pontificate, we can take a more sober look at his leadership than was possible during the universal euphoria that followed him during the weeks and months immediately after October 16, 1978.

The Pope is in many ways an extraordinarily attractive man. His charismatic personality, manly good looks, and willingness to take strong, often unpopular positions give him an aura of positive leadership in a confused world. His scores of mass-appeal journeys abroad have given his papacy a visibility and a local impact never known before.

Yet, he remains an enigma, and, at times, he seems a startling contradiction. He seems a fully modern man, yet much of his leadership seems directed backwards to the past.

He seems extremely sensitive to suffering and hurt, yet his insensitivity and lack of compassion towards the cries of pain coming, say, from his priests, from women in the Church, the divorced, or from young people, are almost monumental. It is no accident that 43 per cent of all Catholic parishes worldwide have no permanent priest today. The decline in attendance at mass in North America and Europe is staggering.

While he never fails to make much of the cultures and traditions of aboriginal peoples (in itself a highly commendable stance), he appears to have a total blind spot where the culture and traditions of those who live in the western democracies are concerned. Part of the widespread disenchantment with this Pope in the U.S. today comes from the fact that he shows no appreciation for a culture in which democracy, pluralism, and creative dissent are primary values.

While he has done much to champion human rights and the dignity of personhood the world over, John Paul II has failed to discern the need for openness, for freedom to doubt, for inner, spiritual autonomy – and hence maturity – that the current spiritual quest in North America and much of Europe is all about.

In spite of his embracing of leaders of other denominations and faiths, the past ten years have regrettably shown little if any *substantive* movement by Rome to bring about global, religious harmony. The message still seems to be: "Come back to The Truth and all will be forgiven."

I join those who congratulate the Pope on his accomplishments. But unless he begins to listen as well as to lecture, one wonders how his flock can survive another decade like this.

— Money for God —

I have no doubt there are people who have been helped by the ministry of Oral Roberts. My investigations of faith healers have shown me that, occasionally, the sick are healed through such evangelists, *in spite of* their antics and lack of theological sophistication or even, at times, moral rectitude.

However, when it comes to parting the flock from their fleece, nobody has a more fecund imagination or fewer scruples than "Brother" Roberts. I want to take this opportunity to alert Canadians to his latest scheme. It was brought to my attention by a reader who has been on Roberts' mailing list for years.

Personalized and running to eight pages, the appeal for dollars is labelled a "War-On-Debt." What it amounts to is a callous exploitation of people's angst over the current recession. Roberts tells the recipient he is his "partner and friend." Because he feels so "close" to him, he can say something very personal to him, "with love in my heart and faith in my soul."

Assuming his reader is loaded down by debt and "financial bondage," Roberts addresses him by his first name and asks: "Does the horror of those thoughts keep you awake at night? The burden ... oh, the burden is sometimes too much for you to bear. You wish there was a magical answer...."

The evangelist doesn't have a magical answer. He has something much better, "a MIRACULOUS ANSWER direct from the throne of God to your home." God, he writes, wants to reveal this through his "prophet," none other than Oral Roberts himself. Roberts then quotes some carefully selected Bible passages to prove his contention that God's will is for all His followers to be prosperous. The secret to this is simple: "When you listen to God's prophet and you put God first by giving to Him, a miracle can happen."

What it all boils down to is that Roberts equates giving to God with giving to him and his association. All you have to do, he argues, is to plant a little "seed" by sending in a gift of $100. No matter how much you owe elsewhere, you send in $100, $50, or whatever you can scrape up and do so immediately, "so you can start receiving your miracle harvest to get out of debt VERY QUICKLY."

In case anyone misses the point, the mailing includes a sheet of cardboard with coloured pictures to be cut out and sent in so that Roberts can touch them in healing power and "break the spirit of debt off your life." The pictures show various items – for example a house, with a space to be filled in under "house loan amounts," a car, a credit card, a person in hospital, a couple of young people at college, and so on. The person being solicited is encouraged to show the total amount owed, with a blank space thoughtfully added that says simply "other debts."

It's a pity Roberts didn't think of this "supernatural" war on debt a couple of years ago when he found himself having to plea-bargain his life before God because of his own money problems. George Bush will undoubtedly be sending him a coloured picture of the White House with his nation's staggering, multi-billion-dollar deficit boldly inscribed below for healing.

Frankly, I find this whole exercise to be spiritually dishonest and bordering on blasphemy as well. Jesus Christ would have driven him out of the temple along with the money-changers and the rest. I will personally begin to take Roberts and all his cohorts in the world of television evangelism seriously when they stop this kind of pecuniary plotting and start tackling the ethical and social failures of American life today.

Not one of them has raised a voice in outrage or horror over the hell on earth now being suffered by the Kurds and others in Iraq, the nation Bush utterly devastated and destabilized in his quest for a new world order.

Not one of them has denounced, in the name of God, the furtherance of the obscene "Star Wars" initiative, the continuing sale of arms to Third World countries, or the other U.S. foreign policies that condemn millions of poor and starving everywhere to remain in despair.

The United States is the most loudly religious country in the entire western hemisphere, thanks in large measure to TV religionists like Roberts and his kin. Yet it is sinking fast into a bottomless moral morass.

Every sixty minutes, about two hundred Americans suffer from violent crime. Only thirty years ago, the number was thirty-five per hour. The population has grown 41 per cent since 1960. Violent crime has grown by 516 per cent. The U.S. rape rate last year was fifteen times that of England, twenty-three times that of Italy, and twenty-six times that of Japan.

The per capita murder rate was four times that of Italy, nine times that of England, and double that of strife-torn Northern Ireland. In 1990, 23,300 Americans were murdered – one every twenty-three minutes.

The Senate Judiciary Committee's report, from which these figures come, put the matter succinctly: "The United States is the most violent and self-destructive nation on earth."

Roberts says he wants to heal Canadians. To him (and to his President with his plans for world renewal) we say: "Physician, heal thyself."

— C. S. Lewis —

In the course of one's spiritual odyssey, God, Allah, Brahman, the eternal Spirit behind, through, and under the whole of the cosmos has an uncanny way of toppling all idols that we might worship only Him/Her. Sooner or later we are confronted again with the thrust of the First Commandment: "Thou shalt have no other gods before me." Priests, ministers, saints, gurus galore, theologians, and spiritual giants of every stripe, no matter how wise or manifestly sincere, all have feet of clay. Put your absolute trust in any, and they will ultimately disappoint.

What is true here, of course, is just as true in any other sphere when the culture or one's personal needs elevate other humans to god-like status. It can happen with politicians, athletes, stars of the entertainment world, and a host of others. It can even happen with a spouse or one's own children. It can happen whenever we deify celebrity or material possessions. It can occur when one's health or appearance become the chief shrine at which the soul pays homage.

This train of reflection began when I received a lengthy letter from a former professor at an American university. We met at Oxford in student days and have had a sporadic correspondence ever since. Though we are still both believers and so have the most important things in common, it would be hard to imagine two more different paths. He became a devout Roman Catholic, with all the zeal and ultra-orthodoxy of the true convert. What strikes me most, however, is the way my friend, like many who write to me, relies on C. S. Lewis for his own views on God and religion.

Lewis, the Oxford English don and then Cambridge professor, author of the famous Narnia tales for children and a host of books on Christianity, from *Miracles* and *The Great Divorce* to *The Screwtape Letters* and *The Problem of Pain*, was a great Christian apologist and communicator. He was an eloquent defender of the faith. But, imaginative writer and scholar though he was, he was not a theologian, and there is a certain irony to the way he has become, since his death, a kind of infallible guru to conservative Christians in every denomination. Fundamentalists in particular now treat him as a sort of cult figure, with one American Bible college glorifying him with a large stained-glass window and a collection of Lewis memorabilia and relics.

My correspondent, a former agnostic who was in the navy at Pearl Harbour when the Japanese attacked, became a Christian through Lewis's writings (Lewis too had been an agnostic), and then, at Oxford, they became close friends. They often met at the Eastgate Hotel on High Street, near Magdalen Bridge, for a pint before dinner. I never knew Lewis that well myself, although I belonged for a time to the Socratic Club of which he was the president. I often saw him, pipe in hand, returning from a walk along the Cherwell River or around Christ Church Meadows. He looked a little like the corner butcher, but when he spoke he had the voice and charisma of an angel.

I have long been an admirer of Lewis, and at an early period of my life he meant a great deal to my spiritual growth. However, I always liked his fiction better than his various theologizings or apologetics (the technical word for defending or explaining faith to non-believers). In matters of theology, he now seems at many points somewhat one-sided, even naive. I never cared for his attitude to women.

Be that as it may, the 1990 publication of A. N. Wilson's fascinating biography of this many-sided man (C. S. Lewis: A Biography) has thrown a number of his conservative followers into a genuine dilemma. Their "saint" has now been revealed as a man whose life hardly fits with their preconceptions of what a good, fundamentalist icon ought to be. For example, Lewis smoked like a chimney all his life, both cigarettes and pipe. He was capable of consuming large amounts of beer and wine and loved nothing better than a roistering evening with his students, where the partying males competed in the composition of bawdy ballads.

For thirty years he lived "without benefit of clergy" in virtual servitude with an older woman (Mrs. Moore) who lorded it over him in what can only be described as a relationship with definite undertones of sadomasochism. Then, later in life, he married Joy Davidman, a loud and lively American divorcée whose husband was still alive – "a sinful woman married to a sinful man" as he himself wrote.

The head of the C. S. Lewis Society in Oxford today (there are many around the world) is a recent convert to Catholicism. He is only one of Lewis's many devotees who continues to deny even that Lewis had sexual relations with his wife, in spite of Lewis's own quite earthy written witness to the contrary! For the true believer he must, like the Mother of Jesus, remain a perpetual virgin (virgo perpetua).

None of Wilson's revelations diminish the stature of C. S. Lewis in the least. In fact, nobody who reads Wilson's account with an open mind will fail to be deeply moved and impressed by this story. He was a great and very gifted human being. But he was anything but infallible. He wasn't a saint of some sort. To his lasting credit, you know from reading the story of his life that he himself would have been the first to have warned against any kind of cult.

— Mark and Huldah Buntain —

Mother Teresa's heart attack, in the fall of 1989, confined her to a Calcutta hospital for many weeks. However, although there was extensive media coverage around the world, nobody mentioned the fact that this modern medical facility was founded and built by a couple of quite remarkable Canadians.

It's important to put this on record, not out of chauvinism but because the Reverend Mark Buntain and his wife, Huldah, are to my mind Canadian heroes. Yet very few people in Canada know very much about them. We tend to do a bad job of promoting our own. Mark, who was called "St. Mark of Calcutta" by supporters of his work, died suddenly in July of 1989 at the age of sixty-nine after working with the sick and starving of that city for thirty-five years. He was truly one of the most impressive men I have met, and I have been meaning to write about him ever since learning of his death.

In late 1979, I was sent to Calcutta to interview Mother Teresa, who had just won the Nobel Peace Prize, and to do a Christmas series for *The Toronto Star* called "Christmas in Asia." My photographer and I found the Buntains in the heart of that teeming city where they had first pitched a tent and begun their work in 1954. Today, a splendid school stands there, with a printing plant, a tailoring shop, and an auto-mechanic wing to train the children to earn a living.

Early on, when the Buntains saw that many of the pupils – who were street urchins – were too weak to profit from any course of study, he began a food program that now feeds over ten thousand youngsters daily. In 1977, he built the 120-bed hospital, with its own training academy for nurses and the very latest in medical technology. His basic philosophy was: "Nothing but the best is good enough. We serve a great God so why not expect the best?"

The dramatic story of the Buntains' labours to make a difference in Calcutta, with its enormous social problems, is living testimony to the impact of two people who determined to "light a candle" rather than sit and curse the prevailing darkness. The hospital actually began at the school, with one bed and a single nurse. Soon there were sixteen beds. Then, almost miraculously, Mark got a ninety-nine-year lease on an abandoned cemetery in the city's core. With a daring that characterized his style, he then asked the president of the Architect's Association of India, a member of his church, to design the most up-to-date facility possible. The estimated cost was $1 million and he had no money at all. Buntain took a year off and crisscrossed Canada and the United States, telling of the desperate need. The hospital was opened, fully paid for, in March 1977. The motto over the door says simply, "Jesus heals."

Mark Buntain, a tall, incredibly energetic man, had had three heart attacks before 1979, yet we could barely keep up with him as he led us about. He was born into a Pentecostal family in Winnipeg and was a Pentecostal minister himself. But he was far from your stereotypical, platitude-spouting preacher. The man was practical to his very marrow, and so was his wife. They had no use for those who seek to convert others to their creed but leave their bellies empty or their bodies naked. When they discovered hundreds of little children living beside and picking through the garbage at Calcutta's dump at Buntola – using bits of wire as hooks to salvage something to eat or sell – Mark promptly organized a feeding depot and a school there. His mobile clinics take health care for many kilometres around Calcutta, and there is now a series of clinic-school units scattered throughout many of the outlying villages.

The Buntains put up with hardships we in Canada would find hard to imagine. For example, each had only a pail of water a day for all purposes, from cooking to hygiene. Yet to be with them was to share a joy that was as infectious as it was spontaneous and genuine. You would never guess that this same man, when he first "felt" God was calling him to India's Calcutta, had reacted with total dismay. He told me, "I'm no mystic, but the call seemed very real, and I sure didn't want to go to India. The very thought of going to Calcutta filled me with a kind of cold chill. It was soon after that that the mission board wrote and said that's where they would like us to go."

The Buntains, greatly to their own surprise, fell instantly in love with the city and its throbbing horde of humanity. I so well remember standing with Mark on the roof of the hospital, looking out over the smoke- and dust-filled streets going off endlessly into the horizon. He turned to the photographer and me and said: "I want to stay here as long as God gives me the strength. I'm sorry I've only got two hands and feet to tackle what remains to be done. Calcutta has been cursed by many, but God loves every single person in it – and so do we."

Early in the summer of 1989, Mark Buntain became ill while driving his wife to the Calcutta Airport. He was rushed back to the hospital and pronounced dead a few hours later. I believe we all have a right to be proud of both Mark and Huldah Buntain – Canadian saints indeed.

— Success and Suffering —

The most warped aspect of the "born-againism" being served up by so many evangelists on TV and in many pulpits today is this: people are being led to feel that failure of any kind is not only an unspeakable sin, it is the very antithesis of what the Gospel of Christ inevitably gives. "Accepting Jesus" is presented as the surefire route to instant and constant health, happiness, and success. Like so many other messages in our media-saturated culture, however, this too-easy nostrum founders badly on the rocks of reality.

Certainly Jesus himself had little in common with the celebrities of his time. A ministry that ends on a cross, between two criminals, is hardly a paradigm of glossy, worldly success! Most of his immediate followers, moreover, suffered imprisonment, torture, and death. One can illustrate the point, however, by two examples from much more recent days.

Evangelicals and fundamentalists are among those with the

highest praise for the Oscar-winning film *Chariots of Fire*. They were overjoyed to see a movie depicting an Olympic gold-medal-list who went on to be a missionary in China. They applauded Eric Liddell's courage and witness in refusing to run on Sundays and his testimony that he was "running for God." Nobody, however, knew or seemed to care very much about what happened to Liddell after he went to China and the mission field.

Intrigued, I was eventually able to track down Liddell's widow and talk with her in 1981. She was living in a small village not far from Hamilton, Ontario. She described Eric's heroism and service to others in China both before the war and then while interned in a Japanese prison camp.

It was a tragic tale in the end. Liddell had become very depressed in the camp. He had berated himself for his low spirits and what he felt must be a defect in his faith. Given his evangelical creed, he believed he must somehow be failing God. The thought tormented him. It was only after he died there and an autopsy was done that it was discovered he had been suffering from a large, malignant brain tumour. Obviously, God was with him, whether Liddell felt like it or not. But his was not the success of the effervescent TV preachers, the always-smiling evangelists. He knew the bitter gall of despair and God-forsakenness.

This was also the fate of another remarkable Christian, Joseph Scriven. Most people are unaware that one of the best-known, most-loved hymns of all time, "What a Friend We Have in Jesus," was written by a Canadian who now lies buried near Rice Lake, Ontario. Joseph Scriven (1819-86) came to Canada in 1847 from England. An itinerant preacher and evangelist, he spent most of his time doing works of charity. He eked out a meagre living for himself by tutoring the children of wealthier settlers in the region from Rice Lake to Port Hope and Coburg, just east of Toronto.

My wife and I made a sort of pilgrimage to the small cemetery in the corner of a field where Scriven was buried. As we stooped and cleared the snow and dead leaves from the stone at the head of the grave, we caught sight of a faded inscription on an identical stone lying next to it. On it were the simple, enigmatic words "Scriven's

Sweetheart." Those who are familiar with the story of Joseph Scriven will know that the man who had such fervent faith that he could write "What a Friend We Have in Jesus" lived a life that was plagued by tragedy.

Scriven had graduated from Trinity College, Dublin, in 1844. He immediately became engaged to be married. However, on the very eve of the wedding his fiancée drowned. Years later, he met another young lady, who became "converted" under his preaching, and they fell in love. The young woman, Eliza Catherine Roche, set a June date for her wedding. As a new convert, she had to be baptized first, and so she was immersed in the icy waters of Rice Lake in April 1860. Tragically, she got a severe chill, became very ill, and died some four months afterwards!

Naturally, Scriven was devastated. He continued to preach, to teach, and to visit, travelling for miles on foot, but he became more and more unhappy. Finally, he became seriously ill himself and was confined to a house at Bewdley, at the southern end of the lake.

Joseph Scriven was found drowned in a nearby stream running into Rice Lake on October 10, 1886. A pall of mystery hangs over his death to this day. Some say he threw himself into the waters in a delirium and fit of despondency. Others claim he wandered out of his sick bed and fell in by accident.

In his service to others, he was one of the most Christ-like people I have ever read about. But, from a wholly worldly point of view, he was a loser. That's something to ponder over the next time you watch some huckster-preacher on TV smiling up a storm and promising the moon.

— Politics and Religion —

No arena of concern is more delicate than the mixing of politics with religion. Indeed, there is a vociferous part of the population worldwide that holds fiercely to the view that they ought never to be mixed at all. This is sometimes supported by a vague appeal to the American phrase "the separation of Church and state."

There is a kind of naïvety running through this position that betrays little knowledge of history and even less of the nature of religious commitment. The truth is that since one's religious out-look – and even the lack of one is itself a kind of religion – affects everything we think or do, it is impossible to divorce it from political realities. A religious faith that confines itself to the "soul," while letting the body – and all that flows from being part of a political order – go to hell, is merely a kind of hobby. It is certainly not something one could live, and if necessary, die for.

The Old Testament, the Hebrew Bible, is an intensely political book. Moses' act in leading his people out of Egypt was a profoundly political one. The prophets flayed kings and priests alike.

So too with Christ. I do not accept the ill-founded view of those whose exuberance exceeds their learning and who hold that Jesus was some kind of Che Guevera-type revolutionary. All the evidence points to the fact that he refused the temptation to armed insurrection. He rejected the way of political power for himself. Yet anyone who thinks he and his teaching were not radically political in their impact and in their threat to the Roman overlords hasn't come to grips yet with the full reasons for the Crucifixion. Christ's utter reversal of the values and allegiances of his contemporaries made a collision with both the temporal and the religious powers of the day inevitable.

Once the Emperor Constantine converted to Christianity and took part of the Greek word for Christ as his military standard or "logo" in 312 A.D., the stage was set for a formal marriage of Christianity and empire that was to last into modern times.

Looking at the world today, it is impossible to ignore the way in which, for good and ill, religion and politics are inextricably meshed. It is obvious in both the Jewish and the Arab world. It has been painfully clear in fundamentalist militancy in the U.S.

On the liberal side, the World Council of Churches has been in constant strife because of its support of liberation movements around the world. John Paul II and his Church similarly have an incredibly high political profile at the moment because of the policy of the "option for the poor."

Those who criticize the mixing of religion and politics assume that by taking a position of neutrality on all political issues religious bodies could keep themselves pure. But this is to ignore a crucial fact: not to take a position on, say, poverty, or racism, or violations of other human rights is to have already taken a position! Not to speak out in some situations is to implicitly or tacitly *approve* of evil.

The reason some right-wing American evangelists are so welcome to hold crusades in places such as South Africa or South Korea is that they can be counted on never to raise a voice against oppression. Sticking to what they call "the Gospel," they actually legitimize the work of Satan.

No journalist in Canada has been a stronger defender of the right of Canadian faiths and religious leaders to speak out on political matters than I. Personally, I am proud that on so many issues – from aboriginal land claims to our immigration laws and the economy – the major religions have often become the conscience of the nation.

But it is one thing to defend the right or even the duty of such bodies to intervene in this manner. It is quite another to assume that they are always correct in their criticisms or solutions. They might have much to offer, but infallible truth, especially on complex, politico-economic problems, is not part of it.

No faith and no party can totally identify itself with revealed truth or with the Kingdom of God. That's why there are ordained clergy of different denominations sitting as members of Parliament for all three of our major parties. It is also the reason why I have absolutely no qualms about differing with those of my Church colleagues who now oppose the free-trade agreement with the United States. I have examined their arguments and find them singularly unpersuasive.

I respect their right to speak out. I am grateful that in our system they have also the right to be wrong.

— Out of Touch —

Each of us had one or more bad teachers in the course of our educa-tion. I know I can recall a couple of pedagogical misfits who seemed dedicated to spoiling learning as a kind of revenge for their own incompetence. But you have to have been unlucky never to have had at least a handful of mentors or professors who inspired and encouraged you to seek and grow in knowledge.

The one subject I really felt cheated in was poetry. Your experi-ence might have been different, but it seemed to me there was a deep, ongoing conspiracy from the moment we first looked at a poem in Grade One through to university itself. The object of this secret compact seemed to be to make poetry as boring, dry, and meaningless as possible.

All my English teachers, good and bad alike, were single-minded, almost obsessive, in their resolute devotion to this cause. They analysed and dissected the poems from stem to gudgeon. They droned on forever about the imagery and the metre. They mostly meant well. But somewhere in the process the spirit of the poem, the inner beauty, and its power to illumine or transform ordinary existence was subtly put to death. It was a long time before I grew to appreciate poetry on my own.

I'm certain it's no mere accident that so many people in our urbanized, secularized culture are so extraordinarily literal about everything. They "never weep they know not why." Whatever poetry they began life with as little children – significantly, poetry comes before prose in the cultures of so-called primitive tribes – is drummed out of them before they ever catch a vision of the glory.

Unfortunately, the reason organized religion today is in such sorry shape, and destined to get worse before it gets better, is that what my teachers did to poetry the churches have done to the Bible and to the essence of the Christian faith. They have passed on a dessicated and atomized mish-mash of dogmatic and moralis-tic teachings that have largely missed the spiritual, "living waters" at the core.

When experts point to current church statistics in Canada and predict that by the year 2000 – if present trends continue – regular attendance will be down to 18 or 19 per cent of the population, they are whistling in the dark. From my observations, and from the undeniable fact that in such matters we tend to lag behind the U.K. and Europe by about ten years, my reluctant conclusion is that a figure of 10 per cent or less is much more likely. Count the number of young people at any typical service today and you can chart the graph for yourself.

Young people want life. They want adventure. They want an engagement with the key issues of our time – the environmental mess, world peace, justice for the oppressed of the Earth. Above all, they want meaning, a depth dimension to existence that goes way beyond the external, the prosaic, the materialistic, or the conventional wisdom of vested interests and self-serving institutions. They need to be challenged to their very limits.

Instead, traditional religion often seems to offer them staid and hoary mouthings, answers to questions they're not asking, solutions to problems that pale beside those their intelligence is posing at this crucial moment of human history, and creeds that presuppose a view of the world and our place in it that no longer fits with what they absorb in the classroom or become aware of through the media.

Frankly, being very personal, considering the way my life has been involved in the warp and woof of organized religion from my earliest days, I sometimes wonder at the Grace of God in bringing me through it all. It is difficult being a seminarian and a Christian. It is harder still being a professional cleric and a Christian. Then – attempting something more challenging still – I taught theology at my old college. Try that while remaining a believer! Finally, as a journalist covering all religions and the wider spiritual quest, my grip on the faith got its toughest testing of all.

What I have learned from all of this, and what I'd like to pass on, especially to those concerned with the future of the churches, is that it is crucial to stop every now and then and ask the question: What is truly central and essential in all this talk about God and religion? What is eternal and unchanging in the message and what is merely peripheral, ecclesiastical chaff? That's the only way I know to the "pearl of great price."

Having answered that (and it's a demanding task, not to be sloughed off lightly by repeating old nostrums), the next step is to ask: Okay now, where exactly does the kernel or heart of what this religion stuff is all about bite or touch on my own deepest needs and longings? You see, it's precisely that sort of connection that's not being made today by more and more people. This whole society shouts aloud its spiritual or religious wants and needs for those who can discern the signs. Yet the very institutions supposedly designed to meet and answer those yearnings are being ignored. They will continue to be ignored – deservedly – until they are willing to go back to the basics and then struggle to find relevant ways to communicate them anew.

The churches have been the architects of their own near-demise. It's not yet too late for them to design a different future.

— Blessing Homosexual Couples —

Should the Anglican Church bless the exclusive, lifelong commitment of same-sex Christian couples just as it does those of heterosexuals?

This is not an academic or sensationalist-type question today. It has been discussed in Anglican and other religious circles for some time. The June 1991 issue of *The Anglican*, the official monthly newspaper of the Diocese of Toronto, poses the question itself in a special pro and con feature.

A committed lesbian couple, who are Anglicans, argue for the Church's blessing. A woman who recently left the United Church to become an Anglican argues against such a move. Readers are invited to weigh the matter and let the paper know where they stand.

The woman opposed to the blessing of same-sex unions bases her argument mainly upon the bitter divisions and unhappiness fomented by the decision of her former church to admit gays to full ministry. (The United Church has not taken any formal steps toward same-sex "marriages.")

The lesbian couple notes that the House of Bishops of the Anglican Church, while not approving gay or lesbian "weddings," has made some fairly positive comments about the quality and mutual enrichment of many homosexual partnerships where there is a dedicated decision to remain together.

The pair point out that, while the traditional marriage service states that one of the purposes of the union of a man and wife is the procreation of children, the Church would never turn down a couple because the woman was well past childbearing age. Indeed, it marries couples from time to time where it is already quite clear beforehand – because of some physical disability – that normal intercourse will never take place. You don't have to be capable of or intending to reproduce yourselves in order to have a full Church blessing on your union.

The two other purposes of marriage (as set out in the Anglican Book of Common Prayer) are: the blessing or "hallowing" of the union between the two partners and the "mutual society, help, and comfort, that the one ought to have of the other, in both prosperity and adversity." The lesbian women contend that both of these elements are as applicable to them as to any heterosexual couple. They are finding much joy and personal growth, they say, in their love for each other and feel deeply hurt that their church feels it can't offer complete acceptance, blessing, and support.

I know what the majority reaction to this whole line of thinking will be already. Nevertheless, I think it's important to look at such a proposal with a calm, compassionate, and open mind. There's much to be said for it.

Totally ignoring the extreme promiscuity of one fringe of the heterosexual population, people argue that gays are too promiscuous to be capable of long-term commitments. This simply is not the case. Indeed, given the almost total lack of social, religious, or legal encouragement and underpinning, it's well-nigh a miracle that there are so many of them around, whether in or out of the closet. (It's interesting in this connection to notice how even with all the support from every side given to traditional marriages, the rate of separation and divorce has steadily increased. What would it be like if there were no props or approvals whatever?)

It is not only possible but also potentially mutually enhancing and fulfilling for those whom nature has made different from the majority to make the same kind of commitment to each other as those made in the traditional marriage service. You don't have to be of the opposite sex to promise to love and care for another person exclusively "so long as you both shall live."

The current stigmatizing and ostracism of homosexuals, which leads to so much misery in their lives, including being disowned by families, bouts of self-hatred, and, all too frequently, suicide, is one of the nastier facets of our society. Recognition by the churches of the full humanity and of the spiritual and emotional needs of gay members through a solemnization of gay unions would go a long way towards bringing healing to gays and to homophobics alike.

Finally, if we really care about the AIDS epidemic, we know that as far as the sexual transmission of the disease is concerned there are only two basic ways to impede and then stop it in its tracks. Either people have to remain celibate or they have to keep true to an exclusive relationship with the same partner. Since, under present circumstances in the West – and in distinct contrast to most Third World countries – AIDS is primarily a disease affecting homosexuals, it seems to me that anything the religious institutions can do to encourage people with same-sex orientation to adopt and preserve monogamous relationships should be done without further delay.

The words "marry," "marriage," and "wedding" should be kept for heterosexual nuptials. For gays and lesbians, something simple like "The Blessing of the Union" would do. References to babies could be omitted. The rest of the service could read exactly the same.

— Misplaced Zeal —

Fundamentalists in the U.S.A. are upset over Martin Scorcese's film, *The Last Temptation of Christ* (released in August 1988). Based upon a not-very-good novel with the same title, by Nikos Kazantzakis, the film has a dream sequence in which Jesus makes love to Mary Magdalene.

Bill Bright, arch-fundamentalist and head of Campus Crusade For Christ, ran full-page ads in three major papers offering to buy all rights to the movie for $10 million in order to burn it! This is grossly misplaced zeal. There is absolutely no historical evidence whatever for Jesus having had a sexual relationship with Mary Magdalene – or with anyone else for that matter. However, the fact that religious people go into a rage or a total funk any time such a matter is broached reveals a very serious problem.

In spite of all protests to the contrary, most churches have yet to come to grips with the full humanity of Jesus. This, in part, explains their enormous inability to come to terms with human nature at all, especially in matters of sex. This is slightly amusing since the Bible itself is by no means so squeamish.

Let me introduce you to three women you won't have heard much about in Sunday School. Each is part of the genealogy of Jesus as recorded in Matthew's Gospel. When I tell you who they were and why they were unusual, you'll understand why many clergy prefer to say little about them. They are: Tamar, Rahab, and Bathsheba.

• Tamar: Judah, eldest son of Jacob and head of the tribe that bore his name and ultimately issued in King David and Jesus, found Tamar and gave her to be the wife of the eldest of his three sons, called Er.

But the Lord "slew" Er, we are told, because he was wicked. Since Tamar was still childless, the law said the second son should marry her and "raise up seed" to his older brother. The son in question, Onan, realizing that technically any child born to him and Tamar would be Er's, preferred to "spill his seed on the ground" in *coitus interruptus*.

This "displeased" the Lord, we are told, so He slew him too! This left the third son for the twice-widowed Tamar.

Judah, however, not unreasonably getting worried that he was going to lose the whole lot, kept putting Tamar off and refusing the marriage. Tamar then disguised herself as a prostitute and entrapped her father-in-law into having sex with her. When Judah found out that she had "played the harlot," he ordered her to be burned. She then showed him his signet ring and other ornaments he had given to her when she was veiled as a whore.

Judah realized her "righteousness" and his own fault. There was no further relationship between them, but she gave birth to twins as a result of their encounter. The one that came out first, Phares, became a vital part of the lineage of Jesus, in Matthew's account.

• Rahab: Rahab was a professional whore in the ancient city of Jericho, according to the Book of Joshua. She later became a symbol of faith because of her kindness in hiding the Israelite commandos who went into Canaan to "spy out the land." Later Jewish tradition said she became the wife of the Hebrew general, Joshua.

• Bathsheba: She was seen by King David as she took a bath on the roof of a nearby building. Captivated by her beauty, David seduced her and then, in one of the most devious ploys recorded in Scripture, arranged for her husband, Uriah, to be killed in battle so that he could have her for himself. Bathsheba remained David's *principal* wife until his death.

As the song says, these might be "Bible stories that you never heard before," but the point in referring to them here is neither to titillate nor to shock.

There is a much more serious purpose. Matthew's genealogy follows the Jewish custom of following the male line, yet he includes these three mothers, as well as a fourth, Ruth. Why?

Some scholars point out that all of these women were foreigners rather than pure Israelites. Thus, it is held, Matthew is preparing his readers for the fact that the Christian Church of his day (c. 85 A.D.) is made up of all kinds of people, including non-Jews.

Others, including myself, believe the point is that by including women with unorthodox sexual histories Matthew is combatting slanders that Jesus was born out of wedlock and thus disqualified to be the Messiah.

In any case, I welcome the controversy over the Scorcese film. It is much better to have a debate about Jesus in the media than to have the yawning silence that usually surrounds Him. This silence doesn't denote respect. It means the subject is being wholly ignored as irrelevant.

— Women at the Altar —

There can be no question that, sooner or later, the powers that be at the Vatican will be compelled to surrender their sexist, fortress mind-set and admit the other half of the human race to full participation in every aspect of the life of the Church. One day, under a different Supreme Pontiff, women will be admitted to the priesthood. There will be women priests, bishops, and, eventually, a woman will walk in the "Shoes of the Fisherman" – there will be a woman Pope. All the theological arguments against such a move have been heard now – *ad nauseam*. There isn't one of them that will stand scrutiny.

Not long ago, I debated this issue with the best-selling author and former Jesuit Malachi Martin. Martin, who is Irish by birth, is a fervent champion of the arch-conservative position against ordaining women. But his charm exceeds his logic by the proverbial country mile.

Struggling to make his case, he took refuge in the argument that Jesus told the disciples in the Upper Room that only males could be made priests. Since there is nothing in the Gospels about Jesus ordaining any kind of priests in the Upper Room, let alone an all-male priestly caste, I inquired how he knew that Jesus had laid down this condition. His answer was that the Roman Catholic Church has always simply known what was in Jesus' mind and what he said in secret to his chosen few on the night he was betrayed.

Well, that's convenient but not convincing. It's an example of an egregiously specious speculation. Of course, you can argue that it *might* be true because it seems clear that the Twelve Apostles were all male. However, they were also all Jewish, all non-black, non-Chinese, non-Indian, and so on. It so happens that most of them, if not all, were married men as well!

In the end, Martin did what most of those who agree with his position do when the Bible and theology fail them. He said (and here I am paraphrasing him) that, after all, two thousand years of Church tradition can't be wrong. Most people today, however, both inside and outside the Church, view with proper scepticism the argument that because things have been believed and done one way for centuries therefore they are religiously and ethically correct. You have only to study the Church's attitude to slavery (it approved of it right into the modern era), to religious liberty, or to science to realize that the old way is often very mistaken or even perverse.

In any case, the argument from tradition and history has now been dealt the ultimate death-blow. New evidence currently being examined and published makes it abundantly clear that there were in fact women priests and bishops in the early Church. Just as the early Church knew nothing of the rule of mandatory celibacy for priests, so too it knew nothing of a prohibition against women at the altar.

A distinguished Italian historian, Professor Giorgio Otranto, director of the Institute for Classical and Christian Studies at the University of Bari in southern Italy, has discovered a wealth of material – including paintings, inscriptions, and letters – proving conclusively that women served as priests in the early centuries of Christianity. Recently, on a lecture tour of American colleges and seminaries to present his findings, Otranto told reporters he was a "historian and a believer," and that he was not taking sides in the controversy over whether women should be ordained today. "But considerable evidence exists that women also filled this role," he said.

Otranto illustrated his lectures with photos of newly excavated or restored archeological sites that stunned many in the audiences. They included a fresco of women blessing the bread in a eucharistic rite, painted on the walls of the Priscilla Catacomb in Rome; inscriptions on tombs in France, Italy, and Syria attesting to women priests – named Leta, Flavia, Maria, and Marta; and a mosaic from the Church of St. Praxidus, Rome, showing four bishops, one of whom is a woman, Theodora.

The scholar also showed correspondence of popes and bishops concerning women priests. One, from Atto, an Italian bishop of the ninth and tenth centuries, explains to another priest the existence of female priests and deacons in the early Church: "not only men but also women were in charge of the churches for greater efficiency." The letter goes on to say the ordination of women was stopped by a council in the fourth century. Obviously, then, it was once a fully accepted practice.

The present Pope has forbidden his bishops and clergy to discuss the ordination of women – thereby betraying a sense of fear that sits poorly with one in a position of moral and spiritual leadership. Nevertheless, the subject will not go away. Just a few weeks ago, Most Rev. Kenneth Untener, the Bishop of Saginaw, became the first U.S. bishop to defy the papal ban. He said: "I've studied this, and, as far as my eye can see, I can't see any reason why women should not be ordained. I think they ought to be."

The bishop is right. Hopefully, soon more of his fellows will share his courage and speak out.

— The Word of God, I —

I seldom listen to or watch religious programs unless I have to. The syndrome of "I have the Ultimate Mystery in my pocket" smacks of spiritual pornography to me. Even Billy Graham, for all his integrity regarding money and sex, falls into this trap. But programs *about* religion are another matter. They can be fascinating. The reason for this is that religion, in spite of all distortions, deals with the issues that ultimately matter most to us, whether we are "believers" or not.

It is to religion that the deepest questions belong – meaning, right and wrong, the origins and destiny of humanity, life and death, and life after death. That is why I have little patience with those who blandly pontificate about how one should avoid talking about religion, politics, or sex in polite conversation. What else is there but the boredom of either sports or the weather if you avoid the Big Three? And since, in my view, religion includes sex and politics anyway, one could argue it's the only worthwhile topic, period!

A recent TV show dealt with the question of whether or not the Vatican has too much power over its huge flock. It underlined a fundamental difficulty plaguing Christianity and other world faiths as we get closer to 2000 A.D. The program revolved around three experts – an Anglican, a Lutheran, and a Roman Catholic – who soon made it evident that their own group's view of religion was the right one and all others were, if not perverse, then certainly inferior.

The Lutheran, a professor-cleric from the Missouri Synod, the smallest and most conservative branch of Lutheranism, was the most blatant in his claim to having a monopoly on "the truth." According to him, the reason there are so many different brands of Christianity is that all the other groups read their own interpretations into the Bible. His group alone allegedly simply allows the Bible "to speak for itself." In his view, the Bible is an exceedingly simple collection of writings directly put down at God's command. When you read it "objectively," its truth passes straight into your mind and heart with no human additions, interpretations, or subjective colouring. When confronted with the possibility that his group also might have their own slant or selectivity in reading the Bible, he vehemently denied it.

This is a fatal form of tunnel vision: the inability or unwillingness to face the fact that no matter what claims are made about any sacred writing to be the Word of God – Jewish, Islamic, Buddhist, or Hindu – the Scripture itself comes to us in the word-signs of a specific, *human* language. As such, it is open to, in fact demands, interpretation. This means that subjectivity, or bias if you like, is unavoidable. It is part of the human condition. We bring ourselves, our needs, our prejudices, our hopes and fears to everything we do – from writing a column or painting a picture to understanding any book, however holy.

You'd think that this fact alone would bring a sense of humility and tolerance to all faiths, never mind the fact that they all claim to teach the essential unity and equality of humankind under God. But, sadly, it doesn't. In the case of Christians, the claim of any church to be the only one to truly understand the Bible seems palpably ridiculous.

For example, Jesus spoke only Aramaic, we believe. His sayings were remembered by Aramaic-speakers and only later translated into Greek in what became known as the New Testament. Most of us, however, read all of this in an English or French translation. We are thus already twice removed from the original. And, at each stage of translation, a sifting and changing occur.

Thus, while Jesus spoke of himself as the Son of Man and preached the Kingdom of God, Paul knows the one term makes nonsense in Greek and the other wouldn't be understood by his largely non-Jewish audience anyway. So he avoids both terms almost entirely in his epistles. In fact, comparing the Gospels themselves, New Testament scholars can see how, even in the earliest handing down of the oral traditions about Jesus, including his sayings, there were constant changes, adaptations, and interpretations going on. Read any good introduction to the New Testament for yourself and you can easily confirm this.

There is no question, for example, that the theology of Luke is different from that of Matthew. So too are some of his sources. Mark's concerns and slants are vastly different from those of John. Read one Gospel and then, soon afterwards, the other; you can check this for yourself without any specialized skills. Each of the four Evangelists sees the Christ-event from his own unique perspective. Each faces a different audience with quite different questions and needs – and so writes accordingly.

— The Word of God, II —

Malcolm Muggeridge, the former editor of *Punch* who became known as "St. Mugg" for his strong views on religion, came to faith rather late in life. In the end, he threw himself into the arms of the

236 — RELIGION TODAY

Roman Catholic Church and, true to form, espoused doctrinal positions more conservative than those of the Pope himself.

With his wicked wit and his superb writing style, Muggeridge could make even the most preposterous – or iconoclastic – arguments seem plausible. As an interviewer and debater he had few equals.

Once, in a conversation in a Los Angeles hotel, I queried his extremely negative assessment of media in general and television in particular, especially as set out in his book *Christ and Media*. I asked: "How can you describe TV as a totally fraudulent medium when you yourself for years have been – and still are – a leading performer and writer for the tube?"

His eyes twinkled mischievously and he replied: "I like to think of myself as a piano player in a brothel who, for the general edification of the patrons, occasionally plays 'Abide With Me'."

I was to hear him tell this story several times thereafter, and it always got a laugh from audiences eager to see the media lampooned or lacerated. The only problem with it, however, was that as an illustration it really failed to speak to the point. It made you chuckle, but the contradiction remained.

I was reminded of this the other day when I heard about an Anglican minister in a small Ontario town who was trying to convince his congregation of the (to him) foolishness of not taking the Bible literally. To illustrate, he told of an incident the previous week when he had left his car at a garage for repairs.

He called the mechanic a few days later and inquired whether the car was fixed. "It is," came the prompt reply. So the cleric walked down from the rectory to the garage a few blocks away – only to find his car still in pieces.

"I thought you said it was ready," he told the mechanic. "So I did," the man replied. "But I never thought you'd take me literally."

I'm told this anecdote, like Muggeridge's, elicited much laughter. Nevertheless it would be unfortunate if the congregation concluded from it that the only direct and commonsense way to understand the Bible is to take it all literally!

You'd think that by now most educated people would be aware that any such simplistic approach to so complex and varied a work as the Bible is headed for disaster from the start. Parts, to be sure, are intended to be taken quite literally. But most of the Bible is couched in the language of symbolism. The context makes it quite clear which mode is being used.

When you realize that the Christian Bible is not one book but sixty-six books written over a time span of nearly one thousand years, by vastly different authors, in widely differing settings and life situations; when you reflect that it is actually a library of every literary form, from poetry and drama to codes of law, history, Wisdom sayings, and letters – it makes no sense at all to take every passage or verse in exactly the same way.

Indeed, you can only truly speak of religious experience and of God by indirect means – by means of stories, images, or myths. What is ultimately being described is a dimension of reality that is only hinted or guessed at in our normal patterns of thought and speech. This is precisely why Jesus habitually used parables to speak of God's Kingdom or about his Father in heaven. Yet to hear most fundamentalists talk you'd think God was in their pocket, so to speak. I find their literalism – and their assumed, overly friendly or too-casual *bonhomie* with the Deity – quite scary. They need to be confronted.

The next time someone tells you they take the Bible literally, "from cover to cover," you might ask them when they last took part in a stoning. Adultery is not unknown in fundamentalist circles, and the literal Bible penalty for it is death by stoning. The death penalty, in fact, is laid down for a whole range of comparatively minor offences.

I have never noticed that ultra-conservative churches have dozens of people around missing hands or eyes. Yet, if they took literally Jesus' sayings about cutting off hands or plucking out eyes whenever they "offend" you (cause you to stumble or sin), there'd be an awful lot of self-mutilation going on.

Similarly, when Jesus says "I am the door" or "I am the true vine, you are the branches," he is plainly not talking literally about doors, vines, or branches. In fact, being literal here, as so often, means that one misses entirely the inner meaning that is being conveyed.

Carl Jung once said that the greatest failure of Christianity has been in not understanding the nature of its religious symbolism. He's right. We have been too literal, too prosaic, and the healing power of the Christian mysteries has too often been swallowed up by death.

As Paul wrote: "The letter kills; it is the Spirit that gives life."

— The Meaning of Myth —

Few people give much thought to one of the cardinal truths about humanity. We live by myths, myths of all kinds. Discover the basic myths of any race, tribe, or culture and you have the key to their values, goals, and sense of meaning. Smash those myths while putting nothing in their place and humans become alienated, sapped of vigour and creativity.

What has happened in the western world is that all the old myths are crumbling. People of all ages, but particularly young people, feel bewildered and lost. The myth of inevitable human progress has been found to be an illusion. The myth of a science-created Kingdom of God has foundered on the realities of pollution, poverty, and nuclear peril. The Communist world's myths – for example, the classless society – have similarly shipwrecked.

Drugs, the frenetic quest for pleasure, the lust for status symbols – from the right brand of sneakers to pretentious, heavily mortgaged homes – all of this underlines the illness of our times. We have become Eliot's "hollow men ... headpiece filled with straw."

Contrary to popular thought, myths are *not* fairy-tales. For example, to say that the story of the temptation of Adam and Eve by a serpent in the Garden is a myth is not to say it isn't "true."

It's not historically true. It's a symbolic or mythical way of stating the spiritual truth that humanity chooses to disobey God. It is an imperfect attempt to explain the awareness of the human heart that it is often "out of sync" with its Creator.

The truly great myths flow from the depths of the unconscious. They are rooted in the intuitive, imaginative side of our nature. Their main function is to explain for us our place in the cosmos, our relationship to nature, to the space-time continuum – and to God. They're not always benign. The unconscious has its dark side too. Hence the myths of apartheid or of Hitler's Aryan Empire.

One of the reasons that the myths of the Judeo-Christian tradition are losing their power for the masses today is that we have lost the ability to think symbolically – that is, mythically. The successes of science (though science too has its own mythical elements) and our dedication to linear, left-brain thinking have meant that we approach all myths from this angle. But once you do this, you miss the whole thrust. What's more, the myth itself begins to seem ridiculous. The typical attitude is: "That story can't be scientifically or historically true, therefore it's just a lot of nonsense."

Tell people that the story of Jonah and the whale or the account of the Tower of Babel are myths and they assume they must then be dismissed as meaningless. The same is true of the creation story in Genesis. The truth that we come from the "hand of God" and that we are made in God's image is of crucial importance for human self-knowledge. Take the details of the story literally, however, and you'll end up throwing out baby, bath water – everything.

My concern is that the entire Christian myth is fast reaching this point of unbelievability and thus of irrelevancy as the year 2000 looms.

I know there are millions who would be offended to hear there is anything mythical about their faith. They're not the ones I'm addressing. There is little gained in disturbing those who are "at ease in Zion." What matters is to bridge the gap of understanding for the many more millions who can't make any sense of the traditional faith of their forebears.

For them, at least two things are necessary. The old myths have to be taught and understood mythically. That is, we need to relearn how to think in terms of symbols, parables, and other imagery. When one talks about God, one *must* speak this way, because you are dealing, by definition, with the indescribable.

Second, the old myths have to be rethought and updated. You can't order the unconscious to produce fresh myths on cue. But we can learn to listen and watch. The Bible calls it "waiting on the Lord."

I believe that behind all the details of the Christian story lies the most sublime myth in the history of our species. It is larger than Christianity and it predates it, too. It says that God is incarnate or enters the spirit of everyone "coming into the world." The baby at Bethlehem is in a deep sense every baby. His Resurrection is the precursor of ours. "Heaven" means to be one day face-to-face with the Source of our Being – to come home.

We are *all* spiritual beings, this myth maintains. The challenge is, then, to "become what you are." The implications of this for a world of peace, unity, and justice are unlimited.

— The Good Samaritan —

Three days before Laurier LaPierre, then a Vancouver broadcaster, made front page news with a public affirmation of his homosexuality, I was a guest on his talk show on CKVU-TV.

He began by listing some of the most contentious moral issues before church and society today and then, in his usual forthright, ebullient style, he queried: "It's the Bible that's really to blame for all the confusion, isn't it?"

I know what he was driving at, but I had to disagree. The problem, I said, is not with the Bible. It's the way people use or abuse the Bible. You can either use the old hunt-and-pick method, snatching out this or that verse to suit your particular argument – in which case you'll "prove" anything you like – or you can approach it with a serious attempt to understand its overall thrust and message.

To do the latter means understanding the context of any specific passage, its historical setting, the original intent of the author, and the life situation or problem being addressed. Then and only then can true dialogue with the Bible really begin, as we wrestle with it in the light of reason and our own experience.

The Bible is not a collection of "proof texts" but rather a living witness that engages us, mind and heart, at the point of our immediate, spiritual journey. Any other view of it leads to incredible distortions and a harshness completely foreign to the kind of God revealed in its pages.

Here's an example of what I'm talking about: When somebody does a good deed – say, giving a total stranger a boost with jumper cables when their car won't start, or shovelling the snow for an aging neighbor – we say: "What a Good Samaritan!" And, according to the Concise Oxford Dictionary, the primary meaning of Samaritan in the English language is a "genuinely charitable person."

However, let's think a bit. The Parable of the Good Samaritan, from which this expression comes, is undoubtedly the best known of all the stories told by Jesus. It was told, according to St. Luke (the only Gospel writer to record it) to answer the question: "Who is my neighbour?"

The account (Luke 10:29-37) tells the familiar tale of the man who fell among thieves on the road to Jericho. (I have walked this road through the Judean wilderness myself and can testify to how lonely and deserted a route it is even today.) Various religious figures see the man wounded and in need, yet pass by on the other side. Then a Samaritan comes along, tends his bleeding body, puts him on his own donkey, takes him to an inn, and leaves money to cover his expenses.

It seems simple enough. When Jesus says: "Go and do thou likewise," it seems he is urging everyone to go out of their way to help others. There's nothing very startling in that.

However, here is where knowing the context and the historical references make a world of difference. To understand the full, explosive impact of Jesus' teaching here you have to know something about who the Samaritans were and what their relationship was with the Jews. To say it as briefly as possible, they hated each other. Their mutual hostility was so great it was proverbial. To be sure (as is always the case where deep enmity and prejudice between races or other social grouping persists), each side thought it had good reasons.

The Samaritans were of mixed race – part Jewish, part foreign –

and they had their own temple on a different sacred mountain than Jerusalem. They even held a different view of which books of the Bible were authentic. Jews had no dealings with Samaritans, and the Samaritans returned the compliment. Both were sure they alone were right, pure and accepted by God. Sound familiar?

The whole point of Jesus' story goes far beyond a pious admonition to help others. What it confronts instead is that whole fabric of myths, lies, and excuses whereby we deny the humanity of those who differ from us. Suddenly the parable becomes both highly relevant to our own contemporary lives – and extremely disturbing to our complacencies.

Suppose that, instead of a Samaritan being the hero of the story, Jesus had talked about a gay or a lesbian coming to aid the victim. Suppose he had referred to a Sikh refugee, an atheist, a Fundamentalist, a Communist, a black, an ardent feminist, a prostitute, or a member of any race or creed that happens to be on our personal prejudice list. What then?

It's at that juncture the message becomes a time-bomb instead of a platitude! It calls for radical change, for a new outlook. It's a call away from our smug, divisive judgements on others. It becomes a challenge to enter the revolution of values summed up in Christ's phrase, "the Kingdom of God."

— The Gospel According to Whom? —

Writing essays is still a major part of a university education in the humanities. I remember the first time our freshman class was assigned one – for a professor of English with a reputation for toughness. A few of us were discussing how to tackle this when one chap, a pre-Divinity student who looked very studious but was quite the opposite, tossed off this advice: "All you have to do is find a book the professor hasn't read on the subject and crib from it mercilessly." Incidentally, this chap went on to study theology but never got his degree and eventually did time for fraud in a B.C. jail.

Quite apart from the cheating, his approach was doomed to failure anyway. Professors have read almost all of the books on any topic they propose for essays. What's more, having been a professor myself and having (for my sins) marked hundreds of essays, I can report that you know instantly when a student is copying. You can tell from the content and style that poor old Jones or Smith isn't capable of originating and writing that!

Another form of cheating, still practised, it seems, is when one of the members of the class allows others to borrow from his finished product. Here again, though, there are few teachers who can't spot this fairly quickly. Even if the copiers go to devious lengths to conceal the plagiarism, it always shows. The only interesting problem for the marker is determining which essay was the original and which are the derivatives.

I use these illustrations for a reason. Perhaps surprisingly, they throw light on something that New Testament scholars have wrestled with for many years. When you read the first three Gospels – Matthew, Mark, and Luke – with some care, you recognize that they have a great deal of material (or verses) that is so similar that it's quite obvious somebody was borrowing generously from somebody else. It then becomes a sort of detective mystery trying to unravel who depended upon whom. One of the very first tasks theological students are given today in their study of the Bible is to put the first three Gospels side by side and consider this problem for themselves.

Once you begin this kind of exercise, it soon becomes apparent that Mark is the earliest of the three, and that the other two had it before them and used it liberally in constructing their own accounts. There are many reasons for concluding that Mark was the earliest. These include the fact that it is by far the shortest; there are very few parables; the chronology is vague, to say the least; some of his expressions clearly offended the authors of the other two works and so were toned down or deliberately omitted by them; Mark's Gospel contains more Aramaisms, and so on.

Another way of posing the question as you compare the Gospels is to ask: if Matthew or Luke were first, what was the point of writing Mark at all? But if Mark were the first, it makes perfect sense that someone with access to more material would copy him and fill him out, so to speak, with the extra.

The presently held majority view, then, runs something like this. Matthew and Luke used the bulk of Mark in their own versions. But they also have some stuff, mostly sayings of Jesus, that is common to both of them but not found in Mark. This suggests strongly that they had a second source in addition to Mark from which they also borrowed, and this is called "Q" from the German word *Quelle*, meaning source.

In addition to Q material, each of these two Gospels has some other elements peculiar to itself. Matthew, for example, has parables not in Luke and vice versa. Matthew has the Sermon on the Mount. Luke's Sermon on the Plain is similar but much shorter. Luke has more about the Holy Spirit than Matthew. Matthew has more about judgement and wrath than Luke. We call Matthew's special source "M," and Luke's is called "L."

The final formula for the composition of these Gospels then begins to look like this: Matthew = Mark, plus Q, plus M. Luke = Mark, plus Q, plus L. If you were to put all three Gospels side by side used a different coloured pencil to underline what is common to each, what is common to just two, and what is unique to each, you could do this kind of detecting for yourself.

This, of course, is just a brief look at some of the issues raised in one tiny area of scholarly biblical research. Since Mark was written about thirty years after the events it describes, interesting questions arise as to the various sources behind it as well. Was there an "Ur-Mark," an earlier version of Mark? We don't really know for sure. Tradition says Mark was based mainly upon the preaching of Peter as it was remembered and later written down. But there might have been some written (Aramaic) collections other than Q. And what is called the Passion Narrative, the story of the events leading up to Jesus' death and Resurrection, might also have circulated independently at an earlier date. There are plenty of books available on how we got the New Testament. It's a fascinating subject well worth taking time to pursue.

My purpose here has been to try to whet your appetite, and to show that when someone shouts or argues "It's in the book," they might be avoiding a deeper and more interesting question: "How did it get there?"

PART SIX

SPECIAL OCCASIONS

— Easter, I —

Coming at a time when the Earth is bursting forth from the death of winter into the resurrection of spring, Easter is the most potent myth in the history of human thought.

Unfortunately, in our culture, with its literalist-materialist obsessions, the word "myth" has lost its basic meaning and has come to be equated with fairy-tales, misconceptions, or out-and-out lies. That's not what is intended in calling the Easter Event and the narratives surrounding it a myth. A myth is, as the Greek word *mythos* indicates, a story; not just any kind of story, but a story that takes us beyond what we know into another realm of understanding.

As Joseph Campbell and other philosophers have shown, myths are those stories that deal with the mysteries of life. They arise from the unconscious in response to specific experiences and their function is to relate us to our own innermost Being, to other people, to nature, and, ultimately to the Mystery we call God.

The Christian Church lives from the conviction that God raised Jesus from the dead; that the agony, shame, and defeat of the cross was not the last word; that Jesus' radical commitment to and trust in God and God's Kingdom was finally vindicated. But if we remain simply fixated upon the past or see Easter as something remote and external to our own lives, the power of the myth is lost. Its dynamic for transforming our inner experience evaporates.

A crudely literal approach to Easter is one of the reasons why Christianity is in such imminent peril in our over-developed western world. It is one of the reasons so many, even of the millions who flock to churches on Easter Sunday, fail to come away with an empowering, renewed vision of themselves, their neighbours, or the planet.

The function and purpose of religious myths is to bring about a change of consciousness in each of us. These stories take us beyond our present, limited understandings and free us little by little to be more truly ourselves – for others. Their goal is not more devotion to dusty dogmas or commitment to more pious rituals, however much these may have their proper place. They have a much more practical and vivifying aim: to help us see our place in the cosmos and thus liberate us to live more intensely, more humanly.

That's ultimately what all the great world religions are about. They speak about a Way that leads to life.

The suffering, death and Resurrection of Jesus are about your life and mine. The potency of this myth lies in the fact that it shows us the way in which life itself works. Human life is fundamentally about seeing suffering and death in a new way.

Every fresh step we take, from the very act of being born, to forsaking childhood, to leaving home, to getting married (for those who do), to choosing a career and/or raising children – until death itself – is a form of dying to the past. Similarly, every occasion of spiritual or inner growth – from losing this or that prejudice to gaining any fresh insight into ourselves, others or the world – means a mini-death and a kind of rebirth.

I believe that the Resurrection of Jesus does mean that we, too, shall one day be resurrected to a fully spiritual plane of Being. But the real power of the myth is what it says about life here and now.

Most of us resist the suffering and death inevitably involved in growing into fuller consciousness and fuller life. Our culture is characterized by massive neurotic flights from this bedrock reality. We numb ourselves with everything from mindless television to narcotics – or, just as deadly, a bland preoccupation with the petty. The result is that a growing number have everything and yet feel alienated and empty.

If inertia or a desire for ease and comfort is strangling a deeper impulse in us to follow some vision or dream, it needs to be "crucified." There can be no resurrection without such a "death."

What is true of individuals is true of society. Racism will never disappear unless each racial grouping is willing to suffer the death of its own assumed superiority. Violence will never cease as long as cultures soak in it for their entertainment, perpetuate it in their structures and economies, and put all their trust in it for their security. If we were prepared to "die" psychologically to this sort of hypocrisy and injustice, there would be vastly less actual violent death or its threat around.

If humanity itself is to be reborn – and the future depends on it – old attitudes to war, to patriotism, and above all to nature itself must die.

Nothing less than a planetary Easter is required.

— Easter, II —

I believe in miracles – and that's what Easter is all about.

First of all, as the name itself reminds us, Easter is about the miracle of the whole created universe; it is about the cosmic context in which we all "live and move and have our being."

According to Bede, the "father of English history" (673-735, A.D.) the word Easter is derived from the name of an Anglo-Saxon spring goddess, Eostre. As with Christmas, then, the celebration of Easter has taken the place of a much older pagan festival, which welcomed the rebirth of nature. The giving of Easter eggs and the symbolism of the Easter Bunny, though regarded as frivolous, commercialized hype by some Christians, actually serve to remind us of this crucial link with the basic truths of fertility, birth, and seasonal cycles.

At this level of meaning, Easter belongs to everyone.

There is another level yet at which this day speaks powerfully to persons of every creed and place, but before turning to that we must see its specifically Christian message.

At the core of Christianity lies fervent testimony to a miracle.

As Peter said, in his first recorded sermon: "This Jesus hath God raised up, whereof we are all witnesses."

Make no mistake. From a purely human point of view, Jesus' ministry ended in a catastrophe. He became the victim of the same hatred of "subversion" that haunts those who oppress and mutilate humanity today. He was tortured and impaled on a gibbet by the powers of the status quo. He was denied and abandoned by his closest followers. So much for the Kingdom of God! So much for the power of love!

If that is where the story had ended, Jesus would probably never have made it into secular history at all. The Gospels would never have been written; Paul would never have composed his letters. The "good news" of Easter Day was, is, and always shall be that the same, fully human Jesus who was crucified and tasted death was then seen alive in a radically transformed, spiritual body by the Apostles and other believers.

As I have written elsewhere, "I feel wholly at one with that tradition. In studying the New Testament and the history of the early church, I have examined this Easter faith from every possible angle. That Jesus was given victory over death, that this steadfast trust in his 'Father' in Heaven was vindicated, that love was proven stronger than the bonds of mortality, that here we receive a foretaste of a glory prepared for each and every one of us – and this I believe with all my heart and mind."

Ultra-conservative critics wince when they come across statements like these in my books. They prefer to rush on to the parts where I refuse to jump through their fundamentalist hoops so they can safely cry "heretic." The ultra-liberal critics, on the other hand, are made unhappy by what they take to be a capitulation to unreason and/or superstition.

But there are places and times when the only words appropriate are those of Luther: "Here I stand; I can do no other." This, for me, is one of them.

Whether or not one is or wants to be a Christian, there is another facet to the Easter message and symbolism that touches us all.

As in Tolstoy's great novel *Resurrection*, at issue here is the theme of personal renewal or resurrection. We all as human beings need to be born again. Not in the now-clichéd sense of the so-called Born Again movement. Not just once as in some Road to Damascus conversion. We need to be born again – and again, and again.

What has always amazed and inspired me, both in my years in the parish ministry and ever since in journalism, is the way in which quite ordinary people can "rise again" from disasters or trials of all kinds and do extraordinary things. The deepest meaning of Easter is that the power to transcend our limitations, to be reborn in the face of any problem or tragedy, is available to those who seek it.

This might be the greatest miracle of all.

⤚ Easter, III ⤚

My father, like his father before him, was very musical. He could fetch a tune out of any instrument he touched, from the tin flute he always carried in his pocket to the violin, accordion, and bagpipes.

Having ambitions for his firstborn, he sent me off for violin lessons as soon as I could carry one. To no avail. I proved unwilling to spend time practising, preferring instead to be outdoors on other pursuits.

One day, hearing me play the only piece I ever learned, "There is a happy land, far, far away," he decided my prospects of being a fiddle virtuoso were even farther away and promptly got me a flute. This phase lasted somewhat longer but in the end was an equal disappointment.

By contrast, at the high school I attended, Malvern Collegiate Institute, a pale, slim young man, Glenn Gould, was already attracting national attention. He used to play occasionally at our weekly assemblies.

We admired his prodigious talent but felt rather sorry for him spending all his time practising when there were sports and so many other things to enjoy. We never realized then that by "dying" to social popularity and whatever else teens deem essential he was destined to give a lasting, priceless gift to millions the world over.

This illustrates a principle that is at the heart not just of what it means to be human but of the whole universe. Out of death comes life. Sacrifice brings newness. This is true out in the depths of space, where even at this moment new stars and galaxies are being born as others are being extinguished. It is true in the forests, the oceans, and in our fields and gardens.

In the spiritual life of every person who longs for the fulfilment of his or her deepest yearnings and hopes, this basic law of the universe holds true: without a willingness to "die" to the old, the past, the encumbering, the narrowly selfish, the fearful, the greedy aspects of one's personality or life situation, there can be no resurrection to a new level of consciousness and being.

This brings me to one of the hardest sayings in the whole of the Gospels (second only to the commandment to love our enemies), and that is, that if you try to save your life you lose it; if you are willing to let it go, you save it.

As Mark Twain once said, "It's not the parts of the Bible I don't understand that bother me; it's the parts I do." The meaning of Christ's words is terribly clear. If you want fullness of life, you have to "die" to the narrower demands of the ego.

He's not talking about masochism or a denial of the fact that we are bodily beings. Jesus never preached a false asceticism or a scorn for the good things of creation. The issue is simply whether or not we are prepared to pay the price of being spiritual beings. True humanity consists not in denying our animal nature but in seeing it positively as the vehicle of something higher still. Every time compassion takes the place of indifference or hatred in a human heart, every time a volunteer says no to the desire to seek one's own ease and enjoyment in order to serve someone else, every time a special interest group "dies" to its own wishes for the sake of the wider good, this spiritual law is at work. There is healing and growth, and we are surprised by joy.

This is not airy-fairy, abstract theologizing. It's of colossal urgency and importance in the practical issues of personal and corporate life right now. Think of the unity problem Canada faces as a nation. We will never be one country or fulfill our enormous potential as long as every region, community, and lobby clique stridently insists on its rights, perks, or wishes. The tough reality is that there's a great amount of "dying" to be done by everyone if Canada is to be reborn to oneness and greatness.

The same is true globally, whether we think of the environment or of world peace. Take the Middle East. Unless the great powers – just now most notably the United States – are willing to die to their lust for control, their lust to sell arms, and their overconsumption of oil, nothing much will change. Unless Israel is willing to "die" to intransigence over the occupied territories, and unless the Arab countries can "die" to their desire to see Israel annihilated, there can never be resurrection to a new order.

On Easter Sunday, the occasion of rejoicing for the world's more than one billion Christians, we need to remember that there would have been no Easter without first of all a cross. Our so-called Christian societies today exploit Easter commercially for all it is worth. Good Friday, now a purely secular holiday, passes almost without comment.

The truth is, we think we can cleverly bypass the cross, both personally and corporately. Unfortunately, life itself will not have it that way. Only on the *other* side of "death" lie resurrection, renewal, and spiritual rebirth.

— Easter, IV —

Most Easter hymns, and even the creeds, seem to say that Jesus Christ rose from the dead.

That statement is perhaps shocking. Why use the word "seem"? But there is more. The plain truth of the matter is that, contrary to traditional and popular piety, Jesus Christ did not "rise" from the dead.

People familiar with my work know that I believe the Resurrection of Jesus is central to the Christian faith. They also know that

I personally accept the fact of the Resurrection and believe that without it Christianity makes little or no sense at all.

In spite of this, I still say that Christ did not rise from the dead. Since I do not make a practice of being perverse or contradictory, obviously I feel that something important is at stake. Let me begin, then, by referring to the only documentary evidence we have for Christ's Resurrection – the Bible itself.

The clear message of the New Testament is not that Jesus Christ *rose* from the dead but that he was *raised* from the dead by the direct intervention of an act of God. This is the picture given by the sometimes strange records in the Gospels. It is the express message of the earliest preaching, as given to us in the Acts of the Apostles, and it is the basis for all of Paul's theologizing.

The very first recorded sermon, that of Peter on the day of Pentecost, the "birthday" of the Church, sets the tone for everything else. "This Jesus," Peter says, "hath God raised up [from the grave]."

In the earliest record of the Easter faith in the entire New Testament (1 Corinthians 15:15), Paul says: "We bear witness before God that He raised Christ up...."

Nobody can contradict this. Few things in the Scripture could be plainer. (Although it is true that the King James translation misleads the reader at times by saying that Christ "rose" from the dead when the Greek says "he has been raised.")

But, some will quickly object, isn't this simply a matter of semantics, a sort of "how many angels can dance on the head of a pin" routine?

Absolutely not. The distinction between the idea of a person who abruptly rises from the dead "under his own steam" and the declaration of a miracle wrought by God is enormous. What's more, it's one with significant consequences for the kind of Christianity believed in and practised by the faithful.

The uncritical singing and saying of assertions that make Jesus' Resurrection something he did on his own give the world a Jesus who was invincible, a Superman or god-from-outer-space who pretended to be human but really wasn't. If Christ just waited in the tomb for three days, feigning death but knowing he had only to will it to burst forth as conqueror, the whole agony in the garden, not to mention the cry of dereliction from the cross, becomes a charade.

Indeed, two key Christian beliefs are destroyed by such a view: (a) that (whatever else you say) Jesus was a full, normal human being; and (b) that he really died. His death was no sham, no "playing the game of life with four aces up his sleeve."

One of the reasons Jesus Christ seems remote to so many modern men and women is that the Easter message has been distorted. If, as the New Testament insists, it was God who raised him up – thus vindicating his trust in him and his self-sacrifice for others – then the message is one of joyous hope for all his "brothers and sisters."

It is because he was completely one with us, including his total powerlessness in the grip of death, that Christians can talk about a Gospel or Good News for the world. That's why, when Paul speaks about the resurrection of all humanity, he says explicitly that just as God raised up Jesus from the dead so too shall he raise up everyone.

Easter is a time of hope and celebration because of the spiritual truth expounded by that first Easter: that humanity's ultimate fate is not extinction but resurrection. None of us will leap to immortality because we are God. None of us will burst forth from any grave because we are invincible. We, exactly like Jesus, will either be resurrected by the direct activity of the living God or not at all.

But don't take my word for it. This Easter might be a good time to check out what the New Testament really says – for yourself.

— Easter, V —

T. S. Eliot, in "The Love Song of J. Alfred Prufrock," speaks of squeezing the universe into a ball and rolling it "towards some overwhelming question."

There *is* an overwhelming question confronting us this Easter.

Some will say, "Yes, there is a big question to be faced every Easter: was Jesus Christ really raised from the dead?" We can't minimize the importance of this for Christians. It is bedrock belief. But it is not what I have in mind.

Until recently, I would have argued that the key question at Easter is not so much whether Jesus was resurrected (I believe he was) but whether his ailing Church can be. As Ezekiel once asked, looking over a valley filled with the bones of past armies: "Can these dry bones live again?"

But even that is far too narrow an issue in the face of the world situation today.

The overwhelming question being hurled at us by the universe now is: Can humanity be resurrected, reborn, renewed? Or is it our self-determined fate to be swallowed in an orgy of barbarism such as our most primitive ancestors never dreamed of?

My thinking on this was brought into sharp focus one early spring morning, when all nature was stirring with new life under brilliant sunshine. The ice was not out of the lake yet, but the geese were back, whirring and honking overhead. I saw a fat muskrat swim by in the run-off, a few yards from our front door, as I set out on my walk.

After a couple of miles, I found myself on a high ridge, surrounded by rolling farmland, with a panoramic view of Toronto in the hazy distance to the south.

Suddenly I saw a couple of brown shapes in the corner of a pasture about two hundred metres away. Thinking they were cattle, I kept striding towards them. But as they snapped their heads up to watch my approach, I realized they were deer – five of them.

I stood very still, only moving when they resumed browsing. Soon, I had managed to stalk to within less than fifty metres. The deer had obviously wintered well, and two of the does were pregnant.

They were curious about me, but nervous as well. The largest one, a buck, looked up just as I took another step nearer. In a flash they were leaping the ditch and hedge. Soon all I could see was the graceful waving of white tails as they disappeared from view.

It was a magical moment, made all the more striking because I could see the tall finger of the CN Tower on the horizon as they ran.

Home in my study, a short while later, I was still thinking of the deer when I was brought roughly back to the realities we humans have created. The newspaper on my desk was filled with stories of violence. It was tempting to agree with the hymn-writer who wrote: "Where every prospect pleases, and only man is vile."

At such times it seems we have learned nothing at all from the sacrifices and tragedies of two World Wars, or from the self-evident truth that if we don't learn to live together we will surely conflagrate together. Sometimes it even seems that only a common enemy *from outside our planet* would suffice to shock us into being the global family God intends – and survival demands – us to be.

In spite of all of this, I am not a pessimist. Nor do I accept the fatalism that says that only a *deus ex machina*-type intervention by God can deliver us.

As the species *Homo sapiens*, created in God's image, we have the capacity to forge here either the kingdom of heaven or the chaos of hell. It is a real choice, and it is ours while there is still time. We urgently need prophets to arise and call the nations to true repentance – not to a sense of merely being sorry, but to that change of will that results in a 180-degree shift of direction.

They should begin by flaying the world's great religions for their centuries of failure, for currently being so often part of the problem rather than an answer. As the ancient prophets said: "Let repentance begin at the House of God."

That holds true for Christians at Easter. But it holds equally true for Muslims, Jews, Sikhs, Hindus, Buddhists, and all the rest.

— Remembrance Day —

One of the most moving experiences for me in years of travelling across our vast country is that of standing at the cenotaphs in even the smallest hamlets – from tiny villages in the Maritimes to Prairie towns or remote, northern communities.

You read the names of the youth who died, far from their native soil, fighting an enemy they didn't know, for reasons often only dimly understood, and you feel an immense grief. Pride and gratitude? Of course. But, mostly a numbing, wistful sorrow at human folly and at the insatiable thirst of the gods of war for the blood of the best.

On Remembrance Day, the world pauses briefly to reflect on the savage costs of war and to ponder ways to peace. Each of us, however inarticulate or humble, determines once more that "they must not have died in vain." But even as we do so, we are dismayed by inner fears that it is only a matter of time; that forces far beyond our own, puny control might once again sweep us all into an insane abyss.

Nobody has magical answers or solutions. But I refuse to believe that a thinking species that can probe outer space, split the atom, perform surgery on an infant in the womb, or tinker with the very coding of the basic stuff of human life itself cannot find a way to stop slaughtering its own members in the collective madness of war.

What is needed at this hour, more urgently than ever before, is a rededication, not to this or that religion (because we will never get agreement to that in a million years) but to the sacredness of the human person.

My conservative or fundamentalist friends will immediately cry "humanism" and carry on as though one had committed the unforgiveable sin. But, they are wrong. Indeed, something that saddens me very much is the manner in which these otherwise good and upright folk malign humanism, as if it were the chief philosophy and weapon of the Antichrist himself. In book after book and sermon upon sermon, they load the terms "humanist" and "humanism" with all the freight historically reserved for the most blatant enemies of God, motherhood, and the rest.

But the Christian faith, though often shamefully perverted to bless and sanction war in a way that would have astonished and outraged its founder, is a humanistic religion. It is focused on how to be human oneself and how to treat others as humans. The whole Christian teaching of the Incarnation – of God made human, the

Word made flesh – is about God taking human life and all that pertains to it so seriously that He revealed himself in a thoroughly human Person.

Jesus was a humanist. He told his followers that to do good to *any* human being was to do it to him. He went about freeing people from fear, guilt, and oppression – anything that marred the wholeness of their humanity. Small wonder St. Irenaeus (130-200 A.D.) could write: "The glory of God is man [the human person] fully alive!"

True, a Christian or other religious humanist differs from a secular humanist. The secular humanist is dogmatic in the claim that man is alone in the cosmos and that this world – or *saeculum* (the Latin origin of secular) is all there is. For the secular humanist, man alone is, in the words of the ancient philosopher Protagoras, "the measure of all things."

Such a view is clearly not Christian (nor Judaic) humanism, which hold that our true humanity is only properly understood when seen as God's creation.

The point, however, is that these two kinds of humanism have some incredibly important things in common in their concern for human welfare. The too-fierce critics of secular humanism should heed the much-neglected words of Christ: "He who is not against us is for us."

The time has come for all men and women of goodwill who care about "restoring a human face" to every human on the face of the globe to band together in a united struggle.

As we think about war today, the deadliest, most pervasive foe of the Kingdom of God or true, Christian humanism is not secular humanism but what I, for want of a better term, call "anti-humanism." The real opponent of humanity and of peace now is not the secular unbeliever. Rather, it is all those groups, states, "principalities and powers" that work to dehumanize us all.

Anti-humanism is at the root of exploitative pornography. It is anti-humanism that is at work wherever torture is used or people are brutally oppressed. It is anti-humanism that crushes the poor, demeans women, and abuses children.

Anti-humanism is at the very core of the war mentality,

no matter who tries to justify it with high-sounding rhetoric. You first deny the enemy's humanity, then you can do whatever you like.

As the bugles sound Reveille at remembrance services everywhere, my hope is that we might finally wake from the sleep of the past and join common cause with all who are determined that war indeed shall be no more.

— Christmas, I —

"And the light shines on in the darkness; and the darkness has not overwhelmed it.... That was the essence of light itself, the same light that imparts light to every person who comes into the world." (From the prologue to John's Gospel; my translation of the Greek text.)

At the time of the birth of Christ, there was a unique Jewish sect living at Qumran, overlooking the bitter waters of the Dead Sea on one side and the arid hills of the Judean wilderness on the other.

Ever since the discovery of the Dead Sea Scrolls in caves near the ruins of Qumran in 1947, we have known that these ascetics had fled what they saw as the worldliness of Jerusalem. They were waiting for the end time, when the ultimate struggle between the forces of light and darkness would take place and usher in the Messianic Age.

In using the imagery of light and darkness, they were picking up mythical symbolism that came from Persia – from the Zoroastrians who worshipped Ahura Mazda, God of Light, whose sacred symbol was and still is fire. (Incidentally, it is likely that the Magi were in fact Zoroastrian astrologers or priests.)

But students of religion and mythology know that the deep, human perception that God is "the essence of light" and that there is a cosmic struggle always going on between good and evil (darkness) has roots that are universal and as old as humanity itself. Speaking of Brahman, "the Lord God," the Upanishads or Hindu scriptures, written hundreds of years before the birth of Christ, say: "Thou alone art – thou the Light Imperishable...."

The same awareness lies behind primitive worship of the sun. In fact, it is no accident that when the early Christians wanted to set a day to mark the birth of Jesus they chose a day already long in use by the Romans to mark the *Dies Natalis*, or birthday of the sun. As the shortest day of the year approached, the winter solstice, it was no wonder pagan peoples felt there was a risk the sun might die or be extinguished altogether. By lighting fires, torches, and candles, they encouraged its rekindling and then feasted to celebrate the renewal of the cosmic cycle once again. At this season, when Jews light candles for the festival of Chanukkah or when Christians – active or lapsed – display Christmas lights and gather for festive meals, there are echoes of this vast, primeval drama.

We miss the point, however, if we fail to go beyond the various outward trappings and symbols surrounding any religious occasion to the inner or spiritual meaning.

The quote with which I began says that the Christ Event is a supreme example of the Divine Light coming into this world, a light that is the very source of the light or presence of God in every human being. What's more, it states that, however daunting and oppressive the darkness, it has never (and can never) wholly overcome the light or goodness of God.

We need to hear this. We need to because it's so easy at times to look at the world around us and feel that the darkness is about to engulf us. We read or hear and see the news and are sorely tempted to believe that evil has the upper hand, that injustice, inhumanity, and war are about to eclipse all vestiges of light.

The spiritual meaning of Christmas is that this does not have to be the case. The light has never been put out. Always throughout history, even at the darkest hour, here or there – often in the most unexpected, least esteemed places – there have been flickers of light.

You see, as John's Gospel says, each one of us is a light-bearer. The essence of light itself, God, has kindled the flame in us. It is individuals who keep the faith with that inner light who make the difference in this world. Wherever a cup of cold water is given to the thirsty, wherever compassion of any kind is shown or the burden lifted from the shoulders of the weak and helpless, wherever depravity is resisted or the oppressor is rebuked, whenever justice is defended or the sick in body and mind are healed, and the lonely comforted, whenever truth is spoken or done, there is light – and God is there.

Challenging as it may seem, we are all of us called to be the light of the world as the Divine Light itself channels through us. As the Hindu scripture also says: "The Atman [God within] is the light. The light is covered by darkness…. but when the light of the Atman drives out our darkness, that light shines forth from us and God is revealed."

Darkness still stalks the earth as it did that first Christmas long ago. There is torture and poverty, there is violence against women and children, there is hunger and unemployment. But the darkness has not overwhelmed the light – nor will it ever. The heart of Christmas is not some sentimental or nostalgic orgy of feelings. It's not about eating, drinking, and getting gifts. It's about letting the light be born afresh in the manger of your soul and taking arms anew in the fight against the dark.

— Christmas, II —

In churches around the world on Christmas Eve, countless millions hear some of the most sublime words ever written. I'm referring to the Christmas Gospel reading, the opening verses of John's Gospel:

> In the beginning was the Word, and the Word was with God, and the Word was God. All things were made by him; and without him was not any thing made that was made. In him was life; and the life was the light of humanity…. That was the true light that gives light to every person as he or she comes into the world."

Unfortunately, sublime or not, the great cosmic sweep of this passage and its relevance both for a new spirituality and for a deeper approach to our environment and to each other are too often ignored or missed. Familiarity has bred not contempt but a terrible dullness of hearing.

The fact that it has implications for everyone, and not just those who belong to the Christian religion, has escaped notice for far too long. Actually, there are concepts here that resonate in the sacred scriptures of the Hindus as well as in the highest religious-philosophical thought of all of the ancient Near East.

Simply put, the big question was: How does a transcendent, "wholly other" Presence, God, relate to this transient, material world?

The ancient Hebrews replied in several ways. For example, God "speaks" a creative Word – thus, in the account of creation in Genesis, you keep reading, "And God said, let there be light, let there be a firmament," and so on. God "speaks" to his prophets; in short, God is a communicating Being.

For the Greek philosophers, the divine Logos or Word was the Ground and Source of all things. The Logos was more than utterance or speech, it was the "fiery breath" out of which the cosmos comes; it was imbued with consciousness and rationality; in its subtlest form it was not just the life principle but the "light" of the human mind – our reasoning power. The Stoics, for example, taught that each of us has a "seed" of the divine Logos or Word within us. This was called, significantly, the *spermatikos Logos*.

What is unique about John's Gospel is that, instead of talking about the birth of Christ in Bethlehem, like Matthew and Luke, he puts it into a cosmic context by using this Logos or Word terminology. The Christ Event, he says, is a supreme case of the divine Word – which is the Ground of our creation and "lightens" every single human soul – becoming "enfleshed" or embodied here on earth.

Unfortunately, after this introduction to his Gospel, our evangelist never again refers to the Logos or its importance. Thus, instead of Christians understanding Jesus as the prime example of how the Word becomes incarnate, he becomes *the only, the exclusive* case in history. From this, the exclusive emphasis on Jesus as

God – together with the stress on redemption out of this "wicked" world, the negation of sexuality and the body, and the age-old Christian sense of superiority, not to say outright hostility, to other religions – has developed.

What this passage really says is that this Word has been made flesh in every living thing. The entire universe is its incarnation, and hence every human on the face of the globe is not merely "made in God's image" but is the embodiment of the divine principle of Life itself. The birth of every child is the birth of Christ in the "manger" of our humanity. As John puts it, the Word or Logos of God gives the "light" that illumines "every person coming into the world."

By restricting the "Word made flesh" to Jesus alone, we have lost the clue to our own spiritual natures. If he was divine, so too are we. We are not God but, in a real sense, the stable in which God comes to dwell, would we but recognize it. Paul puts it slightly differently when he says: "In Him we live and move and have our being."

By focusing overmuch on salvation through the Redeemer, we have failed to see that the entire cosmos glows and shimmers with the embodiment, the "enfleshment," of the Word of God. It is not just humans but every stone, every flower, every insect, beast, or fish, the mountains as well as the stars – all things came into being by the activity of the divine Word. This is what Fr. Matthew Fox is talking about in his book *The Coming of the Cosmic Christ*.

Jesus, whose birth we celebrate, is the "fully-enlightened one," or what the Letter to the Hebrews calls "the pioneer or forerunner" of a realized humanity. To follow him is not a matter of slavish imitation but rather, as he did, to follow with abandonment and joy the inner vision of God's gift of the Logos within each one of us.

The Word is indeed "made flesh" each Christmas Eve. But not just in Jesus. In the whole of creation. In you and me!

— Christmas, III —

The real enemy of Christmas is not commercialism or (that hor-rible word!) consumerism. The deadliest foe of a spiritual aware-ness of the meaning of Christmas is a kind of insipid, superficial sentimentality. I'm referring to a sugary-sweet "away-in-the-man-ger" approach that treats the Christmas Story as a nostalgic kind of folk-tale that recalls for a moment the lost innocence of child-hood.

A lot of the frustration and emptiness – in spite of feasting – that now surrounds Christmas flows from a vain attempt to recreate fantasies of Christmas as we imagine we remember it from long ago. Christmas cards with a religious theme, while increasingly rare, contribute to the creeping miasma of unreality. All the figures – from angels to donkeys, Wise Men, and even the Holy Family – speak of cuteness but little else. None of it seems even remotely connected to the realities of life in the 1990s.

This is tragic, because if one can escape the sentimental over-load and look again with new eyes and an open heart, the elements of the Christmas Story that have come down to us from Matthew and Luke have the power to transform the way we see ourselves, others, and the universe itself.

I propose we go afresh to that far-off, crude stable to watch, reflect, and wonder.

There's a small knot of onlookers gathered around the entrance to what in all probability was a cave in the soft limestone of the hill-side. There are some shepherds. (Anyone who knows the Middle East knows that these were, contrary to pop religion, not bearded men but young people, quite possibly all female.) They are very ordinary, humble folk, smelling of sheep and the outdoors. In sharp contrast, several exotic-looking strangers are there as well. They are Magi or astrologers (the tradition that there were three and that they were kings is not in the Bible) who have come from the East, most likely from Persia (modern Iran).

The innkeeper and a couple of women from the inn who might have acted as midwives at the birth are bustling about inside, tidying things up or keeping the idle curious from crowding too closely. There are animals in the stable in all likelihood – chickens, a few goats, perhaps a cow, a donkey or two, and the horses of the inn's wealthier guests. In fact, without their body heat warming the place, it would be dangerously chilly at night on these hills. But animals mean the strong tang of manure in the air and its adhesive presence all about. This is no antiseptic, Christmas card barn but a place where flies and dung are simply facts of life.

At the centre of the scene are a common tradesman (a carpenter), his young wife, and a newborn baby. Tradition and sentiment have conspired to make them totally otherworldly, remote, virtually unreal. The Church has treated Joseph shabbily to say the least. Because of hang-ups about sex, Church tradition got rid of him as Mary's spouse as soon as possible. He is depicted as very elderly and is supposed to have died before any natural consummation of his marriage took place. Mary herself, without warrant in the original story, is held to have remained a perpetual virgin – again because of an unbiblical belief that sex is somehow less than holy. Indeed, some early Church Fathers argued that the Christ child was born without disrupting her virgin state. They held that one who, after the Resurrection, could move through closed doors did not require the normal expansion of the birth canal, etc., to enter this world.

But the Bible confirms none of this. In fact, apart from the belief (quite common at the time whenever great personages were concerned) that this was a virgin birth, there is every reason to suppose Jesus was born in the normal way. There was pain, crying, the breaking of the waters, blood, mess – and then joy. This was not some wunderkind, some magical apparition, but a real baby. This means soiled "diapers" and the usual wailing.

The story includes a strange star about which a lot of romantic nonsense has also been written. Real stars – supernovas, comets, and the rest – don't move and then "stand" overhead; nor do they manage to pick out one place in a village full of homes, shops, and outbuildings. The spiritual meaning of the star (in antiquity stars were always symbols of the birth or death of the famous) is that the whole of the cosmos is involved in what is going on.

It's important in all of this to realize that what the story is saying is that God reveals Himself/Herself in the very midst of the mud, the blood, the pain, and the joy of the ordinary. Nothing could be more common or more human than the birth of a child in surroundings that include all ranks of people, the animal kingdom, the hay and grains of the plant realm, and the heavenly bodies above. Yet something quite uncommon is going on!

If you are looking for spiritual and ethical enrichment this Christmas, keep your eyes fixed not on some esoteric heavenly vision or some supernatural epiphany. Look instead more closely at the "manger" of real life, and especially at the faces of the poor and lonely. Finding the extraordinary in the midst of the ordinary is what Christmas is all about. Emmanuel means "God with us." That's true, and usually it's where and when we expect it least.

— Christmas, IV —

It's time for some critical reflection on the annual global convulsion known as Christmas.

Unwelcome though it may be, let's at least strive for some honesty. The social spasm that now begins on or before November 1 each year is a ritualized tribute to consumerism and self-indulgence on a scale never before witnessed on this planet. The depth of our devotion to these "gods" makes the demands of the most despotic deity of primitive times pale by comparison. No, we don't engage in human sacrifice but we sacrifice nearly everything else – including peace of mind. It is ironic, even blasphemous, to attach Christ's name to this pathology of behaviour that contradicts almost everything he taught, lived, and died for.

I can hear the loud protests already. But it's clear to any objective observer willing to free herself from the prevailing cultural trance that Christmas, as currently observed in the developed world, has very little to do with Christ. All the carol-singing, midnight masses, pious messages, or handouts cannot change this.

However good in themselves, they now merely add a tinselly touch that hides the enormity of what is going on.

The surfeit of shopping and of materialistic hype actually gains a kind of demonic dimension precisely because it is able to pass itself off as a kind of religious event. Sprinkled, as it were, with holy water, it can summon up deep forces of both guilt and enthusiasm that only reinforce what has now become its overwhelming thrust: an orgy of secular worship to greed and mammon.

It is because all of us, whether practising Christians or not, are aware of this split at some deep level of our being that Christmas has become such an incredibly exhausting and depressing affair for the vast majority. We do our best to achieve some kind of inner compromise – by trying to invoke the lost spirit of childhood Christmases in a self-defeating perfectionism or dropping in on a concert or church service. But more and more people are aware of a haunting sense of failure. Nothing they try quite makes it anymore.

Small wonder! It's an impossible task. We know Christ was poor, homeless, and a friend of outcasts. Yet our celebrations, allegedly in his name, serve only to remind the marginalized everywhere just how forsaken and irrelevant they are. There is no room for them in our glittering malls.

They cry for justice in the name of Christ, and we offer charity instead. In Brazil alone, forty babies die every hour from hunger and disease. The homeless and hungry in our own cities cry for this same justice, and we offer soup kitchens and food banks.

Christmas takes its name from Christ but is marked by an assault on the resources of this earth of such a magnitude that it threatens the very existence of his "Father's" world!

There is an emotional rape going on as well. For thousands upon thousands of families and individuals around the world, December, and not T. S. Eliot's April, is "the cruellest month of the year." They have lost loved ones on or around Christmas; they might have a family member in hospital or a home; or they might be alone with nothing but their memories. As a former pastor, I know the suffering felt when from every side the culture tells them they should "don't worry; be happy" because it's Christmas. Yet their agony abides and is intensified.

For the people of Lockerbie, Scotland, and all the loved ones of those who perished in the bombing of PanAm Flight 103 on December 21, 1988, Christmas will always seem a monster from the pit.

My proposal is that our clergy stop their well-meaning but doomed attempt to re-spiritualize Christmas. In fact, if I hear one more cleric bleating about putting Christ back into Christmas I'm liable to choke. It's too late for that.

I'm convinced the time has come *to take Christ out of Christmas altogether* so that this foolish charade can be ended.

Since we haven't the slightest idea when Christ's birthday actually occurred anyway – the early Christians got by without celebrating his birthday at all for about three hundred years – we should move it to another date altogether. I have always envied those Orthodox churches that have their Christmas in early January. They're able to separate the December 25 secular blow-out from the spiritual experience of the Christ Event.

December 25 could then become "Yuletide" or "Xmas" – with "X" meaning the "unknown quantity" to be filled in by each according to his or her whim. The commercialism and consumerism would probably continue around the December 25 celebration, but at least all pretences that this is a Christ-inspired and/or religious feast could be put to rest.

— A New Year's Resolution —

Robertson Davies, novelist and playwright, reminded me in a TV interview the other day of a saying from the Gnostic Gospel of Thomas. In it, Jesus tells the disciples: "The Kingdom of God is all around you and you see it not."

This at once recalled to my mind some words I love. They're by Francis Thompson (1859-1907) in his poem "The Kingdom of God":

The angels keep their ancient places;
Turn but a stone, and start a wing!

'Tis ye, 'tis your estranged faces,
That miss the many-splendored thing.

Thompson, author of the haunting poem "The Hound of Heaven," makes a similar point in the lines:

The drift of pinions, would we hearken,
beats at our own clay-shuttered doors.

I have a reason for citing these verses now. On the first day of each new year, as the year extends before us like a *tabula rasa* – a blank page, or an unmarked field of snow – many of us make resolutions. Some of these, however fine and good in themselves, might have a trivial ring compared with some we might be making.

For example, here is one that has an enormous appeal because it offers such an opportunity for radical change in ourselves and in how we perceive each other and the world around us. In essence, it sums up what the Gnostic saying and the quotes from Thompson are calling for: that we resolve by will and inner discipline to become more *aware*; that we strive by might and main to see the glory around us, even though at times it seems all but extinguished by life's uncertainties or pain.

We need to become more sharply aware of our own inner selves. One of the most lethal dangers of this information age is that our brains and souls become so overloaded that all true thinking becomes impossible. We are so deafened by the cacophony of advertising, entertainment, and what passes for news that we no longer hear any inner voice at all.

So far from realizing that the Kingdom of God within us is our most precious possession – and our most important gift to others – we see and hear it not.

I'm not talking about becoming more self-concerned or self-conscious in the surface sense. I'm concerned about the spiritual riches that lie within each one of us, whether we are believers in any particular creed or not. Whether you call it the "Overself," the "great soul within," or the Kingdom of God really matters very little. The point is that there is much more to every one of us than meets the eye. It's what John's Gospel calls "the light that lighteth every person coming into the world." Other religions and philosophies describe it differently, but there is wide agreement about the reality itself. My suggestion is that in the new year we get to know this part of us more fully.

Ideally, you need solitude and quiet to listen. But it *can* be done on the subway, or anywhere else for that matter. When Jesus once told his followers to enter into their "closet" to pray, he wasn't talking about hiding in the hall or bedroom cupboard to be alone. He was speaking of the closet of one's own, inner space. It's a matter of turning one's awareness inwards and of doing much more listening than we normally do in what is piously known as praying. Real prayer, real inner communion, is "waiting upon God."

Next, we need to become increasingly aware of those around us. Again, this must be understood in a much more profound sense than merely noticing others – though even this for some of us might be a start!

What I mean is becoming more alert to others in their uniqueness and in their own embodiment of the same divine spark we realize in ourselves. Life grows so much richer and full of moments both of grace and of surprise when we stop regarding others as objects and see them with new eyes. One of the reasons why some people seem to be always experiencing synchronicities or serendipities as they move through life is that they try never to take "even the least of these my brethren" for granted.

Finally, the resolve to deepen awareness must include the natural world around us. This is not a matter of some sentimental or romanticized trivialization of nature à la Walt Disney. It's the kind of "new intimacy with the Earth" taught by Fr. Thomas Berry and others who are challenging us to enter a new age of civilization – "The Ecozoic Age."

To quote the sixteenth-century Chinese writer Wange Yangming, "the truly developed person is someone aware that we form one body with heaven, earth and all living things."

To become more aware of this, of oneself, and of others is to become more alive. This is my New Year's wish for all of us.

Date Dr

Printed in Canada